Gardner Webb College Library

D1214360

ECONOMIC MEANS AND SOCIAL ENDS

Essays in Political Economics

ECONOMIC MEANS AND SOCIAL ENDS

Essays in Political Economics

by
ADOLPH LOWE
ARON GURWITSCH
ERNEST NAGEL
HANS JONAS
ABRAHAM EDEL
FRITZ MACHLUP
ABBA P. LERNER
CARL KAYSEN
HENRY C. WALLICH

edited—and with an introduction—by
ROBERT L. HEILBRONER

PRENTICE-HALL, INC.
Englewood Cliffs, New Jersey

© 1969
by Prentice-Hall, Inc.
Englewood Cliffs, New Jersey

All rights reserved.
No part of this book may be reproduced
in any form or by any means
without permission in writing
from the publisher.

13-226860

Library of Congress
Catalog Card Number 76-77482

Current printing (last digit)
10 9 8 7 6 5 4 3

PRENTICE-HALL INTERNATIONAL, INC., *London*
PRENTICE-HALL OF AUSTRALIA PTY. LTD., *Sydney*
PRENTICE-HALL OF CANADA, LTD., *Toronto*
PRENTICE-HALL OF INDIA PRIVATE LTD., *New Delhi*
PRENTICE-HALL OF JAPAN, INC., *Tokyo*

PRINTED IN THE UNITED STATES OF AMERICA

HB
71
E25

To the Graduate Faculty of Political and Social Science

of the

New School for Social Research

INTRODUCTION

As the reader will shortly discover, this is an unconventional book. For one thing, one does not often find economists discussing philosophy or philosophers discussing economics, or, for that matter, economists and philosophers talking to each other at all. For another, the matter about which they are talking is, to say the least, unusual. It might be thought from the title of this book that its subject is some kind of economic program for social change. But the problem to which the contributors of this volume address themselves reaches much deeper than that. It is not a particular economic or social proposal that is tested in these pages, but the more disturbing question of whether economic theory, as it is presently constituted, is in fact a useful instrument to achieve desired social ends of any kind whatever.

Such an unexpected focus of concern for economists and philosophers requires a word of explanation. These essays are all occasioned by a common challenge. Four years ago, Adolph Lowe, Professor Emeritus of the Graduate Faculty of the New School for Social Research, published *On Economic Knowledge*, a book that marked the culmination of a lifelong interest in the relevance of economic theory and economic practice. Since the thrust of that book will be made explicit in the very first essay, I will not attempt to summarize it here. Suffice it to say that the central contentions of the book were two: first, that contemporary economic theory was not—and worse, could not be—an adequate tool for the control of our social destiny because the very premises on which that theory was based were no longer relevant to social reality; and second, that a restructured economic theory might become such a tool if economists understood the changed relationship of theory and reality in the milieu of industrial capitalism, and altered the nature of their procedures accordingly.

As an argument directed at the foundations of social science itself, Lowe's contentions far overreached the normal boundaries of economics. To explore these challenges, two Symposia of philosophers and social scientists from many disciplines gathered at the New School for Social Research in February and March of 1968. To give a theme to the proceedings, Lowe reformulated his ideas in a position paper that set forth his criticism of traditional theory and his proposal for its restructuring along the lines of a Political Economics. This paper then became the target for a series of invited essays that both supported and criticized Lowe's point of view. Finally Lowe himself replied to his critics, summarizing the arguments and emphasizing the problems that seemed to him to require further study.

These papers, rearranged in sequence and edited to constitute an integrated whole, form the body of this book. I do not know whether a reader who follows the contest of ideas that they present will emerge confirmed in his belief in the adequacy of contemporary economics or convinced of the need for its radical reform, but I think it safe to say that few will follow these exchanges without permanently sharpening and deepening their interest in the issues themselves. I was once so incautious as to write that the proceedings of symposia rarely left lasting impressions. I am now happy to offer these essays as the exception to prove the rule.

It remains only to express, on behalf of the organizing committee of Professor Hans Staudinger, Professor Thomas Vietorisz, and myself, our thanks to the many persons who have contributed to this publication. Needless to say, our gratitude goes first to the contributors themselves and to the chairmen and participants in both Symposia. We are only regretful that lack of space prevents the reproduction of the debates themselves or the addition of the considerable number of written comments submitted after the Symposia. We would like to thank as well the Administration of the New School, in particular President John R. Everett and Dean Joseph J. Greenbaum of the Graduate

Faculty, for having helped make possible both the Symposia and the book itself. Finally we must add a word of appreciation to the New School staff, especially to Mrs. Henrietta Greenberg and Miss Patricia Denson, without whose efforts the whole enterprise would have long since foundered.

ROBERT L. HEILBRONER

CONTENTS

CONTRIBUTORS

ADOLPH LOWE is Professor Emeritus at the Graduate Faculty of the New School for Social Research.

ARON GURWITSCH is Professor of Philosophy at the Graduate Faculty of the New School for Social Research.

ERNEST NAGEL is University Professor of Philosophy at Columbia University.

HANS JONAS is Alvin Johnson Professor of Philosophy at the Graduate Faculty of the New School for Social Research.

ABRAHAM EDEL is Professor of Philosophy at the City College of New York.

FRITZ MACHLUP is Professor of Economics and International Finance at Princeton University.

ABBA P. LERNER is Professor of Economics at the University of California, Berkeley.

CARL KAYSEN is Director of the Institute for Advanced Studies, Princeton.

HENRY C. WALLICH is Professor of Economics at Yale University.

ROBERT L. HEILBRONER is Professor of Economics at the Graduate Faculty of the New School for Social Research.

ECONOMIC MEANS AND SOCIAL ENDS

Essays in Political Economics

1

ADOLPH LOWE

TOWARD A SCIENCE
OF
POLITICAL ECONOMICS

The subsequent pages present the gist of my book
On Economic Knowledge,[1] in which I originally formulated my
ideas on the content and method of a Political Economics.[2] This
condensation of a comprehensive argument to its bare essentials
has the advantage of exposing both its strengths and its weak-
nesses. As far as the latter are concerned, published reviews, private communications, and not least my own further reflections
have made me aware of certain shortcomings which, were I to
rewrite the book, would cause me to shift certain emphases,
soften the tone of some critical comments, and stress even more
than I did originally the convergence of my ideas with the trend
of current theory and economic policy. Yet my main thesis stands,
to my mind, intact, and I will attempt to restate it here, hope-
fully in terms that will strain neither the patience of the economist nor the understanding of the noneconomist.

---

[1] Adolph Lowe, *On Economic Knowledge, Toward a Science of Political
Economics*, Vol. 35 of *World Perspectives*, planned and edited by Ruth
Nanda Anshen (New York: Harper & Row, Publishers, 1965). For brevity
I shall use the initials *OEK* when referring to the book in this text.

[2] For an alternative presentation see Robert L. Heilbroner, "Is Economic
Theory Possible?" *Social Research*, Fall, 1966, pp. 272–294.

1

THE CRITICAL VIEWPOINT OF POLITICAL ECONOMICS [3]

Political versus Traditional Economics

The dividing line between Traditional Economics—by which I refer to the standard formulations of economic theory, past and present—and Political Economics, as I denote my own reformulation of economic theory, can best be approached if we begin from two premises that both procedures share.

The first of these is an emphasis on *theory* rather than on taxonomic or historical description as the essential core of the discipline. Both Traditional Economics and Political Economics, in other words, move from a small number of explanatory principles to a large number of propositions about the facts of economic life. Second, both approaches share a common concern with *prediction*. I wish to stress this point from the outset, because the reservations which I have expressed in my book as to the predictive powers of Traditional Economics have occasionally been misinterpreted as a denial on my part of the possibility—or even the legitimacy—of economic prediction generally. Nothing could be further from my intention. Indeed the major incentive in my search for an alternative to traditional reasoning has been the wish to invest economic theory with the power of prediction that I believe it now lacks.

It does not follow from this that the ability to predict should be regarded as the decisive criterion for scientific economics. As the examples of geology or crystallography show, the capacity to predict is not even a necessary attribute in the physical sciences, and much less so in the social sciences, where historical explanation and structural analysis play such a large role. If, nevertheless, the ability to predict today serves more and more as the touchstone of economic science, the reason is pragmatic. By this I mean not only that the application of economic knowledge is conditional on our capacity to foresee the effect of economic actions, but even more that the adequate functioning of our kind of economic system requires *public action* informed of its consequences. In other words, whether economics is, or is not, capable of prediction is no longer merely a methodological concern but a question of cardinal importance for the organization of economic life.

Thus in the search for explanatory principles from which deductions can be made, and in the focus on prediction as the pragmatic aim of the

---

[3] *OEK*, Chaps. 1–4.

analytical procedure, Traditional and Political Economics agree. The roads part when we ask: How can we obtain knowledge of the explanatory principles—be they laws or stochastic regularities—from which predictive statements can be derived?

Traditional Economics, following the procedure of the "hard" sciences, tries to derive its laws and stochastic regularities from the observation of *actual* economic processes and of the *actual* behavior of the elementary units of the economy—buyers and sellers, consumers, investors, etc. Political Economics does not reject this procedure once and for all. It recognizes a limited period of economic history—the period of "classical" capitalism in the decades following the Industrial Revolution—to which the traditional procedure is well adapted. But it finds the predictive usefulness of the so-called "positive" method on the wane during the later development of industrial capitalism, to the point where, under contemporary conditions, the failures of the method seem to far outweigh the successes. Considering the recent progress in econometric techniques, this trend toward decreasing reliability in economic prediction can hardly be blamed on a lack of refinement of prevailing research methods. Rather it looks as if something had happened to the underlying research object itself to make it progressively more refractory to conventional methods of investigation. The nature of this historical change is, I believe, an ever widening spectrum of behavioral and motivational patterns, with the consequence of increasing "disorder" in the autonomous processes of modern markets.

If this is true, we are confronted with a grave dilemma. In the interest of the proper functioning of the modern market, this tendency toward disorder must be counteracted by appropriate measures of public policy. But in order to devise suitable policies, we require a theory capable of predicting the effects of the particular measures we employ. However, it seems impossible to construct such a theory if the observable phenomena from which the explanatory principles are to be abstracted lack that minimum degree of orderliness which is the prerequisite of any scientific generalization.

It is from the horns of this dilemma that Political Economics tries to lift economic analysis. But before showing how this can be done, we should first examine more closely the two presuppositions on which our formulation of the problem rests. One refers to the "minimum degree of orderliness" on whose presence both the practical functioning of an industrial market and the theoretical explanation and prediction of its movements are said to depend. The other concerns the empirical question of whether the actual movements of contemporary markets do indeed fall short of that "minimum," and what may be the reasons for such a "deformation" of mature capitalism.

The Role of "Order" in Economic Theory and Practice

There is probably agreement that in no field of inquiry can scientific generalizations be derived from the observation of truly "erratic" phenomena. This does not imply that a continuum of observations that leads from "perfect order"—meaning invariability of structure and motion—to "perfect disorder"—namely, full randomization of events—is also a continuum of decreasing scientific tractability. Rather the scientifically inexpedient range lies around the middle of the spectrum, since both extremes and their neighboring regions are open to deductive or stochastic generalizations.

As frequently as the extreme of randomization seems to occur in the realm of natural phenomena, in the social world it materializes only in exceptional cases when no interrelations exist among the members of a group: e.g., in a crowd milling around idly. Nor can we, in view of the spontaneity of the units of social groups, expect the other extreme, invariability of behavior, to be the rule over any length of time. Hence, for all practical purposes, the relevant region for social occurrences lies somewhere between the extreme of perfect order and the middle range of erratic behavior, a region in which orderly and disorderly tendencies combine in varying proportions. The critical question for the predictability of autonomous economic phenomena is, then, whether, in a given case, the prevailing degree of orderliness approximates the state of perfect order sufficiently closely to permit the application of a deductive procedure which, taking into account certain disturbance variables, will yield results that fall within a small prediction interval.

There can be legitimate disagreement as to the size of the prediction interval which, in a given case, is still practically useful and thus compatible with orderly structure and motion. Take the problem of a "reference cycle" for industrial fluctuations. It is one thing to predict—even with a considerable prediction interval—the rates of change of output during an upswing or downswing. It is quite another, however, to predict whether a given economic movement will continue or will turn in a direction contrary to the one in which it is headed at the moment when the prediction is made. In the first case there is no doubt about the direction of the movement; the strategic variables at least have the proper arithmetic sign. In the latter case it is the sign itself and thus the direction that is in doubt.

So, too, in micro-economics, when we predict the effect of a rise in prices on, say, supply. If the situation is orderly enough, we can at least assert that a price rise will bring some increase in supply. But the prediction interval may rise to the point where we may be unable to assert even that much—for instance, if price rises induce a speculative *contraction* in offerings. Therefore, to give some precision to the notion of "disorder," I shall henceforth define it as any situation in which we cannot unambiguously predict the *direction of economic change*.

In contrast with much modern theorizing, I feel bound to emphasize the singular importance of such "order" and "disorder" in micro-economic relations. With Professor Machlup I cannot regard any explanation of macro-processes as complete or any prediction of their future course as safe, unless one can demonstrate the particular micro-processes from whose integration the macro-phenomena result.[4]

Thus, in untangling this problem, the crucial matter of order arises at two levels. On the first level, it is necessary for the *behavior patterns* of buyers and sellers to form a mutually compatible and consistent chain. However, for this smooth intermeshing of individual actions to occur—and here we reach the second level—the *motivational patterns* underlying the behavior of individual marketers must themselves be mutually compatible.

These motivational patterns in turn must be understood to result from two separate constituents. One of these constituents represents the strand of purposive intent, of incentives, or, as I call them, *action directives*. Here we have the motives of pecuniary maximization or minimization, maintenance of asset values (Professor Boulding's "homeostasis"), protection of market positions, etc. But there is a second constituent as well. This is the strand of cognition or interpretation by which a marketer grasps the "meaning" of the actions of his fellow marketers or anticipates future market events—in particular, the manner in which his fellow marketers will react to his own behavior—to be subsumed under the concept of *expectations*.

These expectations of the individual actors are of the greatest importance for the construction of a scientific economics because they themselves represent predictions, although they are formed on a "commonsense" basis from fragmentary experience and information. For only if the state of the market shows a degree of order, in the sense defined above, will the economic actors be able to form correct expectations with a high degree of subjective certainty. And only then will their overt behavior patterns dovetail in such a way as to sustain the prevailing order, thus enabling the scientific observer to predict macro-events within practically useful limits. It is this commonsense interpretation of the ultimate "facts"—buyers' and sellers' behavior—by the actors themselves

---

[4] Fritz Machlup, *Der Wettstreit zwischen Mikro- und Makro-Theorien in der Nationaloekonomie* (Tuebingen: J. B. Mohr [Paul Siebeck], 1960).

that so greatly encumbers the work of the economist, a difficulty which the student of molecules and planets, or of cells and organisms, is spared.[5]

However, there is still another complication in the scientific treatment of social processes that must be recognized if the relevance of "order" for economic theorizing is to be fully grasped. I spoke above several times of the "adequate functioning" of the market as a task to be achieved by orderly macro-motions and interlocking behavioral and motivational patterns, possibly supported by measures of public policy. This implies that orderly macro- and micro-motion and thus predictability, though necessary conditions for constructing an economic theory, are by themselves insufficient ones. Assume, for example, a perfectly periodic business cycle in which the same amplitudes and durations of the phases repeated in unbroken sequence, but in which the stagnation phase each time approached the level of zero output and employment. Although such a process would be fully predictable, it would be rejected as incompatible with another kind of "order." This second type of order refers to those macro-states that will accomplish a certain "purpose" or "goal"— in the case above, the steady employment of the average member of the economic society in question and his steady provision with goods and services.

There is no logical argument by which we could refute a radical positivism interested only in the explanation and prediction of market movements "wherever they might lead." But it can hardly be doubted that some notion of the level of *aggregate* provision that is to arise from the interplay of micro-motions underlies the entire history of economic doctrines, even if it has been conceptualized only recently in the theorems of welfare economics. To put it differently, macro-economic states and processes have always been interpreted as something more than mere chance aggregations of events. They have been treated as phenomena of "organization"—whether autonomous organizations such as the self-regulating market, or contrived organizations held together through planned controls.

Therefore, the orderliness of a particular economic event does not consist solely in its regularity and consequent predictability. At the very least the event must also be compatible with the prime purpose of every economic organization—to wit, macro-provision through an appropriate use of available resources. (I intentionally do not speak of "optimum" provision or of the "efficient" use of resources. Over and above a socially accepted minimum of subsistence, in principle any level of output pro-

---

[5] For an extensive treatment of this problem, see Alfred Schutz, "Common Sense and Scientific Interpretation of Human Action," in *Collected Papers*, Vol. I (The Hague: Martinus Nijhoff, 1962), pp. 3–47.

duced by a technically suitable segment of the available resources and distributed in socially approved shares may satisfy the goals of a particular economic system.)

At the same time, once this is admitted, there is no denying that the ongoing "revolution of expectations" in mature as well as developing countries progressively narrows the acceptable range of provision and employment levels. This development is of great importance for the relationship of regularity of motion and predictability to goal-adequacy. At first sight these seem to be quite separate aspects of an inclusive definition of economic "order." As our earlier example has shown, we can have perfect regularity of motion combined with extreme goal-inadequacy. Conversely, so long as low levels of output and employment are accepted as macro-goals, we can conceive of highly irregular and thus unpredictable motions as compatible with goal-adequate states and processes. But since irregular motions are bound to impair allocative as well as productive efficiency, orderliness of motion turns into a prerequisite of goal-adequacy once the socially tolerable provision and employment levels rise above a certain threshold. There is little doubt that, in the mature economies of the West, this threshold has reached the point where a degree of motional disorder that in the nineteenth century would have been accepted with animistic fatalism, is no longer compatible with prevailing welfare aspirations. Or to put it differently: under prevailing conditions, irregular and thus unpredictable economic processes are bound to lead to socially intolerable states of provision.

What Are the Limits of Economic Prediction?

It is the contention of classical and neoclassical economics that, disregarding minor reservations, the decentralized decisions of the marketers, when free of political and contractual constraints, will bring about macro-states and macro-processes that exhibit "order" in this inclusive sense. All micro-movements are supposed to pursue a fully predictable, self-correcting, and self-limiting course, tending toward the establishment of a network of balances conceptualized as "macro-equilibrium," a state which represents the production–consumption optimum attainable with the given resources under the prevailing order of income distribution. We shall presently examine the implicit sociological and technological assumptions on which this optimistic verdict rests. At this point, however, we are interested in appraising the usefulness of classical and neoclassical models as paradigms for predicting the course of contemporary industrial market processes.

Nothing is simpler than to compile a long list of failures in prediction if the above-stated criterion—accurate forecasting of the *direction* of macro- or micro-movements—is applied to the cyclical changes in the United States over the last two decades. I have dealt with this issue extensively in my book,[6] pointing out there that even the showpiece of recent predictive efforts—the Kennedy tax revision—proves inconclusive, since the upturn in investment preceded the actual tax reduction by a year. And the tug-of-war about the imminence of inflation or deflation that rages while this is being written in December, 1966, does not inspire any more confidence in our ability to predict.[7]

In this connection, preliminary results obtained from a forecasting model that postdates the publication of *OEK* teach an even more impressive lesson. I refer to the Quarterly Econometric Model for the United States, developed from Professor Klein's original model by the Office of Business Economics in the Department of Commerce.[8] The model, dealing with the period from 1953 to 1965, has managed to circumvent some of the basic obstacles that usually hamper economic forecasting. It is actually concerned with "postdiction," because a system of simultaneous equations incorporating what are regarded as the strategic cause–effect relationships is tested *ex post* on statistical material available from observations of the past. This procedure has made it possible to assign to the exogenous variables their actual values. Moreover, the results concern the very period that contained the data to which the model's equations were originally fitted. In spite of these special characteristics, both of which carry a highly favorable bias, the predictions of cyclical turning points have consistently proved to be wrong when made more than two quarters ahead.

Still, in trying to account for these failures, the champions of modern predictive techniques offer some weighty counterarguments. Do we not meet with similar difficulties, they ask, in meteorology—difficulties which the workers in that field are confident of overcoming with the improvement of their research tools? Should we not therefore check our impatience in an enterprise like econometrics that is only two or three decades old? Moreover, is it not true that the observations on which the traditional hypotheses are to be tested reflect an empirical state of affairs in which growing imperfections of competition have removed a prime condition of the traditional model: unconstrained freedom of decision-making on the part of the micro-units?

6 *OEK*, pp. 52–56, 60–61.

7 For many more examples and for a discussion of the variety of predictive techniques employed, see Sidney Schoeffler, *The Failures of Economics* (Cambridge: Harvard University Press, 1955), Chaps. 5 and 6.

8 See *Survey of Current Business*, U. S. Department of Commerce, 46, No. 5 (May, 1966), 13–29.

In deference to such apologies I have fallen back in *OEK* on some general methodological considerations that offer certain criteria for the predictability of economic events *independent* of the usefulness of any particular technique. These considerations center in the fact that economic systems are "open" systems in a very special sense.

As conventionally understood,[9] an open system is a configuration in which the interplay of the intra-systemic forces—the core process—cannot be insulated from the impact of extra-systemic or environmental factors. Under this aspect the comparison of economics with meteorology seems pertinent, since in both cases the nature of the research object makes it impossible to subject the intra-systemic variables to artificial isolation in the laboratory. And yet the analogy begs a fundamental question. If what we observe are always the results of the "impure" experiments that nature and history perform for us—experiments in which intra- and extra-systemic variables are inseparably joined—how can we know that there is any independent core process on which a theory can be built?

As a matter of fact, a satisfactory answer to this question can be given as far as meteorology is concerned.[10] There all the forces, however complex their interplay may be, obey the laws of physics and chemistry, laws which themselves have been tested outside the context in which the meteorologist uses them. In other words, the behavior of the elementary variables is not in doubt, and the true problem of the researcher consists in making the set of such variables inclusive enough to cover all essential influences. This is not an easy task, but it is a technical rather than a theoretical one whose solution is greatly facilitated by modern computers.

Alas, the economist has no such means of testing the elementary laws of motion outside of the economic circuit. And even if he had, he would only run up against another difficulty which his fellow workers in the physical sciences are apparently spared. A simple example will illustrate the salient point. To predict the actual movements of a projectile, the physicist must "add" to the impact of the intra-systemic forces acting on a body falling freely in a vacuum the retarding effect of the atmosphere, the deflection due to movements of the air, and the measurable influence of any other relevant extra-systemic factor. Can we, in analogy with this procedure, predict the effect of a tax reduction on aggregate demand by adding to the current flow of spending a flow equal to the size of the tax relief of business and public, minus an estimated amount of this incre-

---

9 See Schoeffler, *op. cit.*, Chaps. 4 and 8. See also Emile Grunberg, "The Meaning of Scope and External Boundaries of Economics," in *The Structure of Economic Science: Essays on Methodology* (Englewood Cliffs, N. J.: Prentice-Hall, Inc., 1966), pp. 148–165.

10 Grunberg, *op. cit.*, p. 151.

ment withheld from circulation, plus or minus any monetary flow which other extra-systemic forces may set in motion or shut off?

Suppose that all these latter influences can be strictly calculated. We will still arrive at a confirmable prediction only if, in analogy with the situation in mechanics, the tax reduction and the other extra-systemic changes *will not in turn affect the behavioral forces that govern the current flow of spending.* But is it permissible to transfer the postulate of "noninteraction" between intra- and extra-systemic forces from physics to economics?

Let us suppose that in 1963 investors and consumers had interpreted the proposed tax cut as a public confession of grave trouble ahead—a response which was in fact feared by some highly experienced governmental experts. The total flow of spending, rather than rising in anticipation of a boom, might then have dropped well below the level prevailing before the tax cut. This is, of course, precisely the manner in which private investment reacted to increased public spending during the New Deal. All this only restates for a specific case what was pointed out in general terms earlier when market expectations were defined as commonsense predictions on the part of the economic actors. For it is just here that all methodological analogies between physics and economics break down. These analogies overlook "the difference between insensitive particles responding blindly though lawfully to blind stimuli, and purposeful actors who 'move' only after they have interpreted their field of action in terms of their goals and their commonsense knowledge." [11] And in these interpretations the impact of the environmental factors plays a strategic role.

As a matter of fact, the interdependence between the forces of the core process and those emanating from the environment is still closer. Not only are all significant *changes* of the extra-systemic variables bound to affect the intra-systemic ones, but even in a *changeless* environment, behavior and motivations acquire their strength and direction from the continuous impact which natural, social, and technical factors exert on what for purely didactic purposes have been set apart as "economic" phenomena. For this reason economic systems are "open" in a more fundamental sense than is true of any physical system including meteorology. Not even ideally can the autonomous economic core processes be treated as closed, and the validity of the results of "mental experiments" based on the *ceteris paribus* condition cannot be taken for granted beyond the particular set of variables from which they are derived. Rather, theoretical generalizations and, especially, predictions are contingent on what environmental factors do to the core factors of behavior

[11] *OEK*, p. 61.

and motivation from case to case. If their impact creates and maintains "order" in the inclusive sense defined above, theory and predictability are assured. But when the uncontrolled impact of the environment tends to induce "disorderly" micro-behavior, the viability of the industrial market, as well as its theoretical comprehensibility, depends on our ability to devise controls that, in fact and not only by methodological fiction, "close" the system against disruptive forces.

Disorder in Mature Industrialism

We now arrive at the crucial issue. It is my contention that orderly motion of the *intra*-systemic variables—behavior and motivation—although characteristic of the early phase of industrial capitalism, no longer prevails in the key sectors of contemporary markets. This is equivalent to asserting that the behavioral and motivational premises on which all classical and neoclassical theorizing rests are progressively losing realistic significance.

The premises in question are, at the behavioral level, the appropriate negative feedback responses that hold all economic motions to an equilibrating course. These responses have been formalized in the so-called "law of supply and demand," and are supposed to arise as the joint effect of two motivational subpatterns: first, the action directive of maximizing pecuniary receipts and minimizing pecuniary expenditures—what in *OEK* has been defined as the "extremum principle"—and second, what is described in *OEK* as "stabilizing expectations"—namely, price expectations with less than unit elasticity, the limit being zero elasticity, and quantity expectations with positive elasticity.[12] As a result, a present rise in price will induce buyers, in the interest of minimizing expenditures, to shift purchases from the present to the future—that is, to reduce demand. Sellers on their part will be induced, in the interest of maximizing receipts, to shift sales from the future to the present—that is, to increase supply.[13]

There is no doubt that these premises underlie all traditional economic analyses, including the main body of the Keynesian system, not to mention the bulk of the econometric models employed for prediction. What is more difficult to demonstrate, having become for this reason the target of a good deal of criticism, is my contention that, on the one

---

[12] Let me add a brief word of explanation for noneconomists. What is meant by this state of expectations is that price changes are expected to be merely temporary, while quantities offered are expected to rise as prices rise and to fall as they fall.

[13] For details see *OEK*, Chap. 2, Sec. 2.

hand, these premises did depict the actual state of affairs in early capitalism, and on the other hand, they do not do so today.

To the extent to which the "facts of life" are to give support to these assertions, it is easier to prove the latter thesis, if only because we know so much more about the behavior and motivation of contemporary marketers. My book enumerates in some detail the many incentives which today contend with the single-valued extremum principle.[14] As the reader can convince himself, this was not meant to deny that a subjective desire to maximize pecuniary receipts is still the dominant action directive of business. *The essential point is that such maximization has itself lost its classical determinacy,* because the time span over which profits are to be maximized can no longer be defined once and for all. In the modern technical and organizational environment, indivisibility of resources, periods of investment and production, the size of financial commitments, etc., vary from branch to branch, possibly from firm to firm, and even in the same firm from time to time. Consequently, *opposite actions, such as an increase or decrease of output, or the raising or lowering of prices, can each be justified as the most promising step for profit maximization.*

The same indeterminacy of the economic time horizon has undermined the stability of expectations, inducing divergent actions even under the rule of the same action directive whenever the evaluation of future market conditions changes. There is, in addition, a disturbing feedback effect from uncertain expectations to action directives, because a lower level of profits that is expected with greater certainty may well become preferable to a higher but less certain one.

Altogether I feel on safe ground in speaking of a wide spectrum of action directives and expectations as prevailing in the modern scene, in stark contrast to the simplistic assumptions of Traditional Economics. If this is granted, it may appear to be a question of minor importance whether in an earlier stage of industrial capitalism actual behavior and motivations conformed more closely to the premises of classical and neoclassical economics. This would indeed be so were it not that the thesis offers important clues to the fundamental causes of the present "disorder" in market behavior and the resulting impasse in traditional theory.

Briefly, the thesis of a more orderly motion of the processes of early capitalism is derived from the recognition of certain social and technical determinants of marketers' motivations, determinants which tended to bring the latter in conformity with the theoretical postulates of the extremum principle and of stabilizing expectations. Among these determinants were, first, the *automatic pressures* exerted on the action directives of the several social strata by mass poverty, unbridled competition,

---

[14] *OEK,* pp. 46–49.

and an intellectual and moral climate favoring the accumulation of wealth, which made the maximization of receipts and minimization of expenditures a condition of economic if not physical survival. A second determinant was the then-prevailing *mobility of resources* that resulted from the smallness and nonspecificity of capital equipment and the newly won "free circulation of labor from one employment to another" (Adam Smith). This mobility very much shortened the time horizon for adjustment to changes in demand and technology—a prime condition for stabilizing expectations in a laissez-faire market. A third and supplementary determinant took the form of what in *OEK* is defined as *automatic escapements*, in particular the rising rate of growth through rapid population increase, a steady stream of innovations, and the opening of new markets. Through constant stimulation of aggregate demand, these escapements compensated for temporary dislocations and strengthened the stability of expectations by limiting the amplitude and duration of cyclical downswings.

It must be admitted that the empirical data referring to the actual incentives and expectations of that period are much too scanty to serve as a reliable test for the above hypothesis, but they certainly do not contradict it. Moreover, the traditional formulation of the law of supply and demand, in which the classical premises about economic motivations are embodied, dominated the folklore of that age and even today expresses the "conventional wisdom" with which the average businessman tries to interpret his experience.

That these attempts are not too successful is not surprising in the light of what was said above about the growing indeterminacy of profit maximization, and about the prevailing uncertainty of expectations. Nowadays, rising prices are often accompanied by rising demand and falling prices, rather than by the "correct" response of falling demand and rising prices. What is important is the fact that such divergences of economic motion from the model of classical and neoclassical economics can be easily understood once we take note of the striking historical changes in the original determinants of action directives and expectations. Practically all the social forces that once combined to exert pressure toward extremum motivation have greatly weakened. The consummation of the Industrial Revolution and the democratization of the Western social systems have liberated the masses from the bondage of extreme scarcity; self-organization of producers and interventions of governmental policy culminating in the public controls of the welfare state have mitigated the fierceness of competition, and the earlier system of cultural values extolling acquisitiveness is giving way to what, by the criterion of the classical laws of the market, must be judged as capricious behavior. At the same time large-scale technology and the long-term financial commitments it demands, coupled with the spread of monopoly in the markets of goods and productive services, are progressively immobilizing the flow of resources, thus extending the time span over which dispositions must be made, as well as reducing the subjective certainty and objective accuracy of business expectations. On the other hand, persistent international tensions and political unrest in many underdeveloped regions, coupled with growing resistance to foreign capital imports in mature economies, hamper the exploitation of vast potential investment opportunities, thus lessening the effectiveness of one of the main escapement mechanisms of an earlier era.

Most of these changes can be taken as symptoms of an affluent society, and as such the inherent "disorder" of modern industrial markets represents a significant victory of Western man over his environment and a breakthrough into a new realm of freedom. However, we have received ample warning that we must not blindly surrender to this liberation of the behavioral forces. If anything, the Great Depression taught us a lesson about what is likely to happen to an industrial market society that is no longer disciplined by the automatic constraints of the past and, at the same time, lacks an arsenal of compensatory contrived controls. The shock of this experience marks the turning point toward Political Economics as here understood, both as a new theoretical frame of reference and a new practice of public policy.

THE CONSTRUCTIVE FUNCTION OF POLITICAL ECONOMICS [15]

The Instrumental-Deductive Method

From the outset it was emphasized that Political Economics, like Traditional Economics, is a theoretical science. As such it tries to derive a past state of the system (explanation) or a future state (prediction) from the knowledge of a given state (initial conditions) and from some "law of motion." The difference between the two approaches lies in the manner in which the law of motion and its more remote determinants are established. In Traditional Economics either they result from a process of induction—that is, from the generalization of observations concerning, say, actual behavioral and motivational patterns—or they are postulated as heuristic principles independent of any observation, as, for example, the extremum principle is treated in "positive" economics. Still, whatever their origin, these generalizations or postulates serve as fundamental assumptions or highest-level hypotheses, and as such belong among the

---

[15] *OEK*, Chaps. 5, 10, and 11.

knowns of economic reasoning from which the unknown states of the system can be deduced.

As our critical comments have shown, Political Economics denies that, under the conditions of contemporary capitalism, either observation of actual phenomena or heuristic postulation can come up with highest-level hypotheses capable of functioning as "once-and-for-all" valid premises from which confirmable predictions can be derived. Rather it insists that the actual forces that rule economic movements and, in particular, bring about a change in their direction, cannot be known *a priori*, but themselves fall in the category of unknowns. Therefore, a major task of Political Economics consists in devising an analytical technique through which these unknowns can be determined.

In order to understand the precise role of this technique, which I have called *instrumental inference* (or, as now seems to me preferable, instrumental *analysis*), we should compare it with the part played by induction in the traditional procedure of the so-called "hypothetico-deductive" method. In the practical employment of this method, emphasis rests on deduction: that is, on the "progressive" inferences that can be drawn from the premises—the alleged laws of economic behavior and motivation—to conclusions concerning past or future states of the system. In other words, once these premises have been established, they are taken for granted, and their validity is no longer checked each time a concrete explanation or prediction is to be undertaken. But this concentration on deduction when it comes to the *application* of a theory must not blind us to the fact that in the original act of theory *formation*, the premises of the deductive syllogism, are themselves unknown and must be determined by a "regressive" procedure from known observations.

In the reasoning of Political Economics, instrumental analysis is equivalent to this original act of regression in the conventional method. It too searches for explanatory hypotheses which subsequently can serve as premises in a deductive syllogism. And it applies the same procedure, arguing backward from a given phenomenon to its determinants. We shall presently see that such terms as "given phenomenon" or "determinant" take on a new meaning in instrumental analysis and that, substantively, we move there in quite another dimension of experience. But awareness of the formal similarity between the hypothetico-deductive method and what is called here the instrumental-deductive method may facilitate the understanding of the latter.

Perhaps the easiest access to the core of instrumental analysis is through the inclusive concept of *order* we established earlier. It will be remembered that this concept combined the "positive" notion of order of state and motion with the "normative" notion of the satisfactory functioning of the economy as a "system"—satisfactory, that is, when judged by criteria such as a stipulated state of resource utilization, aggregate output, income distribution, etc. Now it is a main characteristic of all traditional reasoning before Keynes that in concentrating on the positive study of micro- and macro-motions and the manner in which these individual motions integrated themselves into aggregate states and processes, it treated these states and processes as the more or less inexorable result of unalterable behavioral forces. This did not exclude the *ex post* evaluation of this result under the normative aspect referred to, nor did it rule out attempts to bring the outcome of the autonomous operation of the market in line with accepted welfare goals through measures of public control. But the idea that such goals might serve as *ex ante yardsticks* for the conscious *shaping* of the macro-states and -processes would have been regarded as a collectivist anomaly and as such incompatible with the nature of decentralized decision-making.

It is perhaps the most radical of Keynes' many innovations that he broke with this tradition. The following quote taken from *OEK* expresses what seems to me his decisive turn in the direction of instrumental analysis:

> *Though [Keynes'] immediate problem is the disequilibria and pseudo-equilibria engendered by lapses of the market from the state of full employment, he does not confine himself to merely explaining and predicting these events which have no place in the orthodox model. By demonstrating that equilibrium and equilibration in the traditional sense are the exceptions rather than the rule in the real world, he has restored awareness of the normative character of these notions. And the entire analytical effort reveals itself as ultimately devoted to the task of determining the requirements for the attainment of a macro-goal—full employment—which is postulated independently of actual experience. Moreover, when the major condition for such attainment turns out to be the substitution, in the sphere of investment, of a novel behavioral force for the traditional decision-making of the micro-units, the realm of instrumental analysis has been entered.*[16]

Instrumental analysis is, then, a generalization of Keynes' concern with the requirements for the attainment of full employment; it extends the range of macro-goals, for which the requirements are to be determined, to any conceivable state or process stipulated as desirable. And it systematically analyzes these requirements—or, as we shall henceforth call them, *conditions suitable for goal attainment*—into their macro- and micro-components. In doing so, instrumental analysis "inverts" the theoretical problem by treating some of the knowns of traditional analysis as unknown and, conversely, by treating the major unknowns of traditional analysis—the terminal states and processes—as known. Or to state

---

[16] *OEK*, p. 218.

the same idea in a different form, the traditional procedure of deriving an effect from given causes is transposed into a procedure by which suitable means are derived from given ends. Under this aspect, instrumental analysis can be called the *logic of economic goal-seeking*.[17]

In explicating this logical structure we begin with the *unknowns*. They are enumerated here in the sequence in which instrumental analysis tries to determine them, each subsequent step depending on the successful accomplishment of the prior one: (1) the *path* or the succession of macro-states of the system suitable to transform a given initial state into a stipulated terminal state; (2) *patterns of micro-behavior* appropriate to keeping the system to the suitable path; (3) *micro-motivations* capable of generating suitable behavior; and (4) *a state of the environment* including, possibly though not necessarily, political controls designed to stimulate suitable motivations.[18]

These unknowns are to be determined with the help of the following *knowns:* (1) the *initial state* of the system under investigation; (2) a *macro-goal* specified as a terminal state, either by stipulating the "numerical values of the target variables" (Tinbergen) or by stipulating the qualitative interrelations among the target variables in terms of, say, a Pareto optimum, full resource utilization, or a steady rate of growth; and (3) certain *laws, rules, and empirical generalizations* with whose help the suitability of means for the attainment of ends can be established.

The specific procedure by which the unknowns can be derived from the knowns will be illustrated below in an elementary example. But first a brief comment is due on the role that is assigned here to the macrogoals.

The Terminal State as Datum

The "inversion" of the analytical procedure referred to above finds one expression in the change of role of the terminal state from the major

---

[17] I refrain from calling instrumental analysis a "teleological" method of inquiry because this label is too often used to indicate that a given procedure is incompatible with causal analysis. That the instrumental approach is fully compatible with cause–effect relations follows from the subsequent application of its results to deductive inferences in which the originally unknown "means" appear, after their instrumental determination, as known "causes" of effects to be explained or predicted. At the same time it is true that the suitability of a "cause" as a "means" for bringing about a stipulated goal cannot be judged without knowledge of the goal itself. In this sense a "telos" enters the search procedure by which the suitable means-causes are to be discovered.

[18] In order to establish full generality for this logic of goal-seeking, we must speak of "suitability," "appropriateness," etc., rather than of "requirements," because there are, as a rule, alternative paths, behavior patterns, motivations, and states of the environment which all can serve as means to the stipulated end. Thus we deal with sufficient rather than necessary conditions.

unknown into a datum. This change is less striking if we compare instrumental analysis, as we should, with its methodological counterpart: inductive rather than deductive inference. Still, there remains an important difference between these two regressive procedures, which concerns the nature of the "facts" from which they take their bearings. In the case of induction these facts are *observed* terminal states—namely, the realized effects of causes to be discovered. In sharp contrast, instrumental analysis starts out from a *stipulated* terminal state which (except in the marginal case when the macro-goal is stipulated as preservation of the initial state) is beyond present observation and which, whenever Political Economics fails to solve its problem, may not even become observable in the future.

This is not to imply that the choice of an economic macro-goal is an arbitrary act. In the concluding section of this paper a few words will be said about this problem. But it is intuitively obvious that such a discussion will carry us beyond the realm of facts and factual relations into the region of value judgments—a region in which discursive thinking, and thus scientific inquiry as the modern mind understands it, cannot by themselves offer final answers. At any rate, the processes by which goals are chosen are not the subject of *economic* studies, and in the latter the macro-goals of instrumental analysis would have to play the role of data, even if reason or revelation—philosophy or theology—were able to present us with "intersubjectively demonstrable" criteria.[19]

---

[19] In this context I have sometimes been asked why I had to coin the term "instrumental" analysis instead of simply speaking of "normative" analysis in line with the recent practice of distinguishing between "descriptive" or "positive" and "prescriptive" or "normative" economics. In the latter dichotomy traditional theory is assigned to the first category, whereas welfare economics, for example, is placed in the second. My answer is that I have tried to avoid a confusion which seems to be inherent in the current terminology.

There is little danger of misunderstanding so far as the first category is concerned. But when we classify welfare economics as simply a normative procedure, we fail to take into account that it is concerned with two quite different problems whose solutions require quite different procedures. One refers to the choice of the most desirable objectives or, in another formulation, to the decision as to whether one collection of goods is greater in terms of welfare than some other collection. Such choices and decisions and the establishment of the guiding criteria indeed fall in the normative realm. But this is by no means so with the other problem of selecting the *means* for achieving these objectives or the *methods* of producing the chosen collection. These are issues that are open to discursive reasoning and are thus proper subjects of scientific analysis. This remains true even if the quest is for "optimum" methods of goal attainment. In that case the discovery of the criteria for optimization is again a normative problem. But the subsequent application of such criteria to the selection of means is a purely analytical task.

What instrumental analysis tries to achieve parallels the analytical part of welfare economics—determining the means suitable for the attainment of given goals. And though drawing on the results of normative judgment for one of its *data,* it derives its own propositions by "positive" reasoning.

However, there is another issue connected with the choice of macro-goals that poses a genuine scientific problem. It is mentioned in *OEK* [20] as an afterthought, but deserves stronger emphasis as a preparatory stage of instrumental analysis proper. It refers to the implicit assumption that the different aspirations of a goal-setter are mutually compatible and can be translated into a consistent and realizable set of targets.

For certain types of goals, such as those that are concerned with a rearrangement of employed or latent resources, these prerequisites are in the nature of the case always fulfilled. This is not so, however, if for example a specific level of output or a certain rate of growth is stipulated, especially if the terminal state is further qualified by optimization criteria, such as the maintenance of a certain level of consumption or of stable prices. In all such cases the search for the suitable means must be preceded by a study of the compatibility of the several goals with one another and with the stock of available resources. Fortunately, the various techniques of mathematical programming are providing us with a growing arsenal of tools with whose help the "feasibility" of a program can be established, taking into consideration all encountered and stipulated constraints.

In passing, it should be noted that such complementarity between instrumental analysis and mathematical programming is by no means accidental. Both procedures are goal-oriented, even if the analytical interest of mathematical programming, like that of welfare economics, is more limited. This interest is confined to the technical arrangements through which a stipulated bill of goods materializes or some objective function is maximized or minimized, while it disregards the behavioral and motivational forces at work. Under this aspect the complementarity of the two procedures is mutual: mathematical programming provides the ground from which instrumental analysis takes its bearing, and the latter transforms the technocratic insights of the former into genuine socio-economic knowledge.

What Laws and Rules Link Ends and Means?

No other proposition relating to instrumental analysis has aroused as critical a response as did the alleged contradiction in my asserting, on the one hand, that there are today no reliable laws of economic behavior on which predictions can be based, and, on the other hand, that it is possible to derive, from the knowledge of an initial and a stipulated terminal state, paths and forces suitable to transform the former into the

---

[20] *OEK*, p. 263.

latter. What else is it but a prediction, the critics ask, if a particular behavior pattern is selected as suitable to set the system on a path that will lead to a stipulated goal? Or, more concretely, how does one know that a rise in the rate of investment is a suitable means of promoting employment, or that the incentive of receipt maximization coupled with positive elasticities of price and quantity expectations will be suitable to stimulate investment decisions? To make such statements, is it not necessary to appeal to laws and rules that relate specific means to specific ends, and to derive the latter as effects from the former as causes?

Far from denying any of these propositions, I am in full agreement on this point with my critics, as I have pointed out in several passages.[21] At the same time I have insisted that the laws and rules which permit us to predict what means are suitable for the attainment of a given end are of a nature quite different from what passes in Traditional Economics as laws of economic behavior, such as the law of supply and demand. At this point let me briefly indicate the nature of these differences, and subsequently discuss the details at greater length.

1. The relationship between ends and means is a problem of technology in the broadest sense. Applied to the realm of economics, in which the relation of matter as a means to human ends plays a strategic role, the problem is one of material technology. Therefore, once the ends, including their hierarchical order, are stipulated, the suitability of means is determined, first of all, by the currently known rules of engineering.

2. Knowledge of such engineering rules, and of certain mathematical theorems that permit the determination of suitable quantitative relations, is all that is required to establish both goal-adequate paths and, within a given sociopsychological environment, goal-adequate behavior. Since the question of whether the goal-adequate path and behavior actually materialize is *not* posed at this stage, there is no need for any "laws of behavior" of the type that states: If behavior A occurs, then behavior B will follow. Rather the "law" implied in these engineering rules states: If behavior A occurs, the state C will follow.

3. For the determination of goal-adequate motivations, it is necessary to take into account, in addition to a knowledge of goal-adequate behavior, a psychological hypothesis that relates specific motivations to specific behavior. However, if accepted at all, this hypothesis is of such generality that its validity extends far beyond the economic realm.

4. Only when instrumental analysis regresses to the point where economic motivations are to be related to environmental factors—a step

---

[21] *OEK*, pp. 141–143, 253, Chap. 11 *passim*.

that is necessary if the deductive part of Political Economics is to be completed—does a causal problem arise that is formally comparable with, but substantively quite different from, the cause–effect relations formulated in the laws of Traditional Economics.

Now let us consider these four points *in extenso*.

1. *The role of technology.* In placing the technological aspect of economics in the center of instrumental analysis, I do not wish to intimate that economics is nothing but technology, or that the investigation of man–matter relations is its only concern. Outside of the methodological fiction of a Crusoe economy, all real economic processes are the combined result of technological and sociological forces, so that the man–matter relationships always operate through the prevailing man–man relationships. But this does not alter the fact that, once we have stipulated a definite state of provision with goods and services—that is, a feasible program of production and/or distribution—the search for the suitable means is first of all a study of the suitable materials, devices, and processes—in a word, a technological problem. From this it follows that the sociopsychological forces that must be called upon for the realization of the stipulated program are themselves suitable only to the extent to which they are compatible with, and promoters of, the technological prerequisites.[22]

2. *Engineering rules as instrumental criteria for path and behavior.* Technological relations, such as those that determine the suitability of specific materials, devices, and processes for the realization of a feasible program of production and distribution, are governed by rules of engineering, understood in the comprehensive sense of physical, chemical, and biological manipulations. These rules themselves are derived from the apposite laws of nature, which thus reveal themselves as the ultimate determinants of instrumental relationships. To these determinants the rules governing socioeconomic relations—behavioral and motivational patterns—will have to adapt themselves if the stipulated goals are to be attained.

---

[22] This is not the place to reopen the dispute between the "materialistic" and the "praxiological" conceptions of economic theory. In *OEK*, Chap. 1, Sec. 2, and Chap. 8, Secs. 3–5, I have restated the well-known reasons why the extension of economic theory into a "generalized theory of choice" is bound to deprive it of any substantive content, reducing its propositions to mere tautologies. Professor Boulding's recent inclusion of painters among economic men because, just as the consumer may have to sacrifice "a little ham for a little more eggs in a breakfast," the painter "sacrifices . . . a little red for a little more green" (*Scientific American*, May, 1965, p. 139), has only strengthened my conviction. Or are we to assume that "optimum painting" amounts to maximization of colors by the square inch of canvas? Poor Rembrandt!

In Chapter 11 of *OEK* I have demonstrated this proposition on three test cases: maintaining a stationary process, stabilizing a market economy in the sense of raising it from a level of underutilization to that of full utilization of resources, and balancing a system undergoing growth by assuring continuous absorption of resource increments and of increases in productivity. In particular, it could be shown that application of the pertinent engineering rules to the creation of characteristic equalities and inequalities among the components of the system is all that is required for the determination of the *path*—that is, a sequence of states of the aggregate suitable for transforming the initial into the terminal configuration. I cannot repeat this demonstration within the limits of this paper. All I can do here is to illustrate it briefly with reference to the simplest—but for that reason least realistic—example: stationary equilibrium. For a discussion that goes beyond an elementary exercise, the reader must consult the original text.

For our purposes stationary equilibrium must be understood, not as a methodological device, but as the structural model of an economic macro-goal. What is singular in this model is the fact that the initial state is structurally identical with the terminal state or, speaking in terms of a process, that the path of the system presents itself as a steady sequence of identical states.

Since by assumption we deal with an industrial system in which all productive processes are supposed to require the employment of real capital as an input, the stationary structure of production can be conceived as a three-sectoral model. Disregarding the input of natural resources, we can say that in each sector certain quantities of labor and fixed capital or equipment goods combine to produce specific outputs, the sum of all sector inputs exhausting the available supply of resources so that full utilization is continually maintained. We also disregard the "vertical" order of the stages in which, in each sector, natural resources are gradually transformed into finished goods. The outputs are then all finished goods, which consist of three physical types: primary equipment goods issuing in sector I and capable of producing equipment goods, secondary equipment goods issuing in sector II and capable of producing consumer goods, and, finally, consumer goods issuing in sector III. For simplicity it is assumed that the specificity of the three types of output is absolute.

At first sight one might suspect that all that can be said about the path suitable for maintaining such a stationary process is that there must be continuity of the processes of production in the three sectors. Such continuity—the maintenance of well-circumscribed engineering processes—is certainly a necessary condition, but it is by no means sufficient. Continuity of outputs presupposes continuity of inputs. As far as labor input is concerned, we may conceive of it as a meta-economic issue, treating the steady "replacement" of "worn-out" labor as a datum. We certainly cannot do so with regard to equipment. Rather the assumed tripartite structure of production is a consequence of the technological fact that the provision of equipment is an intra-economic problem, equipment being not only an input but also an output. In other words, continuous output of consumer goods in sector III is conditional on the steady replacement of worn-out secondary equipment through the steady output of such equipment in sector II. In turn, such output of secondary equipment depends on the condition that the primary equipment, which produces secondary equipment in sector II, is steadily replaced from the output in sector I. But sector I can provide such replacement only if its own equipment stock is steadily maintained. This amounts to the further condition that the aggregate output in sector I must be large enough to steadily replace the worn-out equipment in both sectors I and II.

From these elementary observations it follows that, to maintain steady production in the system, not only must each sector produce its respective output, but parts of this output must be "moved" by other engineering processes from the producing sector into some "utilizing" sector. The same is obviously true of the output consisting of consumer goods, whose aggregate must be distributed among the workers of all three sectors. Were we to adopt the classical position which, in some fashion, interprets the output of consumer goods as the "fuel" that rekindles the working energy of labor, the conception of the path as an engineering process would be further strengthened.

In these physical processes in which inputs are transformed and outputs are shifted, definite quantitative relations must be maintained between inputs and outputs within each sector, between the outputs of the three sectors, and between that part of each sector's output which is applied "at home" and that part which is "exported" to other sectors. We can indeed conceive of the stationary path in analogy with a system of triangular trade relations for which zero surplus balances are stipulated. Obviously the size and proportions of the exchanges that bring about such zero trade balances can be determined without prior knowledge of the "forces"—centralized or decentralized decision-making and the respective behavior patterns—through which such balances are established and maintained. In the same manner, the course of the *suitable* stationary path can be derived without any knowledge of the *actual* behavior of the productive agents, on which, of course, the realization of such a path depends. Rather the instrumental dependence is reversed: not until we know the technologically determined path are we able to "select" the behavioral patterns that are suitable to keep the system to that path.[23]

Thus the suitable behavior of human agents, whether they are productive factors offering their services, managers combining these services according to productive requirements, or distributive agents moving the outputs toward their final destination as objects of consumption or replacement, is nothing but a mode of application of the pertinent engineering rules. It throws some light on the merely "subsidiary" role which these human actions play that there is, at least in principle, an alternative means of realizing the engineering requirements: automation. I am using the term here in the general sense of all mechanical, thermal, and chemical manipulations which at earlier levels of technological developments were performed by human actors. For our present purposes it is convenient to imagine complete automation of all processes of production and distribution to the point where human decision-making is limited to goal-setting—that is, to decisions that concern the content of the output menu and the specific techniques to be applied, and to the acts of programming the computers. Whatever probability we may want to assign to the eventual advent of such a regime, its image offers an intuitive confirmation of the fundamental thesis that, once the goal is set, the structure of the path and the operation of the active "forces" suitable for goal attainment—human or subhuman—can be derived from the knowledge of engineering rules alone.

This is not to say that, as long as human decisions participate in the application of these rules, we can disregard the social setting in which economic processes occur when we try to establish path-adequate behavior patterns. To take the two extremes of economic organization—monolithic collectivism and a laissez-faire market—it is evident that the behavior patterns appropriate to centralized command and subordinate execution differ drastically from the anonymous price–quantity manipulations through which the market operates. One can interpret the respective behavioral patterns as elements of a vast information system and thus establish the basis for another analogy with the cybernetics of a fully automated economy. But this must not blind us to the fact that, at least in the present state of our knowledge, the "sensorium" through which human agents communicate, the manner in which their "responses" are elicited, and the secondary responses ("sanctions") which the primary responses draw, seem radically different from the mechanical or electronic stimulus–response relations in an automated system.

---

[23] For details see *OEK*, Chap. 11, Secs. 3–5. For a more extensive treatment, including the quantitative determination of sector ratios and inter-sectoral equilibrium conditions, see my paper, "Structural Analysis of Real Capital Formation," in *Capital Formation and Economic Growth* (Princeton, N. J.: Princeton University Press, 1955). See especially pp. 591–597.

In order to translate the input–output configurations that represent the path into a suitable chain of coordinated actions, we must know the nature of the prevailing signal system and the social rules according to which information is communicated and specific action solicited. But it must be realized that the meaning of the signals through which information is conveyed is by no means intrinsically fixed. In principle, a market is operable just as well under the rule that rising prices indicate excess supply, as under the conventional rule according to which they indicate excess demand. All that is necessary to insure an interlocking of behavior patterns is consistency in the use of the informative symbols.

At the same time it cannot be stated often enough that even such consistency in interpretation can only tell us what action *if taken* will agree with the pre-established path; it cannot assure us that these actions *will be taken in fact*. It is true that even in a fully automated system, goal realization is threatened by mechanical or electronical failures. But the possibility of goal-*in*adequate responses is inherent in a system that must rely for its driving force on spontaneous human behavior.

3. *The nexus between behavior and motivation.*   This indeterminacy at the level of behavioral responses is the reason why instrumental analysis cannot stop short at the study of behavior, but must pursue its regressive course to the level of motivation. In other words, we must inquire what motivations are suitable to induce goal-adequate behavior. Naturally, this step leads beyond the territory where engineering rules dominate, into the realm of functional or dynamic psychology. This is not the place to embark upon a systematic discussion of the relationship between behavior and motivation, and I certainly lack professional competence for such a task. Fortunately, all we need for our purposes is the acceptance of the hypothesis that, in the absence of external constraints, overt economic behavior can be predicted if the underlying action directive and expectations are known. This then makes it possible to infer regressively from a known behavior one or more motivational compounds that are suitable to induce that behavior.

To illustrate this proposition by our previous example, we start out from a behavioral rule formulated in accord with the guidelines given above. Once the stationary path has been established (its establishment is a dynamic process with its own rules), suitable behavior to maintain it consists in routinized repetition of the actions that achieve the physical transformations and shifts prescribed by the pertinent engineering rules. Now we ask what compounds of motivations are suitable for the establishment of such behavioral routine. Focusing on a market system, we come up with alternative answers: either the extremum incentive as action directive coupled with zero elasticity of price and quantity expectations, or homeostatic action directives coupled with the same type of expectations.

For a proof we assume—along the lines of modern stability analysis, of which our discussion is an amplification—that, accidentally, managers in the consumer goods sector raise their demand for secondary equipment beyond their current replacement needs and, possibly, even offer higher unit prices. If the price and quantity expectations of the producers of secondary equipment are positive, the extremum incentive will induce them to expand output. Contrariwise, while striving for maintenance of asset values—a homeostatic incentive—the same expectations will induce them to contract output. Either response, instead of eliminating the accidental distortion, tends to perpetuate it. Only zero elasticity of expectations—namely, disregard of present changes in demand and price—will in either case maintain the stationary relations among the sectoral outputs, and thus assure the stability of the system.

In discussing growth processes, I have come up against a number of quite varied motivational compounds as suitable conditions for behavior in successive stages leading to balanced growth.[24] But once the behavior patterns themselves have been regressively derived from the engineering rules governing the path, it is, in principle, always possible to infer suitable motivational substructures.

4. *The link between motivation and control.* Before carrying our regressive procedure to completion, we had better review what instrumental analysis has proved capable of achieving up to this point. It is meant to serve as an alternative to the traditional procedure by which the intra-systemic forces either are derived by induction or are postulated as heuristic principles. Instead, instrumental analysis derives these patterns by regressively relating a stipulated terminal state to an observable initial state. Furthermore, it does so without recourse to any "laws of economic behavior," but by invoking pertinent "laws of subhuman nature" and engineering rules derived from them.

These claims appear as fully vindicated. Once we know the apposite engineering rules and the social organization that sustains the economic processes under examination (a datum which is included in the knowledge of the initial state), and once we accept the hypothesis that specific behavior can be derived from specific motivational compounds, we indeed arrive at a precise definition of the paths and the underlying behavioral and motivational patterns that connect the initial and terminal states.

But now suppose that we were to employ the patterns thus derived as

---

[24] *OEK*, pp. 301–305.

highest-level hypotheses in a deductive model. Could we expect the conclusions to yield confirmable predictions about the terminal state toward which the system in question will actually tend? The answer is obviously in the negative, since all we can assert with confidence is that the instrumentally valid intra-systemic forces will lead to the stipulated end, *provided that these forces are actually set in motion.* If, however, the forces at work at the time of observation differ from the goal-adequate ones, not only instrumental analysis but any theoretical procedure imaginable is by itself powerless to set "capricious reality" right. Only the *practical act* of altering the autonomous course of the real economic processes by changing the underlying motivational and behavioral patterns can make reality converge toward a state of goal-adequacy.

Even if this statement were to imply no more than the idea that instrumental knowledge is a useful guide for the framing of economic policy, its analytical technique would be vindicated. But much more is at stake. *Prior reorganization of economic reality in line with the instrumental findings is now a precondition for establishing a viable economic theory.* To be specific, once measures of economic policy have succeeded in changing the existing behavioral and motivational patterns into goal-adequate ones, we can indeed apply our instrumental findings in the deductive part of Political Economics. Thus *analysis and political practice appear as inseparately connected steps in the acquisition of economic knowledge;* this is the rationale for the use of the term Political Economics. The instrumental-deductive method of Political Economics now reveals itself as a *three-stage procedure:* (1) "resolutive" discovery of what is goal-adequate; (2) "compositive" prediction of what will happen once goal-adequate forces are active; and (3) the linking together of these two theoretical stages by an intermediate practical stage in which political control makes the actual forces coincide with the goal-adequate ones.

With these comments we have implicitly answered another question: to wit, how to test the theorems resulting from the instrumental-deductive procedure. Since these theorems will be empirically true—and not merely logically consistent—only to the extent to which control succeeds in transforming real states into goal-adequate ones, testing can only be "indirect" through confrontation of the theorems of Political Economics with manipulated experience. But now the objects of experience are no longer "passively observed" as is the case in the traditional procedure. The theorems to be tested will prove true to the extent to which political action succeds in *making* them true.

If anything, it is this linkage of theoretical analysis and political practice that sets Political Economics apart not only from Traditional Economics, but from all conventional theory formation. It introduces an engineering element into the procedure by which knowledge is generated. The methodological implications for other fields of the social sciences and perhaps even for some of the natural sciences are obvious, but cannot be explored here.

In the foregoing remarks we have linked the actualization of goal-adequate motivations to public control. But in doing so we have skipped a problem whose answer is needed to forge this link. What are the specific measures of public control which, in a given situation, are capable of transforming actual action directives and expectations into suitable ones? Though the application of such measures is a political task, the discovery of what measures are suitable for the purpose is certainly a scientific one. And we realize that the work of instrumental analysis is not completed until we have succeeded in regressing from goal-adequate motivations to suitable measures of control.

To tackle this problem, we must first place it in a wider context. When surveying the procedure of Traditional Economics, I advanced the hypothesis that its predictive success during the classical period of capitalism was due to a combination of exceptional environmental circumstances—automatic pressures, resource mobility, escapements—that influenced economic motivations in the direction of extremum incentives and stabilizing expectations. Such a hypothesis implies that it is, in principle, possible to trace a causal nexus from specific environmental conditions to specific economic motivations. Thus the search for an instrumental link between "contrived pressures" of public control on the one hand and goal-adequate action directives and expectations on the other hand reveals itself as a special case of the wider problem of "social causation": that is, the manner in which behavior and motivation generally can be related to the "forces" of the environment, and the strength of this relationship.

Here we are referred to another field of psychology, unfortunately one in which little progress has been made since J. S. Mill pondered the prospects of an "ethology or science of character." [25] There are at least three limitations to the efficacy of external influences on economic motivations. One is the multiplicity of such influences; even a highly intervention-minded public authority can subject only a limited number of them to conscious control. Another limitation consists of the "internal influences" arising from the psychosomatic structure of the individuals concerned, which may successfully compete with the pressures from without. Third, and most important, there is the ineradicable spontaneity of human decision-making, which renders compliance with the prescripts of control conditional on affirmation by the one controlled. Such affirmation in turn presupposes that the intentions of the controllers are rightly

---

[25] *OEK*, pp. 67–68.

understood and, if so, that both the ends and the measures taken are approved.

In the circumstances, it is not surprising that psychology has not yet presented us with any "laws of social causation" on which instrumental analysis could be safely based. However, this does not exclude a few empirical generalizations or rules of thumb that permit us to form an estimate of the probable effect of certain types of control on economic motivations. Thus it seems safe to presume that the effect of control will be determinate and predictable whenever (1) the macro-goal at which control aims and the specific measures it takes coincide with the "freely chosen" micro-goals of the controlled, and/or (2) the sanctions imposed for noncompliance are severe and inescapable.

We shall presently see that these rules impose some limits on the choice of macro-goals. At this point it is worth noting that the impact which controls are likely to have on expectations is more easily predicted than the impact on action directives.

In a regime guided by Political Economics, *control of expectations* has two functions. The first is to spread information about the future course of economic processes among the marketers, thereby rectifying their own independent guesses and reducing uncertainty of expectations below the critical threshold. Second, the content of such public information—that is, the course of events predicted by the public authority—must coincide with a goal-adequate path if the new expectations are themselves to be goal-adequate.

Judged by rule 1 above, there is every likelihood that such control through information will be highly effective. To quote from *OEK:* [26]

> . . . *every marketer is interested in improving his commonsense knowledge about his present and future field of action. Therefore . . . he can be supposed to accept gladly any public information capable of correcting the content of his expectations and reducing the uncertainty of their coming true.*

Nor is there any doubt that public information thus broadcast can be made to conform to the practical requirements.

> *Once it has established the macro-goal and the optimization criteria, the controlling authority can acquire by a process of instrumental inference precise knowledge of the adjustment processes through which the system is to move toward the postulated terminal state. . . . Thus the successive market constellations—the future field of action of the marketers—are known at the moment when the de-*

---

[26] *OEK*, pp. 155–156.

cision about the goal is taken, and can be communicated to the prospective actors as the body of facts on which correct expectations can be built.

No such prestabilized harmony exists for the *control of action directives*. In the short run, the controllers will have to accept the prevailing incentives as data, trying to neutralize any digression from goal-adequacy by compensatory public action. This presupposes a public sector so organized that it can expand at short notice whenever the private sector fails to respond in accord with goal requirements. Over the long run, the transformation of economic incentives is a problem of "education." In this respect the anonymous pressures of the past—poverty and unbridled competition—were probably more effective than "humanized" sanctions of public control will ever be. The former were truly inescapable, whereas the latter can, in principle, be resisted by countervailing political power.

However, we should not underestimate the potentialities of social learning, which have been so impressively demonstrated by the change in attitude toward fiscal controls on the part of the U. S. business community, an educational advance achieved within one generation. The example highlights the significance of an enlightened public opinion that realizes the advantages which suitable micro-responses confer on the marketers themselves. A prime responsibility in this respect falls to economic science. If today we have some reason to anticipate a more cooperative reaction to public controls on the part of all economic strata, this is due not least to the more enlightened instruction that the present generation of economic leaders has received during its college days.

The Probabilistic Nature of Political Economics

Although they do not display the rigidity of engineering rules or the strict nexus that ties specific motivations to specific behavior patterns, there are ascertainable links that relate particular action directives and expectations to particular environmental forces, especially to public control. These links are likely to grow stronger as public understanding of what is required for goal achievement widens and deepens. Predictions about the efficacy of public controls will then prove confirmable in proportion to the strength of those links. However, this does not alter the fact that as long as we deal with humans rather than with robots, "social" causation will be weaker than "natural" causation. Therefore, even if engineering rules and the behavior–motivation nexus make the instrumental analysis of path, behavior, and motivations fully determinate, the last link in the regressive chain—suitable controls—can be established at best only with a high degree of probability.

This reservation hardly touches the instrumental part of Political Economics, whose earlier steps are unaffected by the uncertainties that surround the last step. But it has an important bearing on the deductive part, where the instrumental findings are applied as highest-level hypotheses. It is true that these hypotheses now have an empirical basis that the heuristic principles of Traditional Economics lack. Once the intermediate stage of the political–economic procedure—the activation of controls—has successfully been completed, a new reality confronts us which is "ready-made" for confirmable predictions. Still, the probability limitations that attach to the effect of controls on economic motivations are necessarily transferred to the highest-level hypotheses and thus to the predictive conclusions derived from them. Therefore, the explanations and predictions offered by Political Economics are essentially probabilistic.

From this one might draw the conclusion that Political Economics has little predictive superiority over Traditional Economics, since both are limited to stochastic propositions. Such a conclusion would miss the essential point made earlier, that it is precisely the *degree* of indeterminacy, as measured by the prediction interval, that matters for the practical utility of an economic theory. Under the conditions of mature capitalism, the odds are all in favor of the instrumental-deductive approach. By setting contrived limitations to the "aberrations" of motivational and thus behavioral patterns, Political Economics approximates a state in which "there is one and only one 'mode' around which the observations . . . are grouped in such a way that the mean-square deviation is relatively small." [27]

These considerations make us aware of the important auxiliary role which the probabilistic techniques of modern econometrics play in the context of Political Economics. As we now see, the doubts expressed earlier about the usefulness of these techniques in the framework of uncontrolled or haphazardly controlled market processes refer really to the *data* to which dynamic econometrics is currently applied rather than to the method itself. "Even a market in good working order is likely to exhibit a considerable range of tolerance for minor deviations from the rules which adequate patterning must obey. Determining the actual range of such deviations and predicting the most probable course of the macro-process within this tolerable range will then be a legitimate task of statistical techniques." [28] What was said in a different context about mathematical programming can now be claimed for econometrics: far

---

[27] See Hans Neisser, *On the Sociology of Knowledge* (New York: James H. Heineman, Inc., 1965), p. 90.

[28] *OEK*, p. 117.

from running counter to the procedure of Political Economics, both approaches are indispensable in making the instrumental-deductive method an effective tool for economic practice.

At long last we are in a position to define precisely the logical relationship between Political and Traditional Economics. Traditional Economics is confined to the analysis of that special instance in which the automatic forces of the environment keep the "aberrations" of the motivational and behavioral patterns within the "tolerable" range, tolerable both for the system's steady provision and for the predictability of its movements. We saw, however, that the empirical validity of the ensuing theorems is at best limited to a passing phase in capitalist evolution. Contrariwise, Political Economics, by substituting contrived controls for automatic ones, establishes an analytical frame of reference which, *mutatis mutandis*, proves valid as an interpretation of all historical forms of economic organization. And thus one can assert that, logically, Traditional Economics is really contained in Political Economics as that marginal case in which the state of the environment makes it possible to keep controls near the zero level.

THE ECONOMIC POLICY OF POLITICAL ECONOMICS [29]

Conventional Economic Policy versus Instrumental Controls

". . . [E]ven if most of the building blocks are available, the systematic construction of a Political Economics is a major task, and one that far transcends the scope of this study. . . . Once more it must be emphasized that our purpose is didactic, and that no more is intended than a demonstration of some principles of economic reasoning within a highly simplified frame of reference." [30] In a word, both my book and this paper move on a level of abstraction far removed from the field of economic–political action where the ideas discussed here are put to the real test.

It follows that important work remains to be done at the level of applied theory before Political Economics can serve as a reliable tool of policy-framing. Among the major issues requiring intensive study I mention the proper balance between what in *OEK* [31] were labeled as "manipulative" and "command" controls, a distinction related to, though not identical with, that between indirect and direct controls; the differential

[29] *OEK*, Chap. 5 and 12.
[30] *OEK*, pp. 250, 264–265.
[31] *OEK*, pp. 148–150.

measures suitable for eliciting adequate response from different socio-economic strata; administrative techniques concerning the timing and sizing of intervention; and, last but not least, the political problems that public control of the economic process raises in democratic societies. Needless to add, the answers to these questions are bound to vary with the level of economic development and political maturity.

At this point I will confine myself to clarifying a distinction that was implied in my earlier comments on policy-framing, the distinction between *instrumental controls* and measures of *conventional economic policy*. After all, in a general sense, economic controls have formed part of capitalist organization from its very beginning. Even if earlier measures of intervention were of a piecemeal and *ad hoc* nature, modern monetary and fiscal controls are certainly system-oriented. What then is the peculiar characteristic of instrumental controls?

Conventional controls

> *take the behavior of the micro-units for granted, confining them-selves to modifying the natural and institutional framework within which micro-actions take their course. Making use of a physical analogy one can say that these controls operate like an outside force which compresses or releases a spring but leaves the elastic forces in the spring itself unchanged. In contrast, control as here understood includes a public policy that concerns itself with the shaping of the behavioral patterns themselves—by influencing the purposive and cognitive motivations of the actors immediately or, in a roundabout way, through reorganization of the system's structure.*[32]

This is by no means to deny that measures of conventional policy—tariffs, taxation, or the monetary and fiscal controls of the new economics—are part, and an indispensable part, of the control system as applied by Political Economics. But though necessary, these measures are never sufficient for goal attainment. We can define them as *primary* controls, whose purpose is to modify the field of activity of the micro-units by opening or closing opportunities for transactions. But to be effective as means of goal attainment, they must be supplemented by *secondary* controls, whose purpose is to turn the responses of the micro-units in the right direction. In fulfilling this function, secondary controls cover a wider range than do primary controls, because they must govern the micro-economic response mechanism both when the stimulus consists of actions of other marketers and when it arises from measures of public policy.

After what was said above about the manner in which expectations as well as action directives can be brought under regulating influence,

---

[32] *OEK*, p. 131.

there is little need to detail the entire scope of secondary controls. They extend from information about the goal-adequate path to measures of persuasion and compensatory public action, not excluding in extreme cases even coercion. However, it may be helpful to illustrate their *modus operandi* through an example. Again the tax reduction under the Kennedy Administration can serve as a paradigm.

Though the tax measure was intended to stimulate the general activity of the system, no attempt was made to affect the behavioral responses and underlying expectations of investors and consumers. It was simply taken for granted that these responses would promote the policy goal, although, as was mentioned earlier, knowledgeable experts entertained grave doubts as to the repercussions of the tax cut on business psychology. In the face of such doubts, an instrumental strategy would have made marketers' responses its major target; e.g., by supplementing the tax reduction with a well-advertised standby program of public investment, which would go into effect if private spending did not rise promptly and to a sufficient degree. By thus reducing uncertainty about the trend of aggregate demand, the major obstacle to goal-adequate private behavior would have been removed.

The literature on economic planning contains as yet little systematic exploration of the techniques of secondary control. But a cursory survey of the postwar economic policies of Scandinavia, Holland, or France gives the impression that practical experimentation is in full swing, and that the tenets of Political Economics, though largely unformulated, are in fact widely applied.

The Choice of Goals

I should like to conclude this essay with another word about the focal point of Political Economics: the choice of macro-goals. Earlier it was stressed that Political Economics *qua* economics must accept the stipulated goal or sets of compatible goals as data. This would be no different if, as economists, we were not wedded to "scientific value relativism," but were prepared to commit ourselves to a definite hierarchy of goals with the apex of a *summum bonum,* as offered by rivaling theologies and philosophies. Even then our problem would be the suitability of the means rather than the validation of the ends.

So the problem presents itself as long as we are engaged in the preliminary work of instrumental analysis. But in order to advance to the level of predictive theory, we must, as we saw, pass through the practical stage in which the holders of political authority seek to modify the original institutional environment in accordance with their instrumental findings. This original environment, conceptualized as the structure of the initial state, reveals itself as a logical constraint in the analysis of the goal-adequate path. However, it is no less a practical constraint when the instrumental findings are to be applied. To give an example, it is in principle a feasible task for analysis to establish the path, the behavioral and motivational conditions, and even the controls suitable to transform a primitive subsistence economy into a mature industrial system. But when we ponder the practical application of the controls thus designed, we may come to the conclusion that the institutional transformation required would have to be purchased at the price of a social revolution which, rather than setting the primitive society on the road to development, might well throw it back to a still lower level.

What we encounter here is a conflict between a particular macro-goal and the socioeconomic environment from which the path toward the goal is to start. Stated in general terms, not all macro-goals are intrinsically compatible with any prevailing order of social relations. Whenever a conflict arises, we are compelled to choose between abandoning the goal or the existing order, the latter at the peril of applying means which may defeat the end.

Value absolutists may brush aside such pragmatic considerations, but I must admit that they govern my own thinking as expressed in the concluding chapter of my book. Though I leave no doubt that the instrumental method is applicable to the elaboration of the means suitable to the attainment of *any* macro-goal, be it the size and composition of aggregate output, the level of resource utilization, the rate of growth, or the order of distribution,[33] I have confined the practical test cases selected for detailed investigation to two: full utilization of resources, and balanced growth. Indeed, these particular goals pose problems of great analytical interest. But my choice was ultimately determined by political considerations. These are the only macro-goals which, I believe, are fully compatible with the institutional environment of mature capitalism.

The reasons for this belief are easy to state. Since decentralized decision-making based on private ownership of the means of production is the core of capitalist organization, instrumental controls other than coercion will be effective within this framework only if the aim for which they are applied meets with the *consensus* of the large majority of micro-units. This consensus can indeed be anticipated for the two goals selected, since extending the opportunity for the utilization of present resources (stabilization) and assuring the absorption of newly accruing ones at a rising rate of productivity (balanced growth) seem to offer benefits to all.

---

[33] *OEK,* p. 255.

I am aware that even in the pursuit of these goals, certain conflicts of interest may arise between particular sectors and social strata of the economy. But the ensuing resistance to public interference with the *functional* performance of the economy is certainly minor compared with the likely breakdown of consensus in the face of *structural* transformations such as the central planning of investment and output would require, not to speak of a fundamental redistribution of income and wealth. Fortunately, the politically feasible goals—stabilization and balanced growth— seem to satisfy the basic requirements for restoring to the market of mature capitalism that minimum of "order" in the inclusive sense defined above on which the preservation of the fabric of Western society depends. Maintaining social consensus is a much more difficult and perhaps insoluble task in poor societies, which struggle not only for a more productive order but also for a more equitable one.

But it should be stressed once more that "prudence" in the choice of macro-goals does not limit the universal validity of the scientific procedure of Political Economics, nor can such prudence itself be vindicated on scientific grounds. It expresses a value judgment emulating peaceful evolution even at the expense of uncompromising justice. If this reveals a conservative undercurrent in my thinking, as some critics have insinuated, I must bow to this, as to the opposite charge that my advocacy of political control of industrial capitalism "gives aid and comfort to men who are neither wise nor gentle." Since the political economist *contrives* his research object as much as he *observes* it, he too cannot escape the risks of decision-making.

2

ARON GURWITSCH

SOCIAL SCIENCE
AND
NATURAL SCIENCE

Methodological Reflections on Lowe's
On Economic Knowledge

For a noneconomist to comment on Adolph Lowe's
position paper, or on his book On Economic Knowledge,[1] might
appear to be an odd, perhaps even a preposterous venture. Still
this venture is suggested and in some measure justified by the
very nature of the question under discussion, which may well be
characterized as the study of the methodology of economic
knowledge. As a matter of fact, methodological considerations
play a substantial role in Professor Lowe's presentation; they are
no less important than his discussions of economic matters in the
technical sense. However, the term "method" must not be understood to refer to techniques of research. Rather the term is to be
taken in its etymological sense as denoting access—access to a certain segment of reality—whereby the general orientation and the
style of cognitive endeavors related to that segment are determined. That is to say, Dr. Lowe raises fundamental questions
concerning not only the nature of economic activity, but also the
cognitive approach to that activity. Discussions of this sort lead
unavoidably, albeit by indirection, to very general problems regarding cognitive and scientific endeavors at large. These circumstances have made it easier for the present writer to accept,
with a not too bad conscience, the honor which—as he grate-

---

[1] Henceforth referred to as OEK.

fully acknowledges—was done to him when he was invited to participate in this discussion.

THE SOCIAL ACTOR AND HIS AWARENESS OF THE SOCIAL SCENE

Among the fundamental methodological problems, the first to be considered concerns the basic difference between the social sciences and the natural sciences. There can be no question of renewing the long-standing debate on this topic, or of substantiating in an adequate manner the position here defended. In the present context we cannot go beyond sketching the position A. Schutz [2] has developed with regard to the problem under discussion, without, however, entering into the phenomenological foundations upon which Schutz has elaborated his views. To be sure, Lowe does not make the specific nature of the social sciences in contradistinction to the natural sciences a topic of explicit inquiry, nor is there any need for him to engage himself in such a direction. Still, he not only refers occasionally to Schutz,[3] but his endorsement of Schutz' position is visible throughout his book.

The natural scientist observes and interprets the objects and especially the events with which he deals; he tries to ascertain the conditions under which certain events occur and to express in the form of laws the regularities of their occurrence. Furthermore, the natural scientist contrives theoretical constructs such as "atom," "electron," "energy," and the like, whose purpose is to make possible the prediction of directly observable phenomena or—as we should prefer to state in a more general way—the rationalization and systematization of a wide range of phenomena. The wider that range, the greater is the fruitfulness—i.e., the explanatory value—of the theoretical constructs. It is in view of their explanatory purpose and function that the theoretical constructs are conceived, defined, redefined, or abandoned altogether to be replaced by different ones. That is to say, the theoretical constructs in the natural sciences are entirely at the mercy, although certainly not at the whim, of the scientist. This leads us to the decisive point. The scientist or, to be more exact, the community of cooperating scientists are the only ones to perform the function of conceiving and interpreting. *They, and they alone, observe the phenomena to be explained and conceive of the constructs by whose means the explanation is given.* Neither the directly observable phenomena nor the theoretical constructs interpret themselves, nor have they

---

[2] Alfred Schutz, "Common Sense and Scientific Interpretation of Human Action," especially I, 2 and IV in *Collected Papers*, Vol. I (The Hague: Martinus Nijhoff, 1962).

[3] *OEK*, p. 62.

any comprehension of their behavior or of the field in which their behavior takes place. At any rate, no such self-interpretation or self-com-
prehension is, or need be, imputed to them.

In the social sciences, the situation is very different. To be sure, here
too theoretical constructs are conceived—e.g., the "ideal types" in the
sense of Max Weber; here too predictions and explanations are intended
and sought for, and deductive reasoning plays a considerable part. However, the "objects" with which the social scientist concerns himself, and
whose behavior in any of the relevant dimensions (in the present context,
the economic dimension) he endeavors to explain, are actors on the
social scene. Such actors have a *comprehension of their own* of the situation in which they find themselves, and within which they carry on their
activities.

In speaking of the actors' comprehension, we wish to stress that it
precedes, is independent of, and is different from the interpretation of
the same behavior on the part of the onlooking observer—e.g., the social
scientist who, however, must make allowance for it in his theoretical
constructions.[4] Social actors—that is to say, human beings—pursue certain
goals, "micro-goals," in Lowe's terminology; they have some awareness
of the adequacy or inadequacy of the actions they plan with regard to
their goals. Needless to say, such awareness may be correct as well as
erroneous; it must be added that, as a rule, it is more or less vague, confused, and inarticulate. Finally, the behavior of human beings is determined—still better, prompted—by action directives aiming at maximization or homeostasis or some other state of provision. Such behavior differs
radically from the behavior, blind though strictly lawful, of a material
body under the impact of an external force impressed upon it. This
difference also holds when the human being acts under duress or finds
himself in circumstances under which no choice is left to him. The difference in question consists precisely in the awareness of being under duress
or of having no choice. Even the slave—to take an extreme example—who
has no choice other than simply to obey his master, still has some indis-
tinct and inarticulate awareness of his situation: of himself as a slave, of
his master as powerful, of the dire consequences an attempted disobedi-
ence would be likely to entail. Even in this most extreme of cases there
remains some human spontaneity, though reduced to a rudimentary
form.

To systematize and generalize, but with special reference to the economic sphere, we can say: Factors of two kinds, cognitive and purposive,
enter as determinants into all economic behavior.

---

[4] Therefore, Schutz, *op. cit.*, Vol. I, p. 6, characterizes the theoretical constructs
used in the social sciences as "constructs of the second degree"; see also "Concept
and Theory Formation in the Social Sciences," in *Collected Papers*, Vol. I, p. 58*f*.

Since economic activity involves the transformation of natural resources into finished goods, either to be consumed or to serve as tools for
further production, it requires some knowledge of, or at least some acquaintance with, the regularities of nature, both animate, such as the
growth of plants and animals, and inanimate. Such knowledge is exemplified by the practice of the several crafts. Obviously, the acquaintance in
question is of the commonsense variety; it does not exhibit systematicity
or other distinctive features of scientific knowledge in any strict sense.
Properly speaking, it consists of a set of rather loosely connected "rules
of engineering" or, as we would prefer to say with Schutz,[5] recipes for
action under specified conditions, recipes of merely pragmatic significance, whose justification derives solely from their yielding the results
desired.

Of still greater importance in the present context is the knowledge
the economic actor has of the social scene. He entertains certain ideas,
whether correct or incorrect, about the condition of the market, not only
about its present condition but also, and chiefly, about trends more or less
likely to materialize in the imminent future. The actualization of such
trends may be beyond the control of the individual marketer, although,
in special cases, he might by his actions contribute to their actualization
or else inhibit it. Marketers are able to entertain expectations concerning
imminent economic developments on the strength of their interpretation: certain events (such as a change in supply or demand, rising or falling prices, and the like) might be taken to presage further occurrences.
Economic life, just like social life in general and in all its dimensions,
requires a system of communication or information that is understood by
the participants, whether the information depends upon interpretation
of events in the way just mentioned or takes a more explicit form, as
when it emanates from a planning and controlling authority. Among the
elements conveyed by the system of communication are those that concern sanctions, both positive and negative—e.g., profit or loss in a free
market—that are likely to be attendant upon a certain economic behavior.
On the basis of such knowledge as has just been sketched, the individual
marketer plans his actions so as to make them interlock with, or gear into,
those of other marketers with whom he is going to be involved in his
transactions. For that end he anticipates the reactions that his behavior
is likely to elicit on their part. Allowance for anticipated reactions influences his planning and might sometimes lead to quite substantial modifications of it.

It appears from the preceding remarks that expectations play a considerable role. Being entertained by the actor, not the scientific observer,

---

[5] Schutz, "Some Structures of the Life-World," *Collected Papers*, Vol. III, p. 120.

they are not predictions in any significant scientific sense. Rather they are based on commonsense knowledge, business experience, and the like, and may be said to form part of economic commonsense knowledge. For the actor concerned, their varying degrees of certainty and uncertainty make them a determining factor in economic decisions.

These decisions are guided by action directives of which, according to Dr. Lowe, a certain variety must be taken into consideration. In the first place, there is what he calls the "extremum principle," the principle of maximizing receipts and minimizing expenditures—in a word, the striving for maximum profit. Other action directives might be the desire to maintain a given level of family income or, on the part of corporations, homeostatic tendencies—that is, policies aimed at maintaining rather than increasing their share of the market or the value of their assets. Furthermore, an individual may endeavor to keep his economic activity within certain confines or even to reduce it, in order to be able to devote as much time and energy as possible to other pursuits. Such latitude of alternatives has practical significance only if survival is assured in both the economic and the physical sense. Otherwise, acceptance of the extremum principle is imperative. However, even this cannot be asserted without some qualification: primitive tribes are known to have stagnated at a level of mere subsistence for long periods of time. It appears that acceptance of the extremum principle under the pressure of circumstances that hardly leave any other choice is very different from the propulsion of a physical body by application of an external force. Finally, it is to be observed that a given action directive—e.g., the extremum principle—does not always unambiguously determine a concrete economic action. A rise in price will be followed by an increase in supply only if the price is not expected to rise still more. Otherwise—that is, if the price expectations have greater than unit elasticity—the sellers will, in the interest of maximizing their profits, withhold rather than increase supply. This is mentioned to indicate the inability of the extremum principle alone to serve as the basis of economic theory.

In our attempts to point out the distinctive feature of social science that underlies all its other differences from natural science, we have, while presenting some of Dr. Lowe's ideas, followed the general line of Schutz' reasoning, focusing on the economic sphere. With respect to the latter, it must be added that economic activity is, according to Dr. Lowe, of merely modal significance, its sole purpose being procurement of the material means that are indispensable for physical human existence. In opposition to other human activities, scientific, religious, artistic, and the like, which are of intrinsic and inherent value apart from any results to which they may lead, the overall economic goal of provision is intermediate only; economic activity is a technique of merely pragmatic significance that consists exclusively in permitting the achievement of specific results.

THE LOGIC OF TRADITIONAL ECONOMIC THEORY

Modern economic thought has developed along with modern market society of which it is the theory, and its beginnings follow rather closely the establishment of Newtonian science, the first and classical systematization of physics in the specific modern sense. This is more than a chronological coincidence. As a result of the prestige that accrued to Newtonian science because of its theoretical success, it very soon came to be regarded as the paradigm and model of scientific knowledge, exemplifying scientific endeavor and procedure as such, and therefore thought to be applicable in *all* fields, including those beyond the physical world in which it had first shown its fertility.

Newtonian science starts from a fundamental hypothesis concerning the behavior of any material mass in the presence of other masses: the law of universal gravitation. As a hypothesis, this law receives its validation from its explanatory and predictive function or capacity. The method is *hypothetico-deductive*. From the assumed hypothesis, consequences are deduced that terminate in propositions amenable to direct empirical verification, so that the initial hypothesis appears confirmed by virtue of the consequences it yields. By means of this method, Newton succeeded in explaining a wide range of physical, and especially mechanical, phenomena, one of his biggest triumphs being the derivation of Kepler's laws—that is, the explanation of the constitution of the solar system. From the point of view of the logic of the sciences, it is worth noting that the condition of a system as a whole—a macro-condition—which functions as unknown in terms of the theory, is derived from the behavior of its members—micro-behavior [6]—a behavior supposed to be known, although not from direct observation but on the strength of the initial fundamental hypothesis.

Emulating the example of Newtonian science, modern economic theorists such as Adam Smith start by laying down a principle that governs the behavior of the economic micro-units. This is the extremum principle, which, according to Dr. Lowe, is one of the presuppositions or prerequisites of the law of supply and demand, the other prerequisite being what he calls "stabilizing expectations." [7] The extremum principle appears as the economic counterpart or equivalent of the Newtonian law

---

[6] Needless to say, in the present context the term "micro" has an entirely different meaning from the one used in contemporary micro-physics.

[7] *OEK*, Part 2, Sec. 2.

of universal gravitation.[8] It matters very little whether the extremum principle is interpreted as an expression of an essential feature of invariable "human nature" or is taken as a heuristic principle of purely explanatory and theoretical significance. If this principle is used as the action directive of the individual marketers, as their micro-goal, the law of supply and demand enters into operation, although, as just mentioned, the condition in question is only necessary but not yet sufficient. The law of supply and demand does more than account for micro-behavior. It describes the motion of the market as a whole, the process of adjustment that takes place after a disturbance has occurred in some sector of the market, and, finally, the terminal state of the market toward which the process of adjustment tends. This terminal state is equilibrium: all quantities supplied being equal to all quantities demanded, at the lowest price possible under the prevailing conditions of production. Equilibrium in this sense also includes full utilization of the available resources, human and other. By virtue of the law of supply and demand, the development and growth of the market becomes a transition from one state of equilibrium to the next, which passes through phases of disturbance of comparatively short duration.

In both Newtonian science and classical economic theory, the macro-condition of the system—in one case the constitution of the solar system, in the other case the equilibrium of the market—results *inexorably* from the behavior of the members of the system. Both apply the hypothetico-deductive method by considering a law of micro-behavior and the initial state of the system as known (in the case of the solar system, the initial state is defined in terms of the masses of the celestial bodies on the one hand and, on the other hand, the distances of the planets from the sun and their respective velocities at a given moment of time); both try to deduce from this the laws of motion of the system (e.g., Kepler's laws) and its future states (in the case of astronomy, past states as well). What is deduced is considered unknown or, more precisely, as that which is to become known. In the case of economic theory, the circumstance that the terminal state of the market—equilibrium—is unknown has a particular significance. It is not known to the individual marketers, nor can it be the goal of any one of them. They are striving for maximization of profit, which is more likely to accrue to them during phases of disturbance than under the condition of equilibrium. If the system moves,

---

[8] Lowe (*OEK*, p. 105) also refers the extremum principle to the principle of least action and other extremum principles in physics. However, it seems to us that the principle of least action is, properly speaking, not so much a law of nature, but rather a regulative principle with respect to laws of nature, or a law of laws of nature. Leibniz speaks in this connection of "architectonic principles" (cf., *Tentamen anagogicum, Die philosophischen Schriften von Gottfried Wilhelm Leibniz,* ed. C. I. Gerhardt, Hildesheim, Georg Olms Verlagsbuchhandlung, 1960, Vol. VII, pp. 272*ff.*).

as it does, this is due to its intrinsic dynamics; no master engineer has conceived equilibrium as a macro-goal and then so arranged and organized the members of the system that it attains this goal.

By virtue of its intrinsic dynamics, the market develops in an orderly fashion. "Orderly" signifies not only regularity and predictability, but also what can be called "being in good working condition"—namely, satisfactory provision of goods and services. This is best illustrated by Dr. Lowe's counterexample of a business cycle that occurs and develops in a perfectly regular and predictable manner, but in such a way that periodically a phase of stagnation is reached in which both output and employment approach the zero level.[9] In the natural sciences, if such a result follows from a theory that is in conformity with observed facts, it is to be simply accepted. The case is already different in engineering or in medicine, where a certain level of performance is imposed as a goal upon the machine or the organism, respectively.[10] What is remarkable is that the market, according to classical economic theory, functions so as to "provide a plentiful revenue or subsistence for the people . . . and . . . to supply the state or commonwealth with a revenue sufficient for the public services"[11] without any such goal being imposed on it. In other words, economic activity comes to realize its sole and only purpose—procurement of material means—by virtue of the intrinsic dynamics of the market.

This appears all the more remarkable since the orderly motion of the market is supposed to result, with the same inexorability as that ascribed to astronomical laws, from the autonomous and spontaneous behavior of the micro-units in a free market in which decision-making is decentralized. This circumstance, to which there is no analogy in the realm of nature, is most enigmatic indeed. Suppose that the behavior of the marketers were really spontaneous, so that each one of them followed one or another of the possible action directives, such as the extremum principle, minimization of physical effort, preference for a given status quo, ostentation in the sense of Veblen's conspicuous consumption, and the like, and that furthermore, the individual marketers whimsically and erratically shifted from one action directive to another. Is it conceivable that an orderly motion and state of the market—orderly in any sense whatever—would result? The suspicion arises that the spontaneity in question is spurious, or at least must be understood with some qualification. Spontaneity and autonomy mean absence of external constraint, control, and command. On the other hand, every individual marketer is expected consistently to abide by the same action directive, the extremum

9 See p. 6.
10 OEK, pp. 114 and 120f.
11 A. Smith, as quoted in OEK, p. 117.

principle, without being forced to do so. This assumption underlies traditional economic theory.

Rather than entering into a discussion as to whether the extremum principle is an expression of invariable "human nature" or a heuristic principle, Dr. Lowe takes a glance at the historical, social, and economic conditions in the early period of the development of Western capitalism. The general poverty of the masses and the fierceness of unbridled competition conferred upon the extremum principle the character of imperativeness, further reinforced by the moral climate of the time—the extolling of the virtues of acquisitiveness and thrift and the social prestige associated with economic success. Furthermore, the socioeconomic system exhibited a high degree of mobility—social mobility because labor was shifted from one line of production to another, and technological mobility because of the relative unspecificity of the equipment, comparatively small investments, and relatively short-term financial commitments. Nor must the political conditions, especially in England, be overlooked: a constitutional government protecting the freedom of the competitive market and the freedom of contract. All this, according to Dr. Lowe, made for stabilizing expectations and for the subjective certainty of these expectations, which, moreover, extended over a rather short span of time. Their stabilizing influence could be and was taken for granted, so much so that in the earlier literature of classical economic theory, the importance that expectations have for the theory and the role they play in it was hardly seen at all.[12] At any event, the conditions were realized for the law of supply and demand to enter into operation. During the early period of the development of capitalism in the West, the classical theory of the market possessed a comparatively high degree of empirical validity.

INTRA-SYSTEMIC AND EXTRA-SYSTEMIC FORCES

Since the middle of the nineteenth century, the empirical validity of classical economic theory has increasingly become problematic in the face of periodically recurring serious disturbances, known as the "business cycle." If the market has always recovered from those disturbances, this was due less to its intrinsic dynamics as described by the classical theory, than to what Dr. Lowe calls "escapements": increases in the population, multiplication of innovations, expansion of existing markets and opening up of new ones—all of these under the favoring conditions of monetary stability and a long period of peace (there was no big gen-

---

[12] *OEK*, pp. 48, 72, 176.

eral war during the period extending from the Congress of Vienna to the outbreak of the First World War).[13] Still, the classical theory was adhered to, at least in its essentials, while business cycles, except in the work of Karl Marx, either were not taken seriously or were treated as transient distortions, as epicyclical phenomena for whose explanation a variety of special assumptions and *ad hoc* hypotheses were offered. In the mind of the theoretician of scientific methodology, even though he may not be a professional economist, the necessity of resorting to *ad hoc* hypotheses, by which the theoretical unity of a field of knowledge is put in jeopardy, cannot fail to provoke a feeling of uneasiness. This feeling is reinforced by the fact that the *ad hoc* explanations in question are in rivalry with one another.

In this connection, Dr. Lowe raises the problem of the relation between intra-systemic and extra-systemic forces. To express it in general terms, the problem concerns the manner in which the combination and cooperation of a plurality of forces and factors is to be understood. Because of its crucial importance, his discussion requires and deserves detailed comment. It makes the difference between natural and social science appear in a new light.

If meteorological predictions are so difficult to make and are so beset by uncertainties, this is because of the variety of forces and factors involved, and the great number of variables for which appropriate substitutions have to be made. A simpler case in point is the motion of a body under the impact of gravity through a resisting medium, a case in which gravity is combined with viscosity and which has been definitively solved by Stoke. Intuitively, the simplest case is the deflection of a falling body from its perpendicular path by a strong wind.

In these and similar cases, each one of the forces in question can be studied in isolation under laboratory conditions, where forces and factors other than those under scrutiny are either eliminated (by using a vacuum) or kept constant. Thus the laws that govern the operation of the several forces can be ascertained and formulated. It is assumed and, perhaps, taken for granted—and rightly so, as the theoretical success of the physical sciences testifies—that *each one of the forces under consideration remains strictly the same, obeying the same law whether it operates alone or in combination with other forces and, again, whether it enters into one combination or another one.* Consequently, the cooperation of a plurality of forces means that each force makes its particular contribution to the overall effect which, in turn, is nothing other than the sum total of the particular effects taken together, which can be obtained by

---

13 *OEK*, Chap. 3, Sec. 4. Since the beginning of the First World War and especially since the end of the Second World War, these escapements have been all but closed.

addition and subtraction.[14] Therefore, the difficulties encountered in meteorological prediction are not theoretical, but rather technical, and can, perhaps, be overcome by means of the computer. At any event and quite in general: *if by the combination of intra-systemic and extra-systemic forces a modification is brought about, it is not the forces themselves that are modified by one another, but only the effects yielded and contributed by these forces.*

However, a modification of some forces by others does occur in the social field—e.g., in economics. As a consequence of the development and maturation of the industrial society, the general standard of living has risen so that the extremum principle has lost its imperativeness and the choice of different action directives has become a realistic possibility. Of still greater moment is the gradual immobilization of the system: the increasing specialization and specificity of industrial equipment, the inevitability of long-term financial commitments, and the necessity for the individual decision-maker to extend his planning over longer periods of time. Expectations become increasingly uncertain, especially under conditions of monetary instability and international political tensions such as those that have prevailed since the end of the Second World War, and to some degree even since the First World War. Even if the extremum principle retains its predominance as an action directive or if, for the sake of the discussion, its predominance is taken for granted, a lower level of profit which can be expected with comparative certainty may appear preferable to a higher level in the face of the risks involved in expanding investment and the concomitant large and long-term financial obligations.

This means that under the conditions of a changed sociohistorical environment, the very preconditions and prerequisites of the law of supply and demand are no longer fulfilled—i.e., are no longer in operation. *It is not the case that the economic core process as propelled by intrasystemic forces according to their specific laws is accidentally and transitorily disturbed and deflected from its inexorable course by facts and events originating in the sociohistorical environment. On the contrary, the very forces that are supposed to determine what is called the core process depend upon the sociohistorical environment and, if they are to assume a certain shape, can operate only under certain specific environmental conditions. The forces in question prove to be intrinsically affected by changes in the sociohistorical environment.* Thus it becomes questionable whether the law of supply and demand can still be regarded as *the* law of economic activity, valid in all sociohistorical environments,[15] and,

---

14 This appears clearly in the derivation of Stoke's law.

15 This point has been made by R. L. Heilbroner, "Is Economic Theory Possible?" *Social Research,* XXXIII (1966), p. 288.

furthermore, whether this law, if permitted to take its course freely in a laissez-faire economy, will yield a market in "good working order"—i.e., an equilibrating market, which assures satisfactory provision. In the latter respect, the earlier phases of the Great Depression have provided instructive experience. The question raised admits of a generalizing radicalization. Given the aforementioned relationship between intra-systemic forces and extra-systemic factors, it appears doubtful whether there are, or can be, economic laws at all in the specific sense the term has in the natural sciences: namely, laws valid under all environmental conditions, supervenient accidental disturbances notwithstanding. Raising the question in this radicalized form is nothing less than asking whether the orientation— or better, the style—of theoretical reasoning in the social sciences is not significantly and profoundly different from that in physics and chemistry.

We may be permitted to observe in passing that a similar theoretical situation has arisen in a biological context—namely, in the organismic theory of K. Goldstein. Goldstein also rejects the procedure of adding and subtracting partial contributory effects, emphasizing the dependence of the behavior of the organism upon the conditions in which it finds itself, especially the initial conditions; he insists that it makes a profound difference whether a stimulus is applied to an isolated organ or system of organs or whether the organism as a whole is involved.[16] We mention this in order to show that the *universal* legitimacy and applicability of the style of theoretical thought and explanation proper to the sciences of physics and chemistry—a style that has proved so eminently fruitful and successful in those sciences that its universal validity has come to be considered as a matter of course—is challenged not only in the social sciences but on the organismic level as well.[17] There remains, of course, the difference that while the factors involved and to be allowed for in social science (in the present context, action directives and expectations) are matters of consciousness, such is generally not the case with regard to organismic phenomena.

After this brief digression, we return to our main concern and argument. The result at which we have arrived should not surprise us. It is nothing other than a manifestation of the *essential historicity of human existence*. Behavioral motivations that were effective under certain his-

---

16 K. Goldstein, *The Organism* (New York: American Book Company, 1939); paperback ed. (Boston: Beacon Press, 1963). Summarizing presentations of Goldstein's theory have been given by A. Gurwitsch, "Le Fonctionnement de l'Organisme d'après K. Goldstein," *Journal de Psychologie normale et pathologique*, XXXVI (1939); and W. Riese, "Kurt Goldstein. The Man and His Work," in *The Reach of Mind*, ed. Marianne Simmel (New York: Springer Publishing Company, 1968).

17 This point is elaborately developed by M. Merleau-Ponty, *Phénoménologie de la Perception* (Paris: Librairie Gallimard, 1945), pp. 134ff. Also trans. by C. Smith, *Phenomenology of Perception* (New York: Humanities Press Inc., 1962), pp. 115ff.

torical environmental conditions, and whose effectiveness was favored by them, are no longer operative under different conditions, at least not in the same way. Thus far we have been stressing the modifying influence of the sociohistorical environment upon action directives and expectations. For the sake of completeness it must be added that, if Western industrial society has reached the degree of maturation it exhibits at present, this is due to the market having operated in a preceding phase of industrial development in accordance with the law of supply and demand of classical economic theory. In other words, the operation of the early industrial market, which was made possible by specific environmental conditions, brought about a change in those very conditions. On this example, the dialectics of history can be made visible. By his work, man transforms his sociohistorical world, whose transformation then reverberates on man, transforming him. This implies the denial of an "invariable human nature," though not of invariants of human existence, as, for example, the dependence upon procurement of material means. Such invariants, which are of a rather formal nature, manifest themselves in concrete form by assuming specific varieties. It is the latter that are of primary, if not exclusive, interest to the social scientist.

POLITICAL ECONOMICS AND THE LOGIC OF INSTRUMENTAL ANALYSIS

As long as the market, operating in accordance with the law of supply and demand, is in "good working order," classical economic theory has empirical validity, although this may be of little practical significance. Things change when in a laissez-faire economy the market tends toward disturbances and grave disorders that must be counteracted by public policy. To guide public policy, a theory is required that will permit us to predict the effects of measures taken by the public authorities. The lack of such an empirically valid theory creates a serious difficulty.

To overcome this difficulty, Lowe proposes the idea of *a Political Economics whose theoretical tool is instrumental analysis*. As will presently be seen, the term "Political Economics" is given a specific sense by Dr. Lowe and must not be taken in the sense of the classical term "political economy," a phase denoting the science of economics in general.

Political Economics starts by postulating a macro-goal, a state of the market which, as a rule, differs from its actual state; the task consists in discovering the means ("instruments") suitable for attaining that goal. Among the possible macro-goals are maximum technical efficiency (i.e., maximum output of investment goods, even at the price of reducing drastically the present standard of living); equalization of income and wealth; market equilibrium in the sense of equality at the lowest pos-

Gardner Webb College Library

sible price between the quantities demanded and the quantities supplied; stabilization (i.e., full utilization of all available human resources); and, finally, balanced growth at a predetermined rate. The choice between possible macro-goals and the vindication of the one actually chosen by the public authority pose a serious and important problem which in the present context can only be treated briefly.

A restricting condition may be imposed upon the macro-goal to be chosen, such as the condition that the macro-goal must be one that does not require complete elimination of decentralized decision-making but is compatible with the maximum possible autonomous decision-making on the part of the micro-units. This restricting condition may be imposed for the sake of preserving some measure of personal and political freedom. The very possibility of imposing upon the choice of an economic macro-goal a restricting condition that is essentially noneconomic is grounded in the aforementioned merely modal significance of economic activity. In other words, economic macro-goals are referred to other macro-goals of a "higher order"—e.g., political macro-goals—and are seen under the aspect of their suitability for the attainment of the latter goals. Methodologically speaking, a new instrumental analysis is required which takes its departure from the higher macro-goal and discovers the economic macro-state in question as a suitable means. Obviously, sooner or later, the apex of the hierarchy of goals is reached—that is, goals which are ultimate in that they no longer serve as subordinate means for further and higher ends. The vindication of ultimate goals is a specific philosophical problem which will not be tackled in the present context, since we are deliberately limiting ourselves to logico-methodological questions. We therefore will confine ourselves to stating that the vindication of ultimate goals is neither arbitrary nor a matter of "existentialist decision." Rather it requires a theory of man, more specifically a theory of the abovementioned invariants of human existence. In contradistinction to what holds for the interest of the social scientist, the invariants in question occupy a central position within a philosophical anthropology.

Traditional economic theory considers the terminal macro-state of the market as a *quaesitum*. Since that macro-state results from the actions of micro-units whose behavior is governed by a law assumed to be known, albeit in the form of a heuristic hypothesis, an attempt is made to derive the macro-state from the interlocking actions of the micro-units. Here, as elsewhere, *the hypothetico-deductive method is progressive*. While granting that the macro-state results from micro-behavior, Political Economics differs from traditional economic theory in several respects. In the first place, the macro-state is now treated as a *datum*, as known, although not, of course, in the sense of its being accessible to empirical observation, because, with the sole exception of the case in which the macro-goal is the maintenance of the status quo, it is not an empirically observable fact. Nor is it known in the form of a heuristic hypothesis that has to stand the test of empirical verification of its consequences. Rather, *the macro-state is known because it is stipulated as a goal to be attained.* It must be remembered that the macro-goal chosen is selected out of a plurality of possible macro-goals. Once the choice is made, the question arises of suitable means for the goal's attainment. The discovery of those means, which here play the role of unknowns, is the proper office of instrumental analysis. To enumerate the unknowns in a somewhat systematic order, instrumental analysis must discover: (1) intermediary states which might serve as phases in the process of transition from the actual state (initial state) of the system to its terminal state (postulated as a goal); (2) patterns of behavior on the part of the microunits suitable for keeping the system to its path of transition; (3) appropriate motivations conducive to those patterns of behavior; and (4) measures of control suitable for influencing motivations and, hence, behavior. If Dr. Lowe speaks of "appropriateness" and "suitability" rather than of "requirements," it is because a postulated macro-goal can, as a rule, be attained in alternative ways. In solving its problem, instrumental analysis avails itself of the extant knowledge of laws of nature, biological laws, psychological laws, rules of engineering, empirical generalizations, and rules of thumb. It is worth noting that nowhere in the course of instrumental analysis do there appear laws that could be specified as inherently "economic."

A further difference between instrumental analysis and the procedure of traditional economic theory can now be formulated. While the latter admits of only one pattern of behavior and motivation, Political Economics allows for a plurality of such patterns, considering them according to their suitability with respect to the postulated macro-goal. This requires that patterns of behavior and motivation be treated as unknowns. Finally, in starting from the macro-goal and inquiring into suitable patterns of behavior and motivation on the part of the micro-units upon whose actions the attainment of the macro-goal depends, *instrumental analysis moves regressively* in contrast to the progressive orientation of the hypothetico-deductive method.

On this account Dr. Lowe compares, without, of course, equating them, the regressive inference of instrumental analysis with induction, by means of which hypotheses in the natural sciences are supposed to be derived from empirical observations and experiments. Far from challenging the importance of empirical, and especially statistical, generalizations, we still submit that logico-methodologically speaking, no fundamental scientific hypothesis, such as the law of universal gravitation or the basic laws of thermodynamics, has ever been established by the procedure of induction. Rather they are posited as heuristic principles to be confirmed by the empirical verification of their consequences.

For this reason we propose to compare the regressive inference of instrumental analysis to another methodological procedure, long since known in the history of mathematics—namely, *analysis*, in the specific sense in which, according to Cassirer,[18] it was invented by Plato. The question of whether a certain geometrical figure can be inscribed in another figure is answered in the following way: Assume that the figure is inscribed, and find the conditions under which this is the case and the conditions under which this is not the case.[19] To formulate it in quite general terms: A certain state of affairs, a number, or a geometrical figure exhibiting specified properties is posited as existing (in the mathematical sense) and the question is raised as to the conditions upon which its existence depends. Mathematical analysis is regressive insofar as it moves from a result assumed as accomplished to the conditions which make that result possible. This description, we submit, may be applied fairly well to the procedure of instrumental analysis. Furthermore, mathematical analysis must be carried out anew whenever a special problem is posed. The same holds true for instrumental analysis, which, Dr. Lowe insists,[20] is "an ongoing task of the social scientist," to be repeated with respect to every possible macro-goal because its validity is strictly confined to each specific macro-goal. This is in marked contrast to the hypothetico-deductive method, which (assuming the ideal case of persistent empirical confirmation of the consequences of the underlying hypothesis) proceeds on the basis of foundations laid down and theoretical results established once and for all, and whose progressive movement may well be characterized as "linear" expansion by way of continuation.

Nonetheless, a difference obtains between mathematical and instrumental analysis. After the conditions have been discovered that make a certain mathematical state of affairs possible, mathematical analysis has completed its task, which consists in nothing other than establishing a mathematico-logical nexus. Similarly, when instrumental analysis has discovered motivations and patterns of behavior suitable for keeping the market on a path from one transitory phase to the next until the postulated macro-goal is finally reached, a "logical" nexus of means appropriate to specific ends has been laid bare. However, nothing guarantees or assures the actualization of that nexus, or its application to social reality. Toward this end, a new factor must be brought into operation—namely,

---

[18] E. Cassirer, *Das Erkenntnisproblem in der Philosophie und Wissenschaft der neueren Zeit* (Berlin: Bruno Cassirer, 1911), I, p. 451.

[19] Plato, *Meno* 87a; cf., also J. Klein, *A Commentary on Plato's* Meno (Chapel Hill: The University of North Carolina Press, 1965), pp. 206*f*.

[20] *OEK*, p. 143*f*.

control—whose introduction gives the full meaning of "political" to Political Economics.

By "control," Lowe does not mean measures of fiscal or tariff policy, which only modify the framework within which the marketers operate, but which do not mold their patterns of behavior. On the contrary, it is the behavior of the micro-units and their motivations, both purposive and cognitive, upon which control is intended to have a bearing. Control can assume two forms. One is *command*, as in collectivist societies in which all decisions are made by the central authority, and where the implementation of the decisions taken amounts to little more than the solution of an engineering problem. However, if some measure of autonomous decentralized decision-making is to be preserved, control will be exercised by *manipulation* rather than command. The objective of manipulation is to influence, without coercion, the motivations of the actors, both their action directives and, even more important, their expectations, by removing their uncertainty as far as possible. This is accomplished by public information concerning the macro-goal to be attained, the intermediary states through which the system is supposed to pass on its way to the macro-goal, and measures of direct intervention that the public authority is prepared to take in case of emergency.

By means of control, provided it is effective, the social and economic reality is transformed by being adjusted to the results of instrumental analysis. What at first was *a logical nexus between means suitable for postulated ends* becomes, due to effective control, *a nexus between causes and effects*. Causal, progressively deductive and predictive reasoning is now made possible by the order control introduces into the system. No disorderly system lends itself to theoretical treatment, since disorder may stem from a great variety of causes; this is perhaps the reason for the plurality of explanations proposed for the phenomena of industrial fluctuations. In Political Economics, there is an interplay between theory and practice, insofar as the practice, guided by instrumental analysis, transforms the reality to make it amenable to deductive prediction. In Traditional Economics, theoretical knowledge depends upon the commonsense experience and knowledge of the actors; consequently, it is affected by the uncertainty and ambiguity that besets them. Instrumental analysis makes theoretical knowledge independent of commonsense knowledge, which, moreover, by such means of manipulative control as information, becomes largely determined by theoretical knowledge.

At this point, the difference between Traditional Economics and Political Economics can be expressed in still another way. Traditional Economics moves in only one direction, progressing deductively from a hypothesis to its consequences, from causes to effects. Political Economics, on the contrary, is involved in two movements. In the second movement, as just mentioned, it also progresses from causes to effects—that is, it proceeds deductively. However, the starting point for its deductions is not a hypothesis laid down as a heuristic principle, but rather the terminals arrived at in the first movement, that of instrumental analysis.

Dr. Lowe claims for Political Economics a logico-theoretical advantage over Traditional Economics—namely, that of a higher degree of generality—so that Traditional Economics proves a special case or—as he puts it—a limiting case of Political Economics. In the first place, classical economic theory has concerned itself with the market economy in the specific modern sense, to the almost total disregard of the forms of economic organization in use prior to the rise of capitalism,[21] while in principle all forms of socioeconomic organization lend themselves to analysis in terms of Political Economics. Even within the confines of the modern market society, traditional economic theory, as repeatedly mentioned, considers one action directive only, while Political Economics admits of a plurality of possible directives. Most instructive in this respect is Dr. Lowe's discussion of the law of supply and demand in terms of instrumental analysis.[22] In its original form this law predicts the actual occurrence of a series of events; it states that if the quantities demanded are in excess of the quantities supplied, certain events will happen that will lead to a terminal macro-state in which demand and supply balance. The translation into terms of instrumental analysis is as follows: If the quantities demanded exceed the quantities supplied, and if a terminal state is stipulated in which demand and supply are to balance, then the events in question are suitable means for attaining the goal. During the early phase of capitalist development, when the law of supply and demand had empirical validity, the transition from the hypothetical nexus between means and ends to the categorical one between causes and effects was assured by the pressures and other conditions of the environment. In other words, the historically given forces and environmental conditions assumed the function which in Political Economics is assigned to control in its various forms. Again, as in traditional economic theory, only one action directive is recognized, so only one form of control—the anonymous one—is taken into consideration, whereas Political Economics admits of a plurality of both action directives and forms of control.

CONCLUDING REMARKS

At the outset we insisted upon the cognizance and comprehension the actors on the social scene have of themselves and of that scene. They

---

[21] *OEK*, p. 28.
[22] *OEK*, pp. 145*f*.

pursue certain micro-goals; in these pursuits they are guided by their commensense knowledge of their field of action, in particular, by expectations of events to occur, and also, and even primarily, by actions and reactions on the part of fellow marketers. Political Economics builds on this foundation and supplements it by pointing out that the knowledge and cognizance in question need not be purely passive contemplation. As in his individual life, so in his social existence, man is capable of willing and planning for the conditions under which he wishes to live. By appropriate action he can, at least in some measure, make himself master of his condition. Instrumental analysis serves as a tool toward this end.

For this reason, the significance of instrumental analysis is not confined to economics but, as Dr. Lowe suggests, extends to other fields of social science as well. Political science is a case in point. A certain political condition may be postulated as a goal and a question may be raised concerning the means suitable for its attainment. Among those suitable means, there might well be certain economic macro-states. However, we feel we should not go beyond this hint, having already ventured far enough, perhaps too far, outside the confines of our professional competence.

3

ERNEST NAGEL

METHOD IN SOCIAL SCIENCE AND NATURAL SCIENCE

My role in this discussion is to comment on some questions of general methodology raised by Professor Gurwitsch's pointed analysis of Adolph Lowe's approach to the theoretical study of economic phenomena. To this statement of my task two further remarks should be added. First, like Dr. Gurwitsch, I feel that it would be absurd for someone like myself who is not an economist to evaluate Dr. Lowe's contributions to economic theory, or even to assess the validity of the various factual claims involved in his estimate of what he calls "Traditional Economics." Some of these claims have been challenged by several of Dr. Lowe's professional colleagues, but although their criticisms provide grounds for doubt as to whether he has established these claims, my doubts play no part in what follows and I will assume that the claims are sound. Second, the methodological problems of economic inquiry with which Dr. Lowe is concerned seem to me both important and difficult, but I am not certain that I understand thoroughly the positions he takes on them. Accordingly, although my comments on the latter are sometimes critical, I am not sure whether my disagreements are on matters of emphasis or on matters of substance. Indeed, Professor Lowe is generally quite aware of objections of the sort I will be making to his methodological claims; perhaps the only good reason for my repeating such objections is that he may be induced to restate his rejoinders to them more fully.

I

Professor Gurwitsch presents his sympathetic examination of Dr. Lowe's methodological views in the context of the long-standing controversy over the differences between the social and the natural sciences, and some of my comments must therefore be addressed to this issue.

Let me begin by mentioning, and then dismissing as not in serious dispute, several points on which Dr. Gurwitsch lays great stress: that unlike most of the things and processes studied in the natural sciences, human beings are capable of choosing and pursuing goals; that they hold beliefs, whether well founded or not, both about the ways things happen in inanimate and animate nature and about the comparative adequacy of their own actions for achieving their purposes; that men's beliefs, rules of conduct, and expectations are among the factors that determine their overt behavior; that the specific content of such beliefs, rules, and expectations is not "inherent" to man but is highly variable; and that in consequence the behavior of human beings, whether as individuals or as groups, cannot be explained or predicted as being simply the resultant of "external forces" impressed on them. On all these matters I agree with Dr. Gurwitsch; I also agree with him that no economic theory can be an effective instrument of prediction if it fails to take into account the specifically human factors that enter into the operation of an economic market.

However, it does not follow from these facts alone that the logic of theoretical economics must differ from the logic of theoretical natural science. Viewed formally, the human factors that are at least partly determinative of men's economic transactions are simply one set of "variables" among others that may have to be recognized in formulating some proposed economic theory. To be sure, the identification and investigation of the substantive factors represented by those variables require the use of special techniques that are distinctive to the social sciences. But a similar statement holds for many variables in theories developed in natural science—for example, astronomy, physical chemistry, and genetics each employ techniques of observation and experimentation that are often unique to the discipline. Nevertheless, the logic of theoretical inquiry in these different branches of natural science appears to be common to all of them.

(It is perhaps worth passing notice that, like Drs. Lowe and Gurwitsch, the economist Fritz Machlup acknowledges his indebtedness to Alfred

Schutz' views on the determinants of human action. But as I understand Dr. Machlup's ideas on the logic of theoretical economics, they diverge seriously from those of Drs. Lowe and Gurwitsch. Therefore, agreement on what are the distinctive marks of social reality does not necessarily lead to agreement on what is the proper method of economic theorizing.)

Dr. Gurwitsch also believes that there are other differences between the subject matters of the social and natural sciences, closely related to those already mentioned, that require the use of a distinctive method of inquiry in the former. One of these further differences, to which Dr. Lowe in particular pays much attention, is that unlike the natural sciences, the behavior of the economic system in advanced industrial societies such as ours, as well as that of the micro-units involved in the system, lacks a sufficient degree of "orderliness" for reliable prediction. According to Dr. Lowe, phenomena can be arranged along a continuum leading from "perfect order" to "perfect disorder," with the range of phenomena that are intractable to scientific generalization lying "around the middle of the spectrum, since both extremes and their neighboring regions are open to deductive or stochastic generalizations." He believes that economic phenomena fall into a range "somewhere between the extreme of perfect order and the middle range of erratic behavior." [1]

These are largely factual claims about economic matters, and I will not dispute them. Nevertheless, it would, I think, be premature to conclude that the logic of theoretical natural science (and in particular the hypothetico-deductive method of physics and Traditional Economics) as described by both Dr. Lowe and Dr. Gurwitsch is therefore radically inadequate for the social science subject matter. I venture some cautionary remarks by recalling, in summary fashion, a few pertinent matters, even though they are quite familiar to both Drs. Lowe and Gurwitsch. In the first place, it is demonstrable that no sequence of events embodies an "absolute" disorder: a sequence may indeed be random when judged by some given standard of order, but it cannot be random in respect to all conceivable standards. Failure to find some order—even a practically useful order—may therefore be only temporary. Again, as Dr. Lowe clearly shows, whether a phenomenon is to be counted as unpredictable depends in part on what degree of precision is stipulated for the prediction. Unpredictability is thus not necessarily an intrinsic trait of a phenomenon, but is relative both to currently available knowledge and to purpose. Finally, although no significant generalization may be statable for a *prima facie* erratic phenomenon when a given set of variables is employed, the possibility cannot be excluded that the use of

[1] See p. 4.

a different or an enlarged set of variables may have a more successful outcome. To be sure, the number of variables indispensable for a generalization may be so large as to make the generalization practically useless, but it is not clear how the difficulty can be outflanked by any method of inquiry. As will be noted later, the difficulty is not removed by Dr. Lowe's logic of instrumental analysis.

There is, however, another feature—for methodological considerations perhaps the most important one—which Dr. Gurwitsch believes distinguishes the social from the natural sciences. According to him, in physics and chemistry (though apparently not in biology), the intra- and extra-systemic forces that determine the behavior of a system can each be studied, at least in principle, in isolation from the influence of other forces. Furthermore, since each force continues to produce its effects in accordance with the same laws whether it is acting alone or jointly with other forces, the total effect produced by a combination of forces in a given situation "can be obtained by addition and subtraction." More generally, although the behavior of a system will vary with different combinations of the intra- and extra-systemic forces, the forces themselves are not "modified by one another." [2] But this is not the case in the social sciences. In economics, for example, the forces that supposedly determine basic processes are "intrinsically affected by changes in the sociohistorical environment" and operate only under certain specific environmental conditions. Dr. Gurwitsch therefore doubts "whether there are, or can be, economic laws at all in the specific sense the term has in the natural sciences: namely, laws valid under all environmental conditions. . . ." [3] Theoretical reasoning in the social sciences, he suggests, is "significantly and profoundly different from that in physics and chemistry," because of the "essential historicity of human existence." [4]

How sound is this contrast, and what is its significance for the methodology of economics? Despite its plausibility, Dr. Gurwitsch's distinction between "forces" or "factors" that are modified by one another (as in economics), and those that are not (although their effects may be when the forces are combined with others, as in physics), is not entirely clear to me. Consider one of his examples: Although the motivation factor of maximizing profits (the extremum principle) was significant in determining economic behavior during the period of early capitalism, it has lost its "imperativeness" because of the rise in standards of living and changed expectations. But what is the difference between saying that the factor *itself* has been modified by these other factors, and saying that

, [2] See p. 47.
[3] See p. 48.
[4] See p. 48.

its *effects* are no longer the same as before, either because they are swamped by the effects of the other factors or because the factor is not as pervasive as it once was? In just what way is the economic example different from examples that can be cited from physics? For example, gravitation plays a dominant role in determining the motions of large masses (as in the solar system) despite the presence of electromagnetic forces, but it can be neglected for all practical purposes in the interior of atoms, where electrical forces are the significant ones.

Dr. Gurwitsch suggests that while physical forces are "additive," this is not so for the "forces" in social science or even in biology. However, much depends on the sense in which the word "additive" is used. Thus, the resultant of the joint operation of what John Stuart Mill called "mechanical causes" is the vector sum of those causes; he distinguished such forces from "chemical" ones on the ground that in chemistry the properties of a compound are not "the sum of its separate parts." Nevertheless, there are systems even in physics whose behavior can be predicted as the effect of their component parts and forces, though not simply by using the familiar parallelogram of forces. As the late Wolfgang Köhler pointed out, the pattern of distribution of electric charges on an insulated conductor depends on the shape of the conductor; it is not a simple "sum" of the effects of the inducing charge on unit areas of the conductor. However, the pattern can be predicted on the basis of electrostatic field theory. Again, quantum theory shows that the chemical properties of an atom depend on, and can be explained by, the arrangement of its components and the forces associated with them, but the resultant property is plainly not the vectorial sum of the effects of those forces. Whether in these and analogous cases one calls the forces additive is of little moment. What the examples illustrate is that an unduly narrow view is taken of the method of natural science if it is supposed that the method is inapplicable to situations in which the systems under investigation have a hierarchically organized internal structure.

Finally, granting the assumption that social existence is essentially historical and that economic generalizations in particular are valid only for given sociohistorical environments, it is not evident how it follows that theoretical reasoning in economics must be profoundly different from that used in physics and chemistry. It is surely not a *premise*, when the hypothetico-deductive method (the method Dr. Gurwitsch takes as representative of theoretical reasoning in physics and chemistry) is used in natural science, that the theories adopted for explanatory or predictive purposes are (or must be) known to be true for all sectors of nature and for all time—although natural scientists may hope that currently accepted theories do have a universal scope. On the contrary, a theory may be believed to be valid only for a limited spatiotemporal region—indeed, its scope may be unknown—without thereby impairing its use as an instrument of reliable prediction in some domain. Thus, no one knows today whether the gene theory of heredity holds for forms of life that may exist in other parts of the universe; and it may turn out, as Ernst Mach suggested, that the validity of Newton's first law of motion (which ascribes an inherent property of inertia to all bodies) depends on the actual distribution of masses in the universe, a distribution that may not be permanent. But even if these theories should turn out to have only a limited range of applicability, in certain areas they yield reliable predictions. In short, the use of the hypothetico-deductive method in theoretical natural science does not depend on the absolute invariance of its theoretical assumptions. In point of fact, since the scope of valid application of these assumptions is generally problematic, this method appears to be indispensable for ascertaining how far the scope extends.

Thus far, my discussion of the controversy over the differences between the social and natural sciences agrees with the claim that there are important differences in the subject matter explored and the problems encountered; but the discussion has also tried to show that most if not all of the considerations advanced strongly support the conclusion that no significantly different method of theoretical reasoning is required in social inquiry than in natural science. However, I have paid relatively little attention to what Dr. Lowe regards as the central methodological problem for economics—namely, how to devise a reliable predictive theory if, as he maintains, the behavior of the economic system and of the micro-units in it fails to exhibit a sufficient degree of orderliness. It is this assumed lack of stable patterns of behavior that is the rationale for his proposal of instrumental analysis as the appropriate method of economic theorizing, a mode of analysis which he believes distinguishes the method of his Political Economics from the hypothetico-deductive method of Traditional Economics. I must therefore turn to instrumental analysis.

II

The main features of instrumental analysis in economics can be stated briefly. The analysis takes its point of departure from some postulated macro-goal (said to be "known") for the economic system—e.g., full employment and a steady growth in productivity—although with the proviso that the minimal objective of economic activity must be realized: namely, the "satisfactory" provision of goods and services. The analysis then "deduces" from the postulated goal a series of initially "unknown" means "suitable" for achieving the goal, with the series terminating in specifications of the patterns of motivation and behavior of the micro-units that would be required for realizing the goal. Finally, if (as is generally the case) such patterns are not actually manifested in the autonomous and erratic conduct of the micro-units, controls must be instituted (whether through "manipulation" of the micro-units or by "command") so that a sufficient degree of orderliness in human actions is produced to permit the prediction of their macro-effects. In its quest for means that will achieve a given macro-goal, instrumental analysis undoubtedly takes into account established laws in physics, biology, and psychology, as well as "engineering" rules; however, at least according to Dr. Gurwitsch, nowhere does the analysis require the use of "laws that could be specified as inherently 'economic.'" [5]

Dr. Lowe's solution to the fundamental and apparently insuperable difficulty he believes faces the economist—that autonomous human behavior lacks the stable orderliness needed for developing reliable economic generalizations and for achieving desirable economic objectives—is thus to *create* the needed order and to *sustain* it by deliberate human intervention. The solution is analogous to what might be done if the motions of a body of water were "naturally" unruly and unpredictable: its energies would be channeled by various artifices in order to produce a fairly regular flow. Given Dr. Lowe's assumptions about the "erratic" character of human actions, his resolution of the problem is on the face of it the only possible one; his instrumental analysis can be construed, as he himself suggests,[6] as a method for finding hypotheses concerning the patterns men's motivations and economic transactions should exhibit, so that if those patterns were actualized, the behavior of the economic system could be at least approximately predicted.

Nevertheless, though Drs. Lowe and Gurwitsch make plain the general character of instrumental analysis, their accounts of it also contain what seem to me puzzling things. Let me state some of my difficulties.

1. Dr. Gurwitsch thinks that, up to a point, instrumental analysis in economics is quite like "regressive" analysis in mathematics. However, the use of regressive analysis in geometry to solve a construction problem—e.g., to inscribe a circle in a triangle—presupposes that the properties of the figures mentioned in the problem are fully specified by an assumed set of axioms. Accordingly, the deduction of the series of steps which, if followed in the reverse order, will lead to the inscribed circle, is not made simply from the supposition that the circle has already been inscribed, but from the *conjunction* of this supposition and the axioms. Thus if regressive analysis in mathematics is a paradigm for instrumental analysis in economics, it is not clear how suitable means can be literally

---

[5] See p. 51.
[6] See p. 15.

deduced from a postulated macro-goal (as Dr. Gurwitsch explicitly says they can) [7] unless some general assumptions are adopted concerning, among other things, more or less stable patterns of human behavior. This difficulty remains, even if the requirement of strict deducibility is weakened by replacing it with the demand that the means are only to be "derived" in some other sense from the postulated goal. But if such assumptions are indispensable for the task at hand, instrumental analysis cannot solve the problem of how, in view of the autonomous and erratic actions of men, reliable predictions about economic matters are to be made.

(Incidentally, the conclusion of a regressive analysis in mathematics—in the above example, the conclusion that a circle is inscribable in a triangle in a specified way—is a logical consequence of the axioms, and is therefore deducible from the axioms by "progressive" or hypothetico-deductive reasoning. Except for the fact that the sequential orders in which statements are derived in regressive and progressive analysis are generally different, it is not evident that the logic of the two procedures is different. A similar remark applies to instrumental and hypothetico-deductive reasoning in economics.)

2. Instrumental analysis in economics starts from some postulated economic macro-goal. It would surely not be reasonable to postulate such a goal without considering what it would entail for the economic system. But can we ascertain what are the likely economic consequences of the goal's realization without employing hypothetico-deductive reasoning to trace out the implications of the postulate? And can we trace out these implications without using, in addition to laws drawn from the natural and psychological sciences, some of the laws or assumptions of "positive" economics about the interrelations of economic variables? If, as I suspect, the answer to these questions is uniformly negative, theoretical reasoning in Political Economics is not "profoundly different" from the hypothetico-deductive method of reasoning in Traditional Economics, since the latter seems to be an indispensable component of the former.

Moreover, it would be a gross oversimplification to suppose that economic goals are, or can be, postulated singly. It is certainly more realistic to assume that a plurality of goals is postulated: not only full employment, but perhaps also a stable price level, a certain rate of economic growth, some stipulated distribution of income, and so on. However, it is not self-evident that the goals that may be entertained are compatible with one another, and as Dr. Lowe makes amply clear, it would be irrational to adopt them without first ascertaining by analysis whether or not

---

[7] See p. 52.

they are indeed mutually consistent. But can such an analysis be undertaken without using some theoretical assumptions about the ways in which
the various economic variables are related to one another? Dr. Lowe
himself appears to believe that the answer is in the negative; he men-
tions as one example of an assumption that may be needed in such an
analysis the "law" that a rise in the rate of investment is a suitable means
of promoting employment.[8] Why he thinks that this and other such
assumptions he cites "are of a nature quite different from what passes
in Traditional Economics as laws of economic behavior"[9] is at bottom
obscure to me. There seems to be no doubt that economic laws of some
kind are essential for instrumental analysis, and that hypothetico-deductive reasoning must also be employed in this analysis.

3. In their accounts of instrumental analysis, Drs. Lowe and Gurwitsch
agree that economic macro-goals must not only be mutually consistent
but must also satisfy other restricting conditions. Perhaps the most important of these is that goals must be compatible with the maximum
possible autonomous decision-making by the micro-units. This condition is tantamount to a requirement that the controls which are to be
instituted for realizing the goals should, as far as possible, be achieved
by "manipulation" rather than by "command"—that is, that requisite
changes in men's motivations, action directives, and expectations should
be effected through "influence" instead of through coercion. But how is
such influence to be exercised? Dr. Gurwitsch cites as examples of "influence" (or manipulation) the supplying of "public information concerning the macro-goal to be attained, the intermediary states through which
the system is supposed to pass on its way to the macro-goal, and measures of direct intervention that the public authority is prepared to take
in case of emergency."[10] The efficacy of publicity (or of education in
general) as an instrument for influencing economic micro-units is doubt-
less not negligible. But there are also reasons to believe that publicity
alone, unaccompanied by the introduction of various economic measures
(such as changes in fiscal and monetary policy), is not likely to produce
transformations in human actions sufficient to achieve the postulated
goals. However, Dr. Gurwitsch seems to deny that the adoption of such
economic devices is a suitable form of influence—although I find it difficult to understand why this is so, or indeed how the public authority
can intervene at all, except by exercising overt coercion, if it does not do
so by instituting economic measures. On the other hand, if such measures
are suitable instruments of control by manipulation, it would hardly be

---

[8] See p. 20.
[9] See p. 20.
[10] See p. 53.

reasonable to use them without having some conception of their likely economic consequences, and therefore without assuming some economic laws. In short, I do not see how one can even begin to employ instrumental analysis to find means for realizing a specified economic end unless some laws of positive economics are taken for granted, if only during a given inquiry and for a given economic system.

4. Instrumental analysis in economics can achieve its objectives only if it can find a series of interlocking relations of dependence between a class of human actions which Dr. Lowe calls "controls," and another class of behaviors that constitute the postulated macro-goals for an economic system. As both he and Dr. Gurwitsch indicate, the number of variables that may enter into this chain of relations can be expected to be large; they also call for the consideration of a large assortment of factors, including physical, biological, psychological, and social ones. It is no exaggeration to say that our current knowledge of the requisite relations of dependence is hardly adequate for accomplishing the task of a full instrumental analysis. In any case, to accomplish it the economist would have to expand his customary range of professional concerns to unprecedented dimensions; however, it is problematic whether such an expansion would be the best strategy of research, and whether it could effectively be done. At present, at any rate, Political Economics is an ideal —indeed, a noble ideal that is undoubtedly worth pursuing—but not one that will be realized in the foreseeable future.

4

HANS JONAS

ECONOMIC KNOWLEDGE
AND
CRITIQUE OF GOALS

I am going to deal with a subject which is marginal to Adolph Lowe's scientific work but, as I happen to know, central to his personal concern: the cognitive status of "ends" and, correlatively, the possible "objective" validation of the choices economic policy must make among them to set the terminal goals of its planning. It is obvious to the reader of Adolph Lowe's work that on this matter he entertains the stance of severe abstention which nineteenth-century positivism has made an axiomatic part of the scientific creed, but, also, that he does so regretfully. Although he is keenly aware that economics deals with a sphere of activities inherently governed by ends, and that of late this sphere has come into a new "freedom of choice" among a plurality of possible—i.e., optional—goals beyond the mandatory, basic goal of mere subsistence; that these goals are of such a kind that their realization, transcending purely economic terms, must affect the total condition of man; and that criteria of desirability among competing goals are more necessary the more open the choices and the more far-reaching the decisions to be made (the criteria also become more urgent since to choose between the alternatives, optional as they are, is itself not optional at all)—although he is aware of all these things, Dr. Lowe still denies to his own science, to economic knowledge, the power to provide such criteria and thus the authority to say "yes" or "no" to any ends proposed, except, of course, for verdicts on mere feasibility. To the question, then, of whether economic knowledge is to be the master or the servant of economic policy, the arbiter of its goals or their executor, his austere answer is: the latter. It is the answer of scientific asceticism, observed for the sake of the purity of economics as a science.

Still, Dr. Lowe does not think that the determination of goals must therefore remain a matter of mere irrational preference. What none of the "positive" sciences of man—economics, political science, sociology, anthropology, psychology, biology—can provide, philosophy (not a "science," yet a species of knowledge) is expected to provide: a knowledge of the "good life," objective criteria of choice based on such knowledge, and a justification of ends, ultimate and intermediate. The following composite quotation is, I believe, a fair representation of Adolph Lowe's position:

> *Technological progress has greatly reduced the traditional pressures which left room for one state of economic welfare only. It is granting us for the first time "freedom of choice" [among a variety of feasible goal alternatives. We are thus required to make] specific decisions on ends, for which no economic mechanism offers any criteria. [Economic policy] cannot be derived from intra-economic considerations. It is the political or social philosopher who alone can vindicate the ends. . . . In a society of increasing wealth, decisions on welfare become his explicit business.*[1]

In other words, the comparative worth and obligatory claims of goals are not objects of economic knowledge, and are not to be adjudicated by it; goals are objects of philosophical knowledge, whence economics may borrow them as "givens," as "hypotheses" for its own reasoning. It was in this spirit of economic modesty and faith in philosophy that I, a noneconomist and presumed philosopher, was asked to deal here with the cognitive status of ends and values and, on the basis of what that status is found to be, with the question of valid approbation and condemnation of goals. It is the hoary question of a science of the "good" and the "bad," the "better" and the "worse," for man.

I

Let me say right away that I must, on behalf of philosophy, reciprocate the modesty and disclaim the competence so generously accorded.

---

[1] Adolph Lowe, "The Normative Roots of Economic Values," *Human Values and Economic Policy*, ed. Sidney Hook (New York: New York University Press, 1967), pp. 177–178.

The historical record clearly discourages the expectation that philosophers can demonstrate a *summum bonum*, the ultimate purpose of man, an absolute scale of values, the authority of "oughts," and the like. Nor should economics (or political science, for that matter) be permitted to wash its hands of those questions entirely and, by shifting responsibility for them to the misty court of "philosophy," leave undone that part of the theoretical task—this side of the unattainable absolute—which in fact it can do, which does fall within its terms, and which therefore is part of its own business. Here indeed the so-called philosopher—that is, the thoughtful outsider—simply by being less immersed in the technicalities of the field, less encumbered (less intimidated, I might say) by its conventions, and therefore freer to reflect on principles, may be in a position to rectify the opinion of itself which a science such as economics develops by internal consensus, and perhaps to show that its limitations in the matter of judging goals are not quite as narrow as those which its own presently accepted rigorism or defeatism enjoins on its practitioners.

This at least is the main and not overly ambitious purpose I set myself in this paper: to argue that a definite goal-commitment is constitutive for the economic field as such and therefore implicitly underwritten by any theory of the field; that from this built-in fundamental commitment, some criteria for the evaluation of economic goals derive which are entirely germane to economic knowledge at its most scientific; and that their application goes a long way beyond the primitive, choiceless goal of mere subsistence, extending well into the sphere of that latter-day freedom of choice where Adolph Lowe sees the economist resigned to agnosticism and to awaiting instruction from the holders of power or metaphysical truth. Thus, returning the compliment, the philosopher returns the task where it belongs: to economic knowledge itself. At least concerning what should *not* be—what goals ought to be resisted—the economist may be able to speak with the authority of his theory: no small matter in the uniquely modern situation where the "no" can become more important than the "yes" in answering the massive offer of possible goals with which our novel powers besiege our "freedom of choice."

So far my message, as one of normative duty and competence, will seem to be cheering, in that it widens the conception of economic knowledge beyond the restrictive conception of its mere factual or instrumental assignment. But, alas, my second purpose will be to suggest where the real difficulty lies: *not* in determining the criteria for choosing among goals, where Adolph Lowe sees it, but in providing the matter for the *application* of those criteria—namely, valid anticipations of the final state to which any long-term macro-goal will lead under the novel conditions of total and global impact. In other words, the real trouble, as I see it, is our scientific inadequacy—more than just a temporary inadequacy—to the task of representing, with anything like demonstrative or even inductive certainty, the alternatives between which choices are to be made, if they are to be between ultimate effects and not merely between proximate advantages.

Dr. Lowe seems to think that, since the projected terminal state is of our own designing, conceived and specified by us, we should surely know it. Having laid down its terms ourselves, we are at least certain what it is we are offering for acceptance or rejection, agonizing as thereafter the choice may be, and difficult as may be the task of devising the means for its implementation. It will be my contention that this assumption that we know the final state by defining it through some select features relevant to our choice—an assumption taken over from mechanical engineering—is unwarranted in the field in which the economist must make his projections. And since the adequately defined "final state" is to function as the initial datum, as the "known" in Dr. Lowe's deductive-instrumental analysis, my contention means that this analysis will in turn be vitiated if its premise, the goal state (whose availability to knowledge the "instrumentalist" must take for granted), is in fact elusive. I may add that with the same principle of "total impact" operating all along the line, each deductive link (destined, in reverse order, to become an instrumental step, but representing in itself a total state of the system *at the time*) will be rendered equally doubtful in terms of *its* total effect.

What it comes to is that, in the last resort, the directed and "controlled" alternative is cognitively little better off than the "automatically" self-realizing one. In either case the "terminus"—whether projected for planning or merely expected from the observed trend of events—is spotlighted for our vision out of a darkness of collateral unknowns with which it is inextricably intertwined, unlike the terminal states of isolable and repeatable physical sequences. We *could*, I say, judge rationally enough the relative merits of alternative end-states and decide their order of preferability *if* we had their full measure, but we haven't and are reduced to imaginative guessing. And when, on a guess, we do decide for any controlled target-alternative, we cannot gauge the full implications of our own progressive, mediating acts of control and thus predict with certainty their consequences.

This view of the state of affairs almost reverses that of Adolph Lowe. It places within "economic knowledge" what according to him transcends it—viz., standards for goal selection even without knowledge of the ultimate good (here the metaphysician is no better off than he)—and it doubts what he is confident of—namely, the competence of existing social science both to represent goal states adequately and to deduce the intermediate, instrumental states cogently. This skeptical reasoning, of course, applies only to the long-range, large-scale goal perspectives which our self-propelled technological powers press on us with their inherent trend to go "all the way," to carry each possibility to its extreme conclusion; and it is these quasi-utopian, quasi-eschatological perspectives, rather than the measured alternatives of our short-range, deliberate planning, that are the "goals" about which we will someday have to decide before they decide about us.

The paradox of our having to decide about ends we don't understand, about hypothetical and incompletely specified, yet unavoidable alternatives, will prompt some concluding surmises on the cautionary rather than "instrumental" role of economic theory and policy in our journey into the unknown.

II

I will now go step by step over the ground staked out in the preceding statement of purpose and try to argue the conclusions provisionally summarized there. What I have first to deal with is the alleged gulf between scientific truth and ends, obviously related to the concept of "value-free science" that is axiomatic to Adolph Lowe as it is to the scientific fraternity as a whole. "It is intuitively obvious," he writes, "that such a discussion [viz., concerning the choice of an economic macro-goal] will carry us beyond the realm of facts and factual relations into the region of value judgments—a region in which discursive thinking, and thus scientific inquiry as the modern mind understands it, cannot by themselves offer final answers." [2] Not final, perhaps, but what science offers final answers on anything? Does "not final" amount to "none at all"?

Let us clarify the relation of values and ends (or goals); they are by no means the same, although they are often confused. We will begin with ends. An end is that for whose sake a thing exists and for whose production or preservation a process takes place or an action is undertaken. Thus a hammer exists for hammering, a digestive tract for digesting and thereby keeping the organism alive and in good shape; walking is done to get somewhere; a court of law sits in order to administer justice. Note that the ends or goals said in these cases to define the things or actions in question do so independently of their status as values, and that the statement of these ends does not involve value judgments on my part. I may deem a state of nature without hammers preferable to the state of civilization where nails are driven into walls; I may deplore the fact that

---

[2] See p. 18.

lions are not vegetarians and therefore disapprove of digestive systems geared to the carnivorous mode of sustenance; I may think it better for people to stay where they are instead of always going elsewhere; I may take a dim view of any justice served by courts of law—in brief, I may consider all those ends as worthless in themselves; nevertheless, I would still have to acknowledge them as the ends of the objects in question, considered on their own terms, *if* my description of them has been correct. Adopting, as it were, the "point of view" of the objects themselves, I may then proceed from the recognition of their intrinsic ends to judgments on their greater or lesser adequacy for the achievement of those ends, and I may speak of a better or worse hammer, digestive condition, locomotive performance, or judiciary institution. These, indeed, are value judgments, but they are surely not based on value-decisions or goal-choices of my own: they are derived from the being of the objects themselves, based on our understanding of them, not on our feelings about them. Thus we can form the concept of a specific "good" and its opposite and the grades in between for different entities and contexts of entities—provided that, and to the extent that, we can recognize "ends" as properly belonging to the nature of the things themselves.

And here, of course, arises the first and most sweeping challenge to the claim of an objective value-knowledge: Can we rightly attribute ends to the nature of things? Of any things, if not of all things? As is well known, the answer was "yes" for a long time with the full backing of natural philosophy, and it increasingly has become "no" with the rise of modern natural science and *its* philosophy. Our query, of course, raises the problem of teleology. In the long-dominant Aristotelian view, the things of nature were activated by principles of goal-direction discernible in their normal modes of operation. This was most obviously so, of course, in the animate sphere, but by hypothesis also in inanimate nature; and again not only for each class of entities according to its specific nature, but also for their totality—i.e., the universe as a system of self-sustaining order assuring the balanced coexistence of its parts. In terms of such a view, it was possible to speak of realization, approximation, and frustration of natural ends; of perfection and imperfection; and of a rank order among those ends according to value criteria derived from the teleological stratification of the system itself. The "good," in other words, and the distinction of lesser and greater goods, had a foundation in the knowable nature of things—i.e., in their particular natures and the nature of the whole.

To be sure, even such a theory of reality leaves "man the knower" the freedom to dissociate himself from the value-decision (as it were) of the universe, to counter it with his own, and in *his* order of preference, e.g., to set ignorance over knowledge, feeling over thinking, unconsciousness over consciousness, inanimate over animate existence, disorder over order, not-being over being. In the exercise of his right to dissent, he is free to entertain the wholesale conviction, *"Drum besser wärs, dass nichts entstünde."* But this is the exercise of a private right and does not materially alter the cognitive situation. Once he has registered his dissent from without, and so long as he does not contest the *facts* of the Aristotelian universe, the theoretician must still, *within* its object-field, abide by its evidence and assess degrees of the good and the success or failure of natural activities on *its* terms—i.e., according to its intrinsic system of ends *as perceived*, even if not approved. Without endorsing these ends (or indeed their very principle), he should yet arrive at the same evaluations as he who, in addition to perceiving, also endorses them. The qualified value verdicts *ex hypothesi* ("given this universe . . .") should not differ from the verdicts delivered absolutely in the case of personal identification. This would then be a pure case of separation between subjective and objective value judgments—i.e., between my own preferences and the immanent standards of the object; it woud be a "value-free" science deferring to an object which by its teleological nature is not value-free at all and therefore demands of the knower the consideration of value as integral to his knowledge. This holds independently of whatever answer be given to the rather outsized question concerning the universal nature of things: it simply says that with objects *of a certain type*, provided there are any such objects, descriptive theory turns of itself into normative theory. The question is: Are there such objects?

The crucial concept here is that of "ends," without which the concepts of norm and objective value would be meaningless. The story of how, since the anti-Aristotelian beginnings of modern science, "ends" have come to be thrown out of the scientific account of reality, indeed of our very idea of reality, is too well known to need retelling. Suffice it to recall that first, in Galilean–Newtonian mechanics, inanimate nature was purged of teleological principles and, stripped down to "efficient" causality, was left alien or neutral to value. Then, with Darwinism, the same thing happened to animate—i.e., organic—nature, the original home ground of final causes and the exemplary object of teleological understanding. Working with the mere mechanics of random mutations and natural selection, Darwinian evolution made reason out of the "folly" (as Voltaire had still called it) "to deny that the eye is made to see, the ear to hear, the stomach to digest": precisely this *is* denied, and we are bidden with all the authority of Science to look upon seeing, hearing, digesting, and, in sum, "living," as *de facto* functions, but not purposes, of structures that came about without the causality of purpose. And so we have to strike the "digestive tract" from our sample list of teleological entities.

At this point we may briefly stop to survey the different meanings of "value-free" that have emerged in our discussion. In the expression "*wertfreie Wissenschaft*," it means an injunction, an "ought" addressed to the scientist: that he should not allow the values of his own option to intrude into and color his reading of the evidence and his reasoning about the evidence. This is nothing but the ideal and duty of objectivity, and on this there are no two opinions. But beyond this self-evident rule, "value-free" may also express a theoretical proposition concerning the nature of things or what is knowable about things. It then implies that not only should the scientist keep from importing his own values into the subject matter; he also should not expect value-information from the subject matter. Neither as prejudgments nor as resultant judgments do values have a place in the universe of science. It is only a secondary point, making little difference in the practical effect, whether this is to be understood as an ontological or an epistemological statement. In the first and prevalent sense, the object itself is claimed to be value-free— that is, alien or neutral to value; this means, when extended to *all* objects, that "value" in its very being is merely subjective and has no objective status whatsoever. In the more cautious epistemological sense, the proposition is skeptical rather than dogmatic, contending that values, whatever their ontological status, cannot be known (i.e., demonstrated or even defined) scientifically, and for this "agnostic" reason they are assigned to the sphere of mere belief.

In any case, it is the propositional (not just the admonitory) meaning of "value-free" which we see emerge with the progressive ejection of "ends" from the field of natural science. With regard to "nature" itself, we saw this movement culminating in Darwinian biology. From there the story goes on into the behavioral sciences. Fortunately, we need not follow it any further; nor need we take a stand on whether this goal-indifferent view of nature is the definitive truth. We can afford to grant it summarily without prejudging our particular subject. For whatever the final word about the status of ends in the scheme of things (and it surely has not been spoken yet), when it comes to the type of thing exemplified in our initial sample list by "court of law"—i.e., when it comes to *human institutions*—there is no room to doubt that these institutions have been brought about by the causality of purpose and are kept alive by that causality alone. Ends are indeed their *raisons d'être*, and how well they serve them is a consideration wholly germane to their nature—a nature *defined* by a "what for." Here we have no choice but to accept the "subjective" aims, with which "in view" they were instituted and are being operated, as "objectively" constitutive of their existence and essence. Not even the meaning of their names could be explained without reference to the "what for." Economics falls in this category. As an instituted system of human activities, it has its inherent goal or goals and is subject to evaluations of its adequacy to serving those goals.

I do not believe that there is disagreement on this truism with Adolph Lowe or any other economist; nor is there disagreement on what is at least the first inherent goal of the economic sphere: the provisioning of its members with the physical goods necessary to sustain their lives or, at the very least, to sustain the collective life composing the economic sphere itself. Dr. Lowe's problem begins with the situation created by modern technology, the (allegedly) assured *solution* of this primary provisioning task and the expanding *latitude* for goals and goal alternatives (and applicable methods) *no longer determined* by the dictates of natural necessity. This situation of freedom produces practical anarchy in the selection of goals and epistemological anarchy in their evaluation. It is the problem, bless our hearts, of affluence.

At this point there emerges in Dr. Lowe's reasoning an intriguing coincidence between the question of goals and that of determinism—i.e., between the chances for economic theory to be scientifically predictive and its chances to be normatively prescriptive. Former pressures, so he argues, endowed the economic process with a quasi-mechanical determinacy which permitted economic theory to approximate the logical form of natural science as well as its predictive power. At the same time, the one "categorical imperative" of economic activity, which theory could do nothing but affirm, provided an unquestionable intra-economic norm for evaluating that activity in given instances and, if need be, for prescribing to it its proper course. With emancipation from those pressures through technological progress, both predictive and prescriptive certainty vanished. Under the condition of excess productivity, the economic process lost its constraining determinacy, and economic theory its purported likeness to physics. And the monism of the one imperative goal that was as normatively binding on theory as it was actually dominant in practice gave way to a pluralism of elective goals, for which—as they transcend the only goal that economics validates *per se*—economic theory fails to provide criteria. This means, alas, that economic theory enjoyed normative competence when it did not need it—viz., when circumstances themselves saw to the observance of the "ought" and even, through their deterministic mechanics, guaranteed the automatic implementation of its goal in the final outcome; and that it lost normative competence just when it really began to need it—viz., when goals became elective and circumstances no longer acted in lieu of human choice by their objective causality. I do not raise the question of whether there ever really was— as economic liberalism assumed—such a "pre-established harmony" between causality and the good, in virtue of which economic science *eo ipso* coincided with economic wisdom (as prescriptive knowledge of ends) and in which by the same token wisdom was practically redundant because unwisdom (or laissez-faire) led to the same effect. My concern is with the new dispensation where both the monism of effect and that of goal are gone, the passing coincidence between them (if ever it existed) is ended, and knowledge concerning the intrinsic good of ends, now anything but redundant, is deemed to fall outside economic knowledge altogether.

I now propose to argue that in fact there is more normative competence (and thus responsibility) left to rational theory in the new situation than this picture suggests, or, put differently, that the original and incontestable "categorical imperative" of the economic realm, properly understood in its implications, remains logically effective in yielding criteria for goal selection even after the seeming fulfillment of its primary goal.

To state the obvious, let us first recall that the fact of economics is grounded in the primary biological fact that we live by *metabolism* and are thus creatures of need. But by saying "need" I am already naming something more than a mere "fact"—i.e., more than the physical truth that food, oxygen, etc., are causally necessary for organic existence to go on and must therefore be provided *if* it is to go on. I am saying that this ongoing is "willed" by the organic subject, with no "if" about it, since "to be" for the subject is to be engaged in the business of insuring its being through metabolism: *therefore, because* of the involvement of *interest,* the necessary means to that effect (i.e., to keeping up the metabolic process) assume for it the quality of "needs." Their pursuit thus expresses the basic self-affirmation of life, which—because it is not simply assured, but requires metabolism—becomes a purpose in itself. This purposive affirmation, an *a priori* "option," underlies all economic activity as the pervading commitment of the whole field, and its acknowledgment is the tacit premise of economic theory. Whatever the private misanthropic leanings of the individual thinker, he has *qua* economist adopted this affirmation without which there would be no economic life. Thus economic theory embodies from the outset the transfactual element of endorsing what is itself another transfactual element—viz., interest in being. In that sense it is in value-consent with its subject, reaffirming its intrinsic affirmation.

Next, still elaborating the obvious, we remember that "provisioning" requires "providence": i.e., looking and planning ahead. Here again economic theory, bound by the initial affirmation, must endorse the imperative, "Be provident," and judge economic actions in its light. But here the questions arise: provident for whom? and how far ahead? Pondering these questions, we realize how inappropriate the Robinson Crusoe model is for representing even the most elementary economic situation, not so much because of the absence of companions—and thus of the whole aspect of cooperation, exchange, and distribution, important as this is— but because of the absence of children and thus of a relevant time dimension and of responsibility for the future. Surely there would be no economic life to speak of without care for the offspring. The needs of terminal individuals could be attended to in a makeshift manner. Crusoe, or even a whole company of shipwrecked sailors, could live from hand to mouth and have to answer only to themselves if they chose to emulate the cricket rather than the ant. "Let us eat and drink, for tomorrow we are dead," is a perfectly eligible maxim for mortals without a future; but with newborns rising and the unborn waiting in the wings, the "we" has an indefinite time spread, and "tomorrow" means an ever extending future. The self-affirmation of need, then, includes affirmation of this continuity, and this means *responsibility*.

Thus it must be stressed that metabolism is only half of the biological premise underlying economic life; the other half is reproduction. Through this counterpoise to mortality, with its powerful commitment, a horizon of self-transcendence is added to the reference of need and interest: self-preservation is widened into preservation of progeny; needs beyond one's own become an integral part of concern; and with the unique length of human childhood and dependency, what would otherwise be short-range and merely optional providence in the service of self-interest becomes long-range providence enjoined by responsibility.

Now "responsibility" surely is a transfactual, normative category, and we claim that it is as germane to economics as is "self-interest." Both have the dignity of immanent principles. Stating them, we are saying more than that people, as a matter of fact, wish to stay alive and wish their children to stay alive; and more than that, in fact, they act to provide for both. Our contention is twofold: that "responsibility," deriving from the fundamental *fact* of reproduction, is as *constitutive* of the economic sphere as is (by general admission) "self-interest" or "need," deriving from the fundamental fact of metabolism; and that therefore it is as *normative* to the economist for the evaluation of economic behavior and the critique of economic goals as "need" is usually agreed to be.

The scientific economist may balk at this. While he will hardly dispute the claims for need and self-interest, which indeed have a long and honorable standing in classical theory, he will tend to regard "responsponsibility" as a category imported from the moral sphere, not indigenous to economics *per se*, and therefore not scientifically entitled to normative use in economic theory *qua* economic. He may be willing to grant that people do wish their children to stay alive, besides wishing to stay alive themselves, and he will count this in with the various actual motivations to be reckoned with in explaining and predicting economic behavior; but under the individualistic or atomistic tradition of his craft he will shy away from admitting that this "wish" or commitment is integral to the economic purpose and thus binding upon it.

Nevertheless, he surely must admit that this commitment was originative of the economic purpose in historical fact. The initial economic unit, the family, owes its rationale to the rearing of the young; no economic order of any elaboration could conceivably have evolved without it (or some equivalent social arrangement) or, once evolved, make sense without continuing devotion to its own regenerative perpetuity. Thus on purely *descriptive* grounds the economist must accord to transindividual providence and responsibility the status of being at the root of economic reality, and must acknowledge them as being of its very essence; however, when he does, he must also accord them the *prescriptive* status of providing an intra-economic principle of valid *judgments* on economic policy, including the choice of goals. Where the *raison d'être* of a field is teleological in its nature, as is the case here, its recognition assumes of itself normative force.

How fruitful is this principle for the setting or critique of economic goals? Perhaps we can find out by first asking how far into the future responsible providence extends. This depends on the causal scope of our actions and the attainable reach of our rational foresight. Both of these were formerly small and have lately become tremendously enlarged. This alone suggests that we now have more to say on economic goals— viz., long-term goals—than any former age. The size and "totalistic" style of our ventures in the sign of technology force us to face their remote outcome conjoined with all the collateral effects. In these conditions the principle of responsible providence operates not so much in the positive prescription as in the critical examination of goals—practically as a principle of restraint. There is no dearth of goals in the modern situation of unbound powers clamoring for actualization, nor is there a dearth of means; what now claims our attention are the dangers lurking in the actualization of the goals and the uses of the means.

The *a priori* object of an unconditional economic imperative is the continued possibility of the economic system itself; not necessarily of the given system, but of a viable economy as such. This was hardly a consideration in former times. With all the ups and downs of capricious nature, the good old Earth could be trusted to endure and to regenerate the conditions for future life, even patiently to repair the follies of man. Modern technology has changed this radically. Thanks to this technology, we live in an era of enormous and largely irreversible consequences of human action, in an era of what I call the total and global impact of almost any of the courses we embark upon under the conditions of technological might; and we must anticipate that these courses, once set in motion, will run self-propelled to their extremes. In these circumstances, the otherwise abstract obligation to preserve for posterity the conditions necessary for an economy as such, turns into a fairly concrete principle for normative judgment—i.e., for approval or rejection of policies. The *a priori* imperative whose positive form might be, "Act so that the effects of your action are compossible with the permanence of an economic order," is for purposes of critical application better expressed in the negative equivalent, "Act so that the effects of your action are not destructive of the possibility of economic life in the future," or simply, "Do not compromise the conditions for an indefinite continuation of some viable economy."

This, I submit, is a relevant, nontrivial, and highly topical rule for decision-making (or decision-checking) in the novel state of our affairs. It is, of course, reminiscent of Kant's "categorical imperative." I cannot properly discuss the logical relationship here, but I may point out at least some of the differences. Kant's imperative enjoins us to consider what would happen *if* the maxim of my present action were made the principle of a universal legislation; the self-consistency or inconsistency of such a *hypothetical* universalization is made the test for my *private* choice. But it is no part of the reasoning that there is any probability of my private choice in fact becoming universal law—indeed, real consequences are not considered at all, and the principle is one not of objective responsibility but of the subjective quality of my self-determination. Now the criterion of consistency seems at first to be similar in our imperative. But there the "universalization" is by no means hypothetical—i.e., a purely logical transference from the individual "me" to an imaginary, causally unrelated "all" ("*if* everybody . . ."); on the contrary, the actions subject to our imperative have their universal reference in their actual scope of efficacy—they "totalize" themselves in the progress of their momentum and thus are bound to terminate in shaping the universal dispensation of things.

Then, since this concerns things that will eventuate "in the long run," there is the *time* horizon, which is entirely absent in the instantaneous logical operation of the Kantian imperative; whereas the latter extrapolates into an ever-present order of abstract compatibility, our imperative extrapolates into a predictable real *future* as the open-ended dimension of our responsibility.

Finally, "consistency" here takes in the interplay of all the conditions making up the final situation under the vast complexity of "the real": it involves foresight saturated with empirical content, requiring the fullness of our factual knowledge, and thus escapes the often-noted vacuity of the Kantian consistency rule. The rule that economics must watch over its own continued possibility is therefore decidedly nontrivial. Before illustrating this by some hypothetical applications, I wish to reiterate its claim to normative authority: the new imperative embodying the principle of responsibility (new, because the occasion for it has only recently arisen) is as unconditionally self-validating as was the immediate-subsistence imperative of pretechnological economy that is allegedly being superannuated through success (I wonder for how long?); it fills the vacant place of the latter with a long-range criterion pertinent to the goal-indulgence of our technologically powered success economy. Its concrete application is, of course, to our interaction with nature, into which our economic pursuits precipitate us on an unprecedented scale and in ever increasing depth; and "nature" here includes human nature together with the animate and inanimate environment.

Everyone can think for himself of the kind of issues which arise here, and which the economist is duty-bound to make his business, unaccustomed as he may be to them. That they are the economist's business follows both from the fact that they originate in economic practice that is actually under way (and assumed as a datum in his own projective reasoning) and from the fact that they will recoil upon the economic possibilities confronting the inheritors of the present run of things. In this connection one thinks first of the physical side—i.e., of the whole intricate ecological complex, now decisively affected by what man, in the pursuit of his economic goals, is doing to his terrestrial environment. The large-scale perspectives opening up here were recently dealt with at a meeting of the American Association for the Advancement of Science, and they can only be called alarming. Biologists and physicists warned of an "ecological crisis" which this planet is approaching under our stewardship and "which may destroy its suitability as a place for human society." Already, so the same speaker (Professor Barry Commoner) holds, the environment is being placed under stress "to the point of collapse." I resist the temptation of dwelling on the impressive examples and arguments advanced in support of this apocalyptic view. They range from outright despoliation over pollution to the very endangering of the earth's oxygen supply. The points to be emphasized are (1) that since such anticipated and by no means fanciful developments have an indubitably economic causation as well as a final economic effect, the economist is concerned with them; (2) that the challenge they pose qualitatively exceeds the more traditional question of exhaustion or preservation of local resources; and (3) that in facing this challenge there is nothing "value-free" about economic science: on the contrary, the principle of responsibility for future life, indigenous to economics, becomes the source of categorical, normative judgment.

To take one imaginary example, suppose that a proposed rate of industrial growth, perfectly feasible and desirable in itself, involves a rate of fuel-burning that brings into play the so-called "hothouse effect" —i.e., the trapping of thermal radiation under a carbon-dioxide layer that forms in the upper atmosphere. Suppose that calculations show that this in time will raise terrestrial temperatures to a point where the polar ice caps begin to melt; and that once started, this is an irreversible and self-accelerating process with the end-result (ignoring all other consequences of the climatic change) of raising the ocean level enough to submerge vast continental areas on this globe, thus leading to incalculable catastrophe in economic as well as other respects. Surely then, with such a prospect demonstrated as certain or highly probable, the simple imperative that no economic policy is right whose eventual outcome defeats the prime purpose of all economy will bid the economist to place a normative interdiction on the policy in question whatever its intermediate benefits may be even over a considerable interval of time.

This is a relatively simple case involving the plain alternative of physical preservation or ruin; it can be decided without regard to any specifically *human* qualities whose presence or absence may affect the viability of the economic order that either promotes or suppresses them. Even here, though, the decision-maker himself must muster more than correct information and clear thinking: he must exercise the moral virtue of resisting the lure of immediately desirable results in deference to the command of long-range responsibility. To sacrifice proximate expediency to the consideration of what will be when we are no more is in itself a moral stance, implying a sense of commitment and strength of self-denial. We claim that these are intrinsic in the meaning of the economic undertaking as such and therefore invokable as "oughts." And the lengthened range of our responsibility, a *novel moral horizon,* is precisely the normative correlate to the entirely novel lengthening of the effective range of our projects and of the theoretical range of our foresight. This much, then, of the *exercise* of "human value" beyond the merely cognitive is implicit in the adequate practice of economic theory, even where, as in our example, no *consideration* of human values beyond the physical enters into the goal-decision itself.

This, however, is the case when we include *human* nature in the "nature" affected by our projects, and when we remember that man himself is among the "economic resources" which must be kept intact and functional. We then are forced into considerations of a subtler kind, as in the following example—again a hypothetical one. Suppose that technically a state of "full automation" is possible which would abolish work for the overwhelming majority of the population and that therefore a process now initiated toward this target would terminate in a state where humanity consisted mainly of taskless state pensioners, "employed" to consume. Further suppose that for such a state to endure, a high degree of orderliness and "good behavior" would be required of its beneficiaries. Finally suppose that psychology or neuropathology—or generally the "science of man"—can show that the very state of affairs which requires this condition precludes it: for instance, that mass idleness of this sort, the lack of function, purpose, and structuring through work, must give rise to forms of anomie or even collective insanity which would wreck the system—in brief, that the latter is self-contradictory in that it demands a maximum of rationality while fostering a maximum of irrationality. Here again, the theoretical economist must advise against a course that would lead to this contradiction. Scientific insight will of itself become normative. (Whether it will be listened to is an entirely different matter. I personally believe that the warner would be doomed to a Cassandra role.)

One could think of more sophisticated and perhaps more likely examples of this kind—e.g., that the system will predictably dry up the source of *knowledge* on which it rests by failing to regenerate the delicate, intellectual, and partly ascetic virtues necessary in the all-important scientific–technocratic elite. The point is that the human condition in all its breadth, and therewith the consideration of "human values," form a legitimate part of hardheaded economic reasoning, because of the kind of goal states toward which economic developments nowadays move either by design or by their own self-propagating direction.

True, those human values do not figure *per se* in this reasoning—i.e., with their own authentic claims, but merely as part of the criterion of viability—i.e., of the question, "Does it work?" But "viability" here has become rather a comprehensive concept in which the technical aspect of consistency and compatibility tends to merge with the humanistic aspect of man's well-being. For there is some reason for being confident that, *understood in this breadth*, the criterion of "compatibility" will safeguard, along with the functional viability of the system, also the conditions for possible human wholeness. To express it the other way around: we may not unreasonably assume that by *avoiding* the one-sided extremes of the goals that lead to functional self-contradiction, we shall also avoid the crippling distortion of man and keep at least the human potential intact. The chances for preserving the integrity of that potential may well coincide with the precepts of sober economic wisdom.

One may object that these precepts are of a restraining or prohibiting kind only, telling us what not to do, but not what to do. True, but it is at least a beginning. We may remember that even the Ten Commandments are mostly "don't's" and not "do's." Moreover, the negative emphasis fits the modern situation, whose problem, as we have seen, is an excess of power to "do" and thus an excess of offers for doing. Overwhelmed by our own possibilities—an unprecedented situation, this—we first of all need criteria for rejection. Perhaps we cannot know what the *summum bonum* is, but we can surely know, when presented with it, what a *malum* is. We recognize evil even when ignorant of the good. Thus, granted that heightening and enhancing life is the goal, on economic and other terms, we may well be uncertain what constitutes such "heightening" according to the true idea of man; but we are not uncertain of what constitutes a stunting of man's image or a mutilation of its very base. Thus I do not think that in the case of economics there is really such a schizophrenia between the economist as a scientist and the economist as a person as is sometimes asserted; there is a convergence between intra-scientific and human norms, and no lack of objects for a legitimate "yes" and "no" *valid by both at once.*

But what if the assumption of such a convergence is overoptimistic? If, indeed, functional viability of the most outrageous kind can be bought precisely with the *right kind* of distortion of man and the right kind of mutilation of the human substance? In our theoretical argument we must not overlook the possibility that scientifically armed "human engineering" can credibly promise to tailor man to the requirements of the system and (e.g., by biological and other intervention) to produce the *stunted* humanity required, à la Huxley's *Brave New World,* for the smooth functioning of a projected economic–technological order. Then, instead of disruptive mass insanity (whose prospect might almost be a relief), we would have the adaptive reduction of the sons of Man to behavioral automata that fit the automation of their world. The viability criterion would thus be satisfied—by a caricature of man, to be sure, but still satisfied. Suppose *this* to be demonstrably possible and durable: then our imperative, with its test of mere viability, would be powerless to protect human inviolateness, and the economist—revolting as the picture may be to him—would have *no intra-economic* (i.e., purely *functional*) veto to raise.

Still, the performance of the economist's analytic and synthetic task is not without import for the cause of the values threatened in this perspective. It is his task, after all, to *draw* the picture, to *fill in* all its features beyond the few specified by the policy-makers—that is, to work out what is collaterally involved in the actuality of the goal—prior to the instrumental question of how to achieve it. He cannot shun this task by retiring behind the official terms of his discipline, by pleading that such and such aspects of the picture are not his job, but the physicist's, the biologist's, the sociologist's, the psychologist's. As the compound situation is indivisible, economics is "interdisciplinary" by its nature, and recent developments have merely added to the variety of disciplines the economist must enlist in the execution of his own reasoning—in our case, in the elaboration of the state embodying the projected goal. Having drawn the picture with their help, the economist can show it to the policy-makers and say to them: You can have your target only as part of a package; this is what goes with it, this is what the eventual goal state will look like. Do you want *that?* Given the fact that there is a greater certainty and consensus on what is undesirable than on what is desirable, on the *malum* than on the *bonum,* scientific knowledge can here be of service to concerns beyond its own jurisdiction—if only it is radical and comprehensive enough in its projections and shows far enough ahead where we are moving.

III

And here comes the rub: Can it really do so? The supposition in the preceding considerations was that we do have the requisite factual knowl-edge. In my examples there recurred the phrase, "Suppose that it can be shown . . . ," referring to what biology, psychology, sociology, etc., can predict. But can they predict these things? I am afraid not, except very tentatively and always controversially. The normative strength I spoke of rests on predictive strength—i.e., on the validity of the extrapolation presenting us with the terminal states. But such extrapolations in social science, unlike those in astronomy, mechanics, or physics, can at best be persuasive. A penumbra and then an outer darkness of collateral con-ditions surround the little segment which our extrapolation can spotlight out of the total. What this total will be, we can only find out by letting the thing come to pass; after that, we have retrospective predictions, knowing now, in the light of the result, how it came about (somewhat like the biologist's knowledge of past evolution).

Note that it is the specification of the *goal* state itself, as the correla-tive, complete "environment" of the proposed target condition, which involves us in a predictive task antecedently to the whole *instrumental* level—i.e., to means–ends prediction. There lies the problem for the *ap-plication* of our imperative. The reason for the predictive weakness of all social science (quite apart from the open question of indeterminacy and free will) is the fact that with man and history one cannot make small-scale, repeatable model experiments in lieu of the "real thing." For it is not the isolated causal strand in which we are interested, but precisely the totality of the large-scale, complex conditions, and the only labora-tory for testing hypotheses about *this* is reality itself—i.e., history in its true dimensions and true time span. For here numbers, configurations, and durations are not only quantitative but qualitative variables. The molecule remains the same whether it is in the company of few or many;

whether it has gone through this or that thermal motion, been part of this or that chemical compound, whether for a short or a long time, in this sequence or that, here or there, often or once. Because of this invariance, we can create for it small-scale, purified, repeatable, experimental situations from which valid generalizations can be drawn. This is not so in the social sciences, whose objects lack this substantial insensitivity to circumstances. There the purified, vicarious paradigms do not work. Where, then, shall the social scientist get his "empirical generalizations"? From past history? Even if it has something to teach about its own recurrent patterns, its generalizations would no longer hold for us. For the basic novelty of our condition is this: Whereas the agricultural revolution with which civilization began, followed by the urban revolution, established a *fact* which lasted substantially unchanged for several millennia, the scientific–industrial–technological revolution of the modern age did not establish a fact but started a *movement* which continuously creates new facts that always carry in themselves the germ of their own overcoming. But a sequence of unprecedented and nonrepetitive change—which is what we are living in—simply offers no basis for empirical generalizations of any extended scope. And extended scope is precisely what we need today and did not need before.

Such is the inductive side of the matter. The deductive side would look no better, even if the logical premises for it were given. For even supposing that the sequence of novelty is in ultimate truth deterministic, and moreover, that all the single, operative causalities and the law of their combination were known—in short, if computation were possible "in principle," the order of complexity to be dealt with would defy all human computation. Nothing less than *total* projection will do here for relevant prediction, with integration of all the interacting factors that will compose the future state—human and extra-human, material and mental, natural and institutional, rational and emotional, biological and technological (this last, incidentally, means anticipating future inventions—i.e., making them now). This is clearly a task which no existing science can handle and probably none ever will. The computer that could process all the data combined would have to be of cosmic dimensions, so mathematicians assure me. In fact, of course, we would have neither all the variables to be put into that monster computer nor the sophistication to program it. (Not to mention the paradox that, since the computation is undertaken in order to enable us to change its result—i.e., to offer us alternatives—we have introduced an anti-deterministic element into a purportedly deterministic scheme.)

Returning once more to the inductive side, I repeat that only the full-scale "experiment" would be valid in yielding the desired "empirical generalization": full-scale in numbers, span, and above all *time,* which is a prime reality in human affairs. But we cannot experiment with mankind. When we have run our experiment, the deed is done and we cannot return to the initial state. Its having been done creates a new condition. We may be wise after the fact (e.g., find that it should not have been done), but it cannot be undone; history is unrepeatable and we cannot start over again. Our knowledge would come too late. Our generalization would be good only for a repeat performance of the universe.

IV

Where does that leave our imperative, which we found to be non-trivial indeed and of indubitable validity in itself, but which we now have also found to be of uncertain applicability, since its theoretically compelling application requires a certainty of foreknowledge which we lack? If the projection of the total end-state can at best be hypothetical and must always be elliptic, the normative decision the economist is to make will lack strict scientific cogency. It cannot be more valid than the forecast on which it is built. It may still be as persuasive as the forecast itself, and since we are dealing with the best-informed extrapolations that can be had, this persuasiveness can be great indeed. But even the best-informed extrapolations, shot through with guesswork as they are, are contestable and will be contested by disinterested and interested opinion alike. Worse still, the mere appeal to the incontestable fact that "we don't really know" can be used as a license to try out the critical course anyway if its short-range advantages are tempting enough. Here then the principle of long-range responsibility requires that *the fact of ignorance be incorporated in the imperative itself,* and that the normative role of the economist become wedded to the Socratic role of stressing our ignorance. In the face of the quasi-eschatological situations toward which the potentials of our economic–technological processes point, ignorance of the ultimate implications becomes itself a reason for responsible restraint.

The forethought of our ancestors could, in the general shroudedness of the future and with the modest causal scale of their doings, get by with Mr. Micawber's pious expectation that "something will turn up": no use to worry our heads with the very distant, the future will take care of itself, our grandchildren will cross the bridge when they come to it. We cannot afford the Micawber attitude anymore. For we live under a new dispensation and a new responsibility. By the mere scale of its effects, modern technological power propels us into goals of a type that was formerly the preserve of Utopias. To put it differently, technological power has turned what ought to be tentative, perhaps enlightening plays of speculative reason into competing blueprints for projects, and in choosing between them we have to choose between extremes of remote effects. The one thing we can really know of them is their extremism as such—that they concern the total condition of nature on our globe and the very kind of creatures that shall, or shall not, populate it. In consequence of the inevitably "utopian" scale of modern technology, the salutary gap between everyday and ultimate issues, between occasions for common prudence and occasions for illuminated wisdom, is steadily closing. Living now constantly in the shadow of unwanted, built-in, automatic utopianism, we are constantly confronted with issues whose positive choice requires supreme wisdom—an impossible situation for man in general, because he does not possess that wisdom, and in particular for contemporary man, who is intoxicated with his power.

There is, then, one wisdom left to us: that of realizing the inadequacy of our foreknowledge to the scope of our actions. The imperative that incorporates this realization bids us to be cautious—i.e., to forgo a use of our power which, for all we know, may lead to runaway effects of excessive and ungovernable magnitude. Accordingly the economist's normative role is to warn of *eschatological situations as such*, and thus of policies apt to lead to them. Armed with all the tentative knowledge of what could be, yet unable to predict what *will* be, he will have to counsel against courses too pregnant with extreme possibilities.

In conclusion, then, we have this to say about the rational, normative critique of goals. Our "imperative," founded upon the principle of responsibility, and in its straightforward form supposing our knowledge of consequences, must be adapted to the fact that this responsibility now extends into the unknown. The first mortal sin in economic policy is *"après nous le déluge"*; the second, to *risk* the possibility of deluge for our grandchildren on the excuse of ignorance ("Who knows what unforeseen remedies will appear in time?"). The knowledge of our ignorance, plus the knowledge of the *possibilities* we might be setting in play (this indeed is a knowledge), should beget the corollary imperative: Do not gamble with goals that are too big—and so resist the drift toward them. For although there may, in principle, be cases of good eschatological "terminals"—i.e., a desirable millennium—the chances for apocalyptic ones are immeasurably greater. Thus, in the present state of our affairs, and for some time to come, an advisable principle for normative decision may well be healthy fear of our own Promethean power.

5

ABRAHAM EDEL

ENDS, COMMITMENTS,
AND
THE PLACE OF IGNORANCE

A general philosophical reflection comes to mind, which I would like to raise before going on to my assigned role of commentator on Professor Jonas' paper. There is, I think, increasing recognition among philosophers that even the most general categories arise and function within a context of theoretical problems, and are subject to modification if they complicate rather than help resolve those problems. Perhaps then it is the means–ends cut itself that needs central reconsideration. Perhaps it is this categorial structure itself that is cracking under the strain of the difficulties it generates. It seems to me that Professor Jonas' paper can be interpreted as underscoring the cracking by carrying to the limit the dilemmas in which we are placed. If so, it is implicitly inciting us to revolt against the tyranny of the means–ends model as applied in social science, and in this respect I find myself in a large measure of agreement. But, of course, among philosophers it is not only agreement but the ground of agreement that is significant—for different grounds, like different formulas, may soon incline in different directions beyond the range of the immediate data. And so just as Professor Jonas will not let the economist be quit of his commitments *qua* economist—indeed this is a central part of his argument—so I cannot be quit of my critical responsibility *qua* critic.

89

In pursuit of the general reflection, let me first make clear my own perspective on the fact–value problem that lies at the base of the concerns before us, because it has hardened the means–ends distinction as a theoretical framework and often has even been assimilated into it. My attitude is not without ambivalence. On one hand, I regard the fact–value distinction as a categorial cut into two quite obscure categories, of which the first is highly metaphysical and the second is an artificial construct that puts into one bag an extremely varied set of human phenomena, ranging from bare approval to complex judgment. On the other hand, I do not mind using the distinction for any job that it does efficiently. It is highly useful for preventing the smuggling of purposes and interests into an apparently neutral concept or field—for example, it prevents speaking of "needs" as if they were a factual question rather than the discovery that certain nonsatisfactions produce certain undesirable consequences; or again, it prevents speaking of "adjustment" without recognizing the implicit approval of the state of affairs to which adjustment is desired.

But customs inspection is no substitute for production, and the categories of customs inspection will not run a productive enterprise, either ethical or economic. I want to emphasize three points:

1. The distinction between science and ethics is not equivalent to the one between fact and value; science and ethics each contain both facts and values.

2. The distinctive problems of establishing policy or justifying action rarely raise the question of drawing value conclusions from purely factual data. Typically, they involve going from some facts and some values to *other* values. The unbridgeable gulf may exist, but we rarely have to go where it lies.

3. Some other categorical cuts may be more important for the problem of the relation of science to ethics. For example, the cut between the determinate or definite and the indeterminate or indefinite (in the sense of the extent to which answers can be furnished to questions) runs across the fact–value dichotomy; while many questions of fact are no doubt more easily answered than questions of value, some questions of value are more easily answered than some questions of fact. I therefore do not have to destroy the value–fact dichotomy, although future analysts may decide in the long run that it was just another dogma, of anti-empiricism this time, mistakenly popularized by empiricists. I simply find it less relevant to our problems.

These considerations will indicate the large measure of my agreement with Professor Jonas. He too finds value commitments on both sides of the science–ethics fence. He also finds factual difficulties on both sides. Moreover, his argument leans very heavily on the question of the extent of the indeterminate, both in the picture of the end and in the ascertainment of the means. His three topical arguments are as follows:

1. Economics is not without certain basic commitments which open the way readily to vast responsibilities.
2. Even then it cannot really do the factual job because the goal state it requires is too elusive.
3. We must therefore adopt a policy of caution for our journey into the unknown.

My comments will raise the following corresponding questions:

1. Who defines the economist *qua* economist?
2. If the means–ends model is so helpless here, cannot some other model be found to do better?
3. How do we decide whether the dangers of cautious inaction are greater or less than the dangers of bold action?

I

Economics, we are told, no longer offers us simply the means of subsistence; the growth of novel powers has reached the point where we have the massive offer of all sorts of goals—we have but to choose and economics will be our willing servant. But, Professor Jonas argues, philosophy in fact cannot furnish the wanted list of ends. He urges us, however, to take heart: at least some commitments are inherent in the economic enterprise as an instituted system of human activities.

The first such commitment, which was imperative in the age of scarcity, is "the provisioning of its members with the physical goods necessary to sustain their lives." [1] With affluence there came a pluralism of elective goals and so an absence of criteria of choice in economics itself. Professor Jonas goes on to argue that the original categorical imperative expresses the basic self-affirmation of life, and he pushes on from the provisioning of the present generation to making provision for the next generation. It is easy, especially in the integrated large-scale operations of the modern world, to show the growing scope of these responsibilities once they are assumed. Care for the existence of future generations makes us afraid of handing on a plundered planet; once human nature is recognized as affected, criticism of workability and viability comes to embrace the whole humanistic aspect of man's well-being.

With the values that come marching on apace, I have no quarrel. But in this case I want to be the customs inspector. For there is a touch of the old economic appeal to reasonable self-interest in the way Professor Jonas constructs a categorical imperative for the economist: "Act so that the effects of your action are not destructive of the possibility

---

[1] See p. 75.

of economic life in the future." [2] Again we are told, "The rule that economics must watch over its own continued possibility is therefore decidedly nontrivial." [3] For a bit it sounds almost as if the physicist were being told that he could not do research on a cobalt bomb *qua* physicist since if it were made and exploded it would make research into physics impossible! But it will not help us much to go into such questions as to whether it would be a logical contradiction for an economist reading Professor Jonas' paper to decide that economists interfere too much in the order of things and that therefore as an economist he is committed to working for the abolition of economics! For Professor Jonas is really talking about economists only in relation to the economy itself.

Who or what constitutes the field of economics? Is it a "subject matter," in whose account we will find defining postulates with value presuppositions? Or is it professors in the universities taking care that their departments do not shrink? Or a minister of the economy in a government, carrying out dominant party policy? Or a U. N. division such as the Food and Agriculture Organization, seeking to encourage production and distribution on a global basis?

And what is "the economy"—a set of activities of people? Where are we extracting the responsibilities? The "field of economics" is a very strange abstraction. Nor will the history of definitions of economics help us; they have at times confined themselves to the laws of the distribution of scarce means to ends, and have not been incompatible with a Spencerian sacrifice of the subsistence of a large part of a population in the name of evolution, or with leaving the subsistence of many to religious charity.

In fact, Professor Jonas is arguing not from the existence of economists but from economic enterprise as an instituted system of human activities. Now human activities express purposes, and so we must either find out men's purposes in these activities or, if we already know them, evaluate them. Presumably descriptive economics, with the aid of anthropology and social psychology, could tell us why men work at what tasks under what conditions and with what expectations. (To a large extent, such aims might be culturally variable.) They also could tell us some of the consequences of these aims. Many of the commitments Professor Jonas describes as inherent in economics could be established equally and even more firmly for all men, not only economists, by a search into the conditions necessary for all or most of the values men hold even when the values differ. Thus the same type of argument that establishes law and order as a minimal goal in political science, or shows

---

[2] See p. 79.
[3] See p. 80.

the imperative character of peace under conditions of contemporary warfare (however diverse and competitive are the goals men will pursue in a peaceful world), can in the present state of the globe justify most of the responsibilities Professor Jonas wants assumed.

But such an argument does not preclude an attempted *evaluation* of goals held. And here I should like to recast Professor Jonas' initial description of the situation that generates the problem. Economics, we were told, had furnished subsistence, but now, with the development of greater power, it needed to be told what goals to pursue, because it lacked criteria for choice. Let us say instead that economics did not merely furnish subsistence; rather it gave us the value of freedom of choice among many possible ends. Thus it contains the positive criterion of free individual choice. Now it is described as a value, not as a problem or the lack of a criterion. Professor Jonas criticizes the value because of its consequences—perhaps he does not think there is wise use for this freedom at present, just as economists themselves may criticize the situation in which consumer demand, stimulated and controlled in effect by unregulated manipulators, produces undesirable results.

This shift in description is not trifling. The same point arises in Professor Jonas' picture of the traditional removal of natural ends in the eclipse of teleology. Somehow this is always construed as the removal of value from the account of the processes. But actually it is a shift in the locus of value, from a presumed species-end to the will-acts of individuals. The rise of individualism is a different value-selection, not a metaphysical conjuring away of value.

I see the strength of Professor Jonas' position, then, not in the proof that economics *qua* economics has certain commitments on pain of self-contradiction, but in the exhibition that in the modern world, empirical relations can be found which show that some minimal human aims entail wider commitments as a consequence than they used to, and that the purposes for which we carry on various types of activity (including specialized study of those activities) must be reconstructed because, at present, the consequences of some of the built-in aims have been empirically discovered to be disastrous.

II

Professor Jonas' attack on the means–ends model is in many respects a crushing one. We can never, in fact, have an adequate account of the end in terms sufficient to weigh all the means and alternatives and choose the best. The goal state that is to be the terminus is "elusive"; the terminus "is spotlighted for our vision out of a darkness of collateral unknowns with which it is inextricably intertwined, unlike the terminal states of isolable and repeatable physical sequences." [4] This theme is developed precisely after Professor Jonas has persuaded the economist to acknowledge responsibility. What would he answer if the economist now invoked Kant's "ought implies can" to reject the responsibilities so elaborately fastened upon him? If he cannot carry them out, how can they be his responsibilities? Professor Jonas argues that the only laboratory for testing hypotheses about the totality is reality itself. The usual scientific method of dealing with isolated parts will not do. And the experiment changes reality: "When we have run our experiment, the deed is done and we cannot return to the initial state." [5] Our knowledge comes too late.

Some of the points Professor Jonas is making here, in his attack on the applicability of the means–ends model, could be restated in Deweyan language. We never really deal with ultimate ends but with focal aims or ends-in-view that are set within a problem context, so that our very pursuit of the end-in-view rests on the hypothesis that its pursuit will help solve the problem. Dewey offers an altered model in which proposed goals are tested on definite criteria posed by the situation, rather than serving as ends in unalterable blueprints; fresh ends emerge in the process, to which the model of policy formation must be constantly sensitive. Whether such a model is helpful depends on how well structured the situations turn out to be, how extensive our theoretical knowledge is of the area, and how manageable the novelties are. Dewey's pluralism would prevent him from seeing the whole human life as the integrated situation which Professor Jonas' dire speculations envisage.

But clearly the issue need not be all-or-none. There are many situations that exemplify the Deweyan model. Some diseases have been intelligently eliminated; in others we find that we have cleared the way for more virulent strains. The life-span has been extended, though fresh problems emerge. It is true that there is greater danger in large-scale experiments, for there is much that we do not know. In really total experiments, there are the dangers of setting off utterly destructive chain reactions. Life is becoming increasingly precarious. But not all experiments are equally precarious. Many have a margin of maneuverability in case they begin to go wrong. A kind of operations-research model is possible in which many fields cooperate and the dangerous variables are kept under constant scrutiny. Perhaps this is like driving a car on rough terrain, as against an automated train on a prepared roadbed.

Professor Jonas might well point out that this begs the question by

4 See p. 70.
5 See p. 86.

assuming the reliable knowledge at issue. But how far is he prepared to carry his argument? I am reminded of G. E. Moore's definition of "right" in *Principia Ethica* as that act which makes the whole world better off than any alternative possible act would have done. Since the definition poses impossible conditions for the knowledge we must have, Moore quite consistently decides that we cannot really furnish any evidence that would be adequate to change any current moral rule. The outcome is that he advises utter conformity to any rule that happens to exist in any community, but only within that community! Professor Jonas' recommendation is not conformity, but neither is it the hope of improving our knowledge and expanding the area of careful experiment. It is rather that the fact of ignorance be incorporated in the imperative itself. What this portends, we must now ask.

III

I am not sure that I really understand how ignorance can be incorporated into the economic imperative. There are several possibilities.

1. The proposal may be recommending a virtue of humility. This is generally said to be characteristic of our greatest scientists who know all the difficulties and shortcomings in what they know.

2. It may be urging caution about specific undertakings. For example, the use of nuclear weapons in war today might unleash uncontrollable disastrous consequences. That we cannot foresee them is part of the grounds for not going ahead. But what about a guaranteed annual wage in America? Would it be irreversible if we adopted it, irrespective of the goodness or badness of consequences—unlike Medicaid in New York State (which proved to be reversible in part) or the nationalization and subsequent denationalization of steel in Britain? Surely the kinds of consequences anticipated play a large part in deciding what risks to take; if so, then knowledge is involved in estimating the extent of ignorance.

3. Perhaps the proposal calls for incorporating only some particular sense of ignorance. There may be various kinds of unknowns—variables in equations that may turn out to have several values, questions not touched by a particular system that is being used, unknown state-conditions to which a well-established theory is being applied, variables whose values cannot be predicted in advance but can be decided in time by an on-the-spot inspection at a given point, theoretical limits indicated by a theory itself, unknowns we do not even know are unknown. The haunting fear that some undiscovered variable is at work may have adequate grounds

in some areas and only an obsessive quality in others—but to distinguish the latter we must have some knowledge about obsessions.

4. Perhaps the proposal is directed only against certain types of experiments—Utopian, as against middle-sized projects. But perhaps it is not the size but the oversimplification that is the issue. Then we should do a study of Utopias to learn the lessons of planning. However, the theory of planning is itself a form of knowledge.

5. Perhaps the proposal may be put in positive form by incorporating not ignorance, but something like *openness*. There is considerable similarity between the proposal and the kind of argument Julian Huxley gives in *Touchstone for Ethics*—that a central task of ethics today is to maintain openness against the kind of hardened closure that makes readjustment on a large scale of changing conditions impossible. We do not want to die out like the dinosaurs. In a given scheme of human self-regulation, this means freedom of criticism, wide participation of various points of view in decisions, flexibility of goals over different generations in a changing world, and so on. Such openness is a characteristic of even some deterministically inclined philosophies. Remember Marx's objection to Utopian socialism and his belief that quantitative changes may produce qualitative leaps, so that we cannot rest on plans but have to be constantly on the watch.

Perhaps in these arguments I am binding or taming what is offered as radical ignorance. I do not think that Professor Jonas is offering "I disbelieve because it is possible" as a latter-day substitute for "I believe because it is impossible." But there is one argument against his proposal that seems to me to be decisive. He appears to be assuming that the consequences of caution are less far-reaching than the consequences of considered action. In human life it is not always so. Perhaps the timid drivers cause more accidents than the rash ones. Those who were so busy arguing against socialism, and who assumed that without intervention the old ways would prevail, missed the impact of the rise of corporate organization. But once we recognize this, then the answer is unavoidable—we need knowledge to certify that doing nothing will not have more disastrous consequences than major experimentation. An efficient administrator may decide to make no decision so that a situation will mature, but it is not ignorance but wisdom that he incorporates into his decision not to decide on that occasion.

I conclude then that as far as the unknowns are concerned, we need to incorporate not ignorance but the study of different kinds of unknowns and their roles; that insofar as attitudes are concerned, both humility and sharp critical power are essential; that insofar as models of decision are involved, we should use those that allow a maximum of flexibility and maneuverability. But as for ultimate attitudes, I think the stress on courageous responsible experiment has more to be said for it than general warnings of caution.

6

FRITZ MACHLUP

POSITIVE
AND
NORMATIVE ECONOMICS

An Analysis of the Ideas

Although there are some economists who "can't be bothered" by such exercises in "philosophy" or "mere semantics," the distinction between positive and normative plays a considerable role in present-day economic discussion. And this has been true for more than 150 years. While for some the distinction refers to a boundary between two branches of a science, for others "normative science" is a contradiction in terms, the discourse of norms or values being by definition nonscientific. The question is, of course, semantic and philosophic, but this does not make it trivial or useless. An elucidation seems worth our while.

Such an elucidation should be both historical and analytical. In the interests of conserving space, I shall confine myself here, however, to a discussion of the analytic questions.[1] The reader

---

[1] When we distinguish analytical from historical semantics, we do not suggest that the former can be independent of the latter. Words have meanings because people have used them to express certain ideas, and the meanings in which words have been used are historical data—though they are derived by way of interpretation, not observation.

If meanings have changed over time and between different groups, historical semantics will present these changes. The task of analytical semantics is largely one of rearrangements: the historical evidence and the chronology are removed and the different meanings are ordered and grouped in a systematic fashion designed to exhibit significant contrasts and relationships,

who would care to pursue the matter on a historical level may, if he is patient, wait for the publication of the history of ideas I am preparing on the issues behind the concepts "positive" and "normative."

When we embark on a methodological analysis of the ideas of "positive" and other kinds of economics, we cannot dispense with semantics. Questions of semantics and methodology are difficult to disentangle.

This is easy to comprehend. If some authors, for example, expound the intricacies of welfare economics, old or new, and conclude that certain propositions are normative in character, whereas other authors have characterized the same propositions as positive, either the difference may be semantic or it may be a matter of methodological interpretation. Obviously, it makes a difference whether "normative" in this context is to mean prescriptive, advisory, persuasive, evaluative, ethical, emotive, instrumental, or political; and whether "positive" means expository, descriptive, explanatory, predictive, nonhypothetical, nonevaluative, nonmetaphysical, nonspeculative, operational, testable, verifiable, nonpartisan, or consistent with agreed premises. But even if authors agree on the meaning of the adjectives, they may still come to different judgments on the character of the propositions in question, for they may not agree on all that is involved.

We shall begin with a brief summary of findings from the historical survey.

THE MEANINGS OF "POSITIVE"

The adjective "positive" has been used, in the literatures of economics, of the social sciences in general, and of the philosophy of science, chiefly to modify the following nouns: economics, inquiry, science, theory, problems, propositions, premises, and conclusions. The meaning of the adjective, however, has varied considerably over time and among different authors. The following list presents a quick review of some of the meanings of "positive" as a modifier of relevant nouns, the nouns being shown in parentheses:

Incontrovertible, unconditional, not merely hypothetical	(conclusions)
Empirical, not arbitrary	(premises of empirical sciences)

---

and thus to aid in the understanding of the concepts in the contexts in which they are used.

Perhaps all this can be said more simply by prohibiting the analytical semanticist from acting like Humpty-Dumpty, whose program was, "When I use a word, it means just what I choose it to mean—neither more nor less." The semanticist may analyze, but not dictate.

Probably true	(conclusions, corresponding to "positive reality")
Free from metaphysical speculation	(stage of scientific development)
Unconcerned with ultimate efficient causes	(science)
Based on facts of immediate perception	(science)
Disregarding psychic and spiritual facts	(science)
Confirmable or at least conceivably testable	(propositions)
Not merely critical or negative	(theory)
Nonpolitical, nonethical	(problems)
Neither normative nor prescriptive	(inquiry)
Not concerned with ideals or precepts	(inquiry)

This list can be reduced to a few pairs of opposites:

> Positive (constructive) versus negative (critical)
> Positive (certain) versus uncertain
> Positive (observable) versus nonobservable
> Positive (confirmable) versus nontestable
> Positive (descriptive) versus prescriptive
> Positive (factual) versus normative

In addition, there are two terms that have been used sometimes as equivalents of positive and in other instances to denote the opposite of positive. One of these terms is *"speculative,"* which for practically all philosophical positivists stands for nonobservable, if not metaphysical, and hence nonpositive. For at least two authors, however (Sidgwick and Keynes), the word meant the opposite of normative–prescriptive and, hence, the equivalent of positive–theoretical. (Thus, they would not approve the pair of opposites used by philosophical positivists: positive versus speculative.)

The other term is *"natural."* In legal philosophy, it modifies "law" to mean norms dictated by reason, social necessity, or divine order, and imposing justice and ethical precepts. In contrast to this "natural law" (of metaphysical origin), "positive law" is formally laid down, artificially instituted, not derived from general principles of justice but formulated in accepted codes, anchored in statute or formal precedent. In scientific discourse, however, "natural law" has meant law of nature, empirically tested and therefore a part of positive science, in contrast to arbitrary construction, mere fiction, product of imagination—hence, metaphysical. (This would contradict the pair of opposites in the language of legal philosophers: positive versus natural.)

THE MEANINGS OF "NORMATIVE"

The semantic record of the adjective "normative" is less voluminous and less bewildering. This is clearly reflected in the dictionaries: *The Oxford Dictionary*, which lists thirteen meanings for "positive," gives only a single meaning for "normative": "Establishing norms or standards." But this overlooks some significant differences in the use of the word by different economists, social scientists, and philosophers.

The most important differences in the meanings of "normative" relate to the degree in which the statements in question are (1) explicit with regard to the norms (objectives, values) to which they refer; (2) focused on the problem of valuation, especially on the problem of comparing particular norms (objectives) with conflicting ones; and (3) concerned with the means and techniques of attaining certain stated norms (ends) which stand high in the value systems of some but not necessarily of the person making the statements.

There are writers who would use the word "normative" to denote all statements that are advisory or hortatory in effect or intent, regardless of whether the underlying values are concealed or clearly stated, the problem of conflicting values is raised, or the objective to be attained is assumed as given and independent of the adviser's personal system of values. Others, however, prefer to remove the tag "normative" from statements that merely describe the means and techniques by which given ends can be attained. And some would remove the tag as soon as the underlying values are made explicit and unambiguous.

"POSITIVE" VERSUS "NORMATIVE"

Disregarding for the moment all other meanings of "positive," and concentrating on "positive" as the antonym of "normative," we may think of two sets of ideas associated with this pair of opposites:

Positive	*Normative*
Description	Prescription
Explanation	Recommendation
Theory	Practice
Theory	Policy
Thought	Action
Laws (statements of uniformities)	Rules (statements of norms)
Science	Art
Factual judgments	Value judgments

| Statements in the indicative mood | Statements in the imperative mood |
| Testable propositions about facts | Nontestable expressions of feelings |

We shall not discuss all these pairs of opposites, some of which reflect misunderstandings, serious or trivial. We should not fail, however, to comment on the grounds on which "practice" and "art" were placed in the normative column.

Let us not forget that the writer most responsible for the wide adoption of the terms "positive economics" and "normative economics" really proposed a triple distinction, not a dichotomy. John Neville Keynes distinguished positive, normative, and practical economics, which are concerned, respectively, with uniformities, standards, and precepts. I find it expedient to follow this tripartite division, at least for some distance.

THE TRICHOTOMY AND THE CHOICE OF TERMS

According to Keynes, positive economics tells you "what is," normative economics tells you "what ought to be," and practical economics tells you "what you can do to attain what you want." [2]

The term "practical" in this context is ambiguous; it disregards two significant differences: the one between action and advice, and the other between general advice for typical situations and specific advice for concrete (unique) situations. If what is meant is advice of a more general nature ("precept"), a more self-explanatory term had better be sought. The frequently used term "prescriptive" is not of great help either. It may prescribe standards, and thus become synonymous with "normative," or it may prescribe actions, and thus be equivalent to "practical." In this case, it leaves open whether one prescribes according to one's own standards (values), those of one's client, or some other stipulated standards. In the first of these possibilities, "prescriptive" would be both normative and practical at the same time. Let us use the term favored by Adolph Lowe, "instrumental," to denote the task of describing and prescribing actions by means of which specified objectives can be obtained.

The term "normative" as one of the triad will be examined later in greater detail, but let us agree at this point that the norms to which it refers are not rules or precepts telling you what to do or not to do to

---

[2] The first two phrases between quotation marks are Keynes', the third is mine, designed to fit what Keynes intended to express.

achieve given ends, but instead ethical (or aesthetic) standards telling you what we consider good or bad, right or wrong. The term "evaluative," referring to systems of ethical (or aesthetic) values, would probably be more expressive of the idea. In any case, in the following discussion "normative" means "evaluative."

GRAMMATICAL FORMS

Positive, normative, and instrumental statements will now be characterized by simple relationships between events A and B, alternatively seen as causes and effects and as means and ends.

Positive: If A, then B;
                    that is, B is the effect of the cause A.

Normative: B is good;
                    that is, you ought to get (strive for) B.

Instrumental: If you want B, A will get it for you;
                    that is, A will be the means for the end B.

Much has been made of the fact that normative sentences can (and ought to be) expressed in the imperative mood, whereas positive sentences would always be in the indicative mood. In the scheme above, both the positive and the instrumental propositions are stated in the conditional form, the positive one taking the cause (A) as the condition of achieving the effect (B), the instrumental one taking the end (B) as the condition for resorting to the means (A). The normative sentence can be translated in a variety of ways: it can be expressed in the indicative mood, in the imperative mood, and in conditional form.

Indicative: B is good; indeed, B is the best.
Imperative: Get B!!
Conditional: (1) If you want the best, you ought to get B.
                    (2) If you don't get B,
                          (a) you don't know what's good for you;
                          (b) you are a fool or a coward; or
                          (c) you will be disliked, despised, or even punished.

It is questionable, however, whether these grammatical modifications are legitimate from a logician's point of view. Logical positivists deny the legitimacy of anything but the imperative mood. Rudolf Carnap, for example, contends that "actually a value statement is nothing else than a command in a misleading grammatical form. It may have effects upon the actions of men, and these effects may either be in accordance with our wishes or not; but it is neither true nor false. It does not assert anything and can neither be proved nor disproved."[3] The contention that the indicative mood is misleading because the value judgment "does not assert anything" is rather pretentious. After all, if I say that I value B, I do assert something about my likes and dislikes. But I know that this does not count for logical positivists; they are not interested in my or your tastes, maxims, or values. If I say, "Kate is the loveliest girl," they want me to express this in the imperative mood, such as, "Kiss me, Kate!"

The translations into the form of conditional statements do not fare much better. One should perhaps admit that forms 1 and 2a are merely attempts to express the value judgment in a more persuasive way. Form 2b tries to reinforce the persuasion by a threat which may influence the addressee by inducing fears of being regarded as a fool or a coward, at least by the maker of the statement. Form 2c goes farther by threatening the addressee with sanctions if he fails to accept the value judgment and to act accordingly. Incidentally, in this form it is not made clear just who entertains the valuation expressed: I; we; the majority of educated people, of voters, or of all people; the government; the prince; the dictator. But even without this specification, the statement seems to make an assertion; the predicted sanctions for nonconformists may in fact be imposed, and thus the statement can (at least conceivably) be tested and confirmed or disconfirmed. Perhaps, though, the statement in form 2c has been promoted from a value judgment to an indicative statement about the morals and codes of a group or society and to an instrumental proposition stating something like this: "If you want to avoid social or legal penalties, you will act to show that you too value B, and thus you will resort to A as the appropriate means for it." In this advisory proposition, B has become an intermediate end—namely, a means for avoiding the sanctions imposed on those who fail to conform with the value judgment in favor of B.

THE LANGUAGE OF THE COOKBOOK

Many discussions of normative science and technology refer to the cookbook or, more generally, to the book of recipes, as an analogy for prescriptive or normative statements. As a matter of fact, recipes in cookbooks (or technological handbooks) are commonly written in the imperative mood, and their authors thus seem to obey the logician's normative statement on the proper grammatical form of normative statements. Some of the most frequently used imperatives in the cookbook are

---

[3] Rudolf Carnap, *Philosophy and Logical Syntax* (London: Kegan Paul, Trench, and Trubner, 1935), p. 24. Partially reproduced in Morton White, *The Age of Analysis* (3rd printing) (New York: Mentor Books, 1957), p. 217.

Have! Cut! Slice! Chop! Wash! Soak! Drain! Shake! Melt! Cook! Boil! Bake! Fry! Add!—all, of course, followed by quantities of victuals to which the prescribed operations are to be applied.

However, each of the sets of imperatives is under a heading, such as "Crab Cakes," "Cheese Omelet," or "Crêpes Suzette." From the logician's point of view, the heading is the premise of a hypothetical proposition, the premise stating the assumed objective. For example: "*If* you want to make a cheese omelet for *n* persons, *take* 2*n* eggs. . . ."

The imperatives of the cookbook are therefore in a grammatical form misleading for the beginning student of logic, though most helpful to the intermediate student of cooking. A logical cook could translate each recipe into a positive statement of cause and effect: "If you take 2*n* eggs . . . you will get a cheese omelet for *n* persons." But since the cookbook is organized and classified, not according to causes, but according to effects or ends, the more appropriate translation would be into instrumental statements about desired ends and required means. That is, to say as I said before, "If you want to make a cheese omelet for *n* persons, take 2*n* eggs. . . ."

This may be the point at which to digress for a discussion of whether a cookbook belongs to the science of cookery or to the art of cooking. The question is much broader, of course. Are instrumental propositions part of an "art"? Is "science" confined to positive propositions?

ART AND SCIENCE

Those who speak of cooking as an art do not mean to say that it is an art to read a cookbook and carry out its instructions, or to prepare without instruction the simple dishes commonly eaten by most of us. They refer, instead, only to the work of those rare cooks who prepare very special meals, using unusual imagination and a fine sense of taste, form, and color. The "art" in this activity lies precisely in their deviation from common practice and from common precepts.

This meaning of art, as a performance superior to that of most practitioners, is contrary to another meaning of art, as a body of precepts for practice; this is one of the dictionary definitions and has been widely used as an antonym of science. Art in this sense is, like science, systematic knowledge, but arranged in a different way, suitable for more immediate practical application. As John Stuart Mill has explained, science is a body of knowledge classified according to causes, and art is a body of knowledge classified according to effects, the causes of which are often the subject of several different sciences.

Bentham's aphorism, that science is knowledge while art is practice, places us right between the two meanings of art just contrasted. Clearly, not all knowledge is science and not all practice is art. Perhaps one may say that highly qualified knowledge (rather than common, everyday knowledge) is science,[4] while highly qualified practice (rather than common, everyday practice) is art. But since virtually all practice, and certainly all qualified practice, presupposes knowledge, it is quite possible, as some writers have proposed, to use "art" and "applied science" as synonymous terms.

Those who define art as practical knowledge have usually failed to differentiate various degrees of practicality and various degrees of practice. There are important differences between, say, a handbook of technology, technological advice in a concrete situation, actual instruction given for immediate activation, and the final, perhaps manual, execution of the instruction. Yet all four phases of practical knowledge, practical application of knowledge, and practice have indiscriminately been called art.[5] (Let us recall Menger's complaint about this confusion.)

An important idea in designating certain kinds of practical activity as art is, I submit, the recognition that these activities presuppose a combination of human qualities that cannot be obtained solely from books or lectures. These activities are "art" in that they call for judgment, intuition, inventiveness, and imagination; they call for skill in making the correct diagnoses and prognoses required for successful prescriptions and good performance. Here lies a real distinction from science, scientific knowledge, and even technology and general practical precepts.

To what extent can it be said that art is normative or contains significant normative elements? Let us recall our resolution to use "normative" as an equivalent of "evaluative"—that is, as referring to standards for judging things as good or bad, right or wrong—and not as rules helpful in the attainment of stated ends. In this sense, art is normative to the extent that the activity in question calls for judgments of value, ethical or aesthetic; it is neutral or nonnormative where no value judgments are involved. In other words, art cannot reasonably be put under the normative heading except after an examination of the value-content of the judgments employed.

That the fine arts and the performing arts presuppose commitment to aesthetic standards goes without saying. The medical arts and the engineering arts, however, may go a long way without giving up their basic

---

[4] See the discussion of the meanings of science by Joseph A. Schumpeter, *History of Economic Analysis* (New York: Oxford University Press, Inc., 1954), pp. 6–11. One of Schumpeter's definitions differentiates scientific knowledge from that of the layman and mere practitioner.

[5] The German word for art is *Kunst*, but the German language offers the compound nouns *Kunstlehre* (for art as a body of precepts, technology), *Kunstregel* (for art as a precept or rule for practical application), and *Kunstfertigkeit* (for art as technical skill).

value-neutrality. The art of making recommendations on economic policy, requiring diagnostic and prognostic skills as well as interdisciplinary intelligence, may likewise proceed on the basis of agreed ethical standards without any violation of the adviser's value-neutrality. The economic adviser practices an art, not because his recommendations serve certain ends desired by people committed to certain values, but rather because his recommendations presuppose so much more than economic science: politics, sociology, psychology, pedagogy, and diplomacy, as well as diagnostic judgment, prognostic flair, intuition, and inventiveness.

One other concept of art may be mentioned here, the one used in grouping the various academic disciplines taught by the nonvocational faculties of our universities. The "arts," in academic parlance, were originally the disciplines of the trivium (grammar, logic, and rhetoric) and the quadrivium (arithmetic, geometry, music, and astronomy). In a series of reorganizations, the universities have reassigned various disciplines among the faculties of arts and sciences. In some institutions the "reading departments" are considered as professing the arts subjects, the "laboratory departments" as professing the sciences. The adjective "normative" is not relevant to such a division of subjects. Sometimes the fields classified as the humanities are regarded as inseparable from commitments to unscientific value systems. This, too, is quite superficial, if not downright wrong. Studies in linguistics or paleography are not any less value-neutral than studies in acoustics or paleontology.

NORMS, VALUES, RULES, PRECEPTS, ADVICE, PERSUASION, AND COMMAND

Be it tedious repetition or proper reinforcement, it may be helpful to sort out, once again, the set of nouns that are related and yet differentiated in meaning: norms, values, rules, precepts, advice, persuasion, and command. (We could add many more, such as instruction, directives, recommendations, and guideposts.)

The idea common to all these nouns is that somebody's actions are to be directed: someone is told what to do or what not to do. Certain differences in connotation are not generally recognized in common parlance, and not always even in learned language analysis. Of course, the differences between advice, persuasion, and command are patent, but the difference between precepts and advice or the differences between norms, rules, and precepts are not.

Perhaps we can agree on the difference between the general or typical and the specific or concrete. Advice, persuasion, and command may refer to both, to typical as well as concrete situations (concrete as to time, space, and persons involved). Norms, values, rules, and precepts are always general, and their application in concrete cases is left to intelligent interpretation. Norms and values refer to systems of valuation which the acting individual or individuals may recognize as valid (cogent or imposed by sanctions) but may not necessarily accept as their own. (After all, persons frequently act in violation of legal, ethical, or religious norms, and in breach of social etiquette.) Precepts, on the other hand, are general advice, directing voluntary action in the interest of or toward ends desired by the decision-makers. Rules may be norms or precepts; the word has not acquired a special sense linking it to only one or the other. Norms, then, are rules of conduct, self-imposed or imposed by coercion or pressures of various sorts, which relate chiefly, though not exclusively, to social objectives, whereas precepts are rules of suitable conduct for the achievement of ends chosen by the decision-makers themselves.

These semantic explications will have justified our previous terminological decision to reserve the adjective "normative" for references to norms or value judgments, and to use the adjective "instrumental" for references to precepts that direct actions designed to attain explicitly stated objectives. In order to safeguard against misunderstandings, we should add that precepts may be used for individual or group action, and for the attainment of individual or group objectives. Thus, there are precepts for householders, telling them what to look out for in shopping, budgeting, borrowing, and so forth; and there are precepts for legislators, telling them what to look out for in drafting legislation to reduce unemployment, to alleviate poverty, to accelerate growth, and to achieve other national goals. A book of precepts is instrumental and not normative in that it tells what to do *if* certain things are wanted but does not say that these things are beneficial or worth their cost.

THE LOGICAL STATUS OF NORMATIVE STATEMENTS

From the survey of the philosophical literature, it has become apparent that normative statements, or expressions of value judgments, do not enjoy an unequivocal status in logic. They are, depending on which logician pronounces the verdict, empirical propositions, analytical propositions, or no propositions at all. The differences in the verdicts are not entirely due to the differences between logical schools, but are also due in part to semantic differences, since the meaning of "normative statement" is far from unambiguous.

There are several possible ways to show that a (supposedly) normative statement is an empirical proposition. "The policies of the United States between 1963 and 1967 indicate that the avoidance of large unemployment was regarded as more important than the removal of the deficit in foreign payments." This is a statement about the system of values held or goals desired by the government (the Legislature as well as Administrations); depending on the acceptance of certain definitional and theoretical relationships, the assertion can be tested and therefore represents an empirical proposition. However, it may be denied that an assertion about values held or shared by certain persons or groups is a normative statement. That "full employment is more important than balance in foreign payments," would be a genuine value judgment. But that "full employment is held to be more important than balance in foreign payments," or is "more important to the government" or "to the majority of the people," is not a genuine value judgment.

"If a reduction in the payments deficit is desirable, but not at the price of an increase in unemployment, then the Congress ought not to increase the income tax." This looks really normative; it even employs the characteristic "ought." Yet, the statement merely asserts that a tax increase will reduce both employment and the payments deficit. It also draws a correct inference from an assumption about relative values. It does not try to persuade anyone to accept this valuation. The opposite assumption might be made, with the opposite inference, and the statement would make the same assertion: "If a reduction in the payments deficit is desirable, even at the price of increased unemployment, then an increase in the income tax is not ruled out." (In this case, the "ought" cannot legitimately be used, because it would presuppose, not only a comparison between the values of reducing the deficit and increasing unemployment, but also a comparative evaluation of all other possible side effects of the tax increase. The assumption in the "if"-clause has not gone that far.) The point is that the (indirectly) asserted relationship between tax increase and payments deficit makes the proposition empirical.

"The American people will resent an increase in unemployment and will not regard it as a fair price to pay for a reduction in the deficit." If we can agree on operational definitions for the feelings predicted in this statement (take, for example, certain replies in an opinion poll), the assertion is conceivably testable and the proposition can be characterized as an empirical one. Thus, it may be denied that a value judgment was expressed. A statement about people's reactions, even if these reactions express their evaluations, is not regarded as normative by most logicians, and surely not by radical empiricists. Indeed, when they speak of the "science of ethics," what they have in mind is an empirical study of observed or observable behavior in reaction to particular events.

That value judgments can be regarded as analytical propositions means that they can be derived by logical inference from stated assumptions—for example, from a convention or resolution about a definite system of values. Given this convention with all its "axiological rules," to use Felix

Kaufmann's phrase, one can deduce whether 3 per cent unemployment with a payments deficit of two billion dollars is better or worse than 4 per cent unemployment with a deficit of only one billion dollars, all other things being equal. The value judgment is true "in terms of given axiological rules" if it was correctly deduced from the axiological system. The trouble with this position, in my opinion, is that there are an infinite number of such value systems, and we have no criteria for choosing among them in selecting the most appropriate "convention."

According to logical positivists, value judgments are no propositions at all. The sentences in which these judgments are expressed "say nothing." A sentence stating that "a reduction of the payments deficit from two billion dollars to one billion dollars is worth an increase in unemployment from 3 to 4 per cent" asserts nothing that can be true or false and, hence, is "meaningless," according to logical positivists. I submit that this formulation of the verdict against normative statements is unduly harsh. The condemned sentence makes perfectly good sense to me, and probably to many others, even if I readily admit that what it expresses cannot be proved or disproved. In order to show the difference between "meaningless" and "nontestable," I propose that we compare the sense of the indicted and condemned statement with that of the following: "A reduction of the deficit is greenish pink and much more erudite and farther east than an increase in unemployment." Even this sentence may make sense if there is a secret code to decipher those words that destroy the sense if they are given their ordinary meanings.

The assertion that a sentence expressing a nontestable judgment is meaningless cannot be tested either, and would therefore be meaningless itself by the standard it proposes. Speaking in a more reasonable language, I find the finding of "meaninglessness" against value judgments presumptuous and overdone. It suffices to say that pure value judgments cannot be tested by empirical procedures and therefore cannot be admitted into the body of positive science.

"POSITIVE" VERSUS "NONOBSERVABLE"

By giving the floor to logical positivists in the discussion of the logical status of "normative," we have unwittingly changed the meaning of "positive": From being the opposite of "normative" it has moved—because the normative is nonobservable and nontestable—to being the opposite of "nonobservable."

The logical positivist or radical empiricist will not recognize that there is a change of meaning involved: Normative equals metaphysical equals nonobservable equals nontestable equals meaningless. For me, these are quite different qualities and, hence, their opposites are different too. I have many witnesses testifying in support of my position. Let me recall a statement of Schumpeter's complaining about these qualifications; [6] the pronouncements of John Neville Keynes, originator of the expression "positive economics"; the comments of Milton Friedman in his essay on the subject; and the remarks of Tjalling Koopmans in his methodological discourses; to mention only a few. For none of these authors is positive economics confined to propositions that are based solely on observable premises and that assert nothing but observable relationships. Some if not all of them would insist on "conceivable testability" as a criterion of eligibility for positive economics; however, the tests may be indirect, through rough correspondence of deduced consequences with observed outcomes, rather than direct, through empirical confirmation of all assumptions, including the fundamental hypotheses.

Rather than expatiate on this issue, I may refer to several earlier statements of mine in which I have attempted to show that propositions in positive economics may—nay, must—be conceived in terms of purely mental constructs, some of which do not even have operational counterparts. [7] Thus, the "positive" in positive economics is definitely not the equivalent of "observable."

"POSITIVE" VERSUS "NONTESTABLE"

I may repeat that many, perhaps most, economists nowadays insist on conceivable testability of the propositions of positive economics, although some are satisfied with indirect tests, applied to the conclusions, and do not require direct tests of the premises. [8]

However, the insistence on empirical testing (as against merely logical demonstration) is not implied in the designation "positive" economics. The designation is given only to separate this body of knowledge from

---

6 "The word 'positive' as used in this connection has nothing whatever to do with philosophical positivism. This is the first of many warnings . . . against the dangers of confusion that arises from the use, for entirely different things, of the same word by writers who themselves sometimes confuse the things" [J. A. Schumpeter, *History of Economic Analysis*, ed. E. B. Schumpeter (New York: Oxford University Press, Inc., 1954), p. 8n].

7 Fritz Machlup, "Operational Concepts and Mental Constructs in Model and Theory Formation," *Giornale degli Economisti*, XIX (*Nuova Serie*) (1960), 553–582; "Operationalism and Pure Theory in Economics," in *The Structure of Economic Science*, ed. Sherman Roy Krupp (Englewood Cliffs, N. J.: Prentice-Hall, Inc., 1966), pp. 53–67; and "Idealtypus, Wirklichkeit und Konstruktion," *Ordo*, XII (1961), 21–57.

8 In addition to the articles cited in the preceding footnote, see Fritz Machlup, "The Problem of Verification in Economics," *The Southern Economic Journal*, XXII (1955), 1–21; and "Rejoinder to a Reluctant Ultra-Empiricist," *The Southern Economic Journal*, XXII (1956), 483–493.

normative and perhaps also from practical or instrumental economics. In other words, the "positive" in positive economics is not meant to be synonymous with "testable."

THE ECONOMIST'S CONCERN WITH VALUES

It now seems well established that the "positive" in positive economics means nonnormative, nonevaluative. Moreover, the meaning of "normative," though perhaps not sufficiently cleanly defined, seems fairly well circumscribed. There is little danger, therefore, that a knowledgeable economist will confuse "value references," many of which he cannot avoid in his studies and reports, with "value judgments" incompatible with his value-neutrality and scientific objectivity. Noneconomists, however, including philosophers discussing the problem of "values" in scientific activity, may easily fall into error. Indeed, we could cite a good many confused dicta of philosophers of science reflecting on the supposed difficulties of purging the social sciences of nonscientific evaluations.

It may, therefore, be in order to examine the many kinds of values and value references with which the economist may have to concern himself. We must find out which ones, if any, are likely to lead him into making normative statements or expressing value judgments inadmissible in positive economics.

My list—may I be forgiven for my irrepressible propensity to produce lists?—has twelve items, referring to valuations by the economist, by those who produce the events he analyzes, by those for whom he makes his analyses, or by those whom he wishes to influence. More specifically, the values of possible concern to the economist are those of individuals as micro-economic decision-makers and micro-political decision-makers (items 1 and 2); of social groups or society as a whole (items 3 and 4); of the government (item 5); of the clients to whom the economist reports (item 6); of the symbolic clients whose "welfare function" he assumes as given (item 7); of his own values in his capacity as analyst (items 8–10); and of his own values in his capacity as adviser and persuader (items 11 and 12). Here is the list:

1. Values (estimates of utility, tastes, preferences) which the individuals, in the economist's models, are assumed to have and by which they are assumed to be guided as micro-economic decision-makers (household and business managers) in reaction to changes in their opportunities.

2. Values which individuals, acting alone or in groups, may reveal as micro-political decision-makers in voting for advocates of certain programs and for changes of constitutional provisions, in writing to

newspapers and legislators, in lobbying, haranguing, demonstrating, or revolting.

3. Values which social groups or society as a whole, represented by writers, speakers, and preachers, leaders in schools, clubs, associations, parties, or communities, or any influential or vocal group, may express and by which the values of individuals as micro-economic decision-makers are shaped or influenced.

4. Values which society, as either anonymous group or political institution, expresses in the form of legal norms, ethical codes, or moral suasion and which operate as constraints on, or even prohibitions or suspensions of, individual preference systems and micro-economic decisions.

5. Values which guide the government (legislators and administrators) in its decisions affecting micro-economic decision-makers by changing through coercive measures or incentives the opportunities open to them.

6. Values of the economist's clients (business firms, trade or labor organizations, government agencies) which he takes as the basis for his analysis, leading to his recommendations of optimal policies to attain their objectives.

7. Values of the economist's symbolic client—the local community, nation, or world community—which he assumes to be given in the form of a "social welfare" function as a basis for his unsolicited policy recommendations designed to serve the public interest thus defined.

8. Values of the economist as analyst which influence him in the choice of his research projects, of the problems to be analyzed, and of the hypotheses to be entertained and examined.

9. Values of the economist as analyst which influence him in the choice of his research techniques and analytical procedures, in the weights he attaches to various types of evidence, in the elegance of his logical demonstrations, and in his eagerness to subject his findings to suitable empirical tests.

10. Values of the economist as analyst which influence him in the choice of his terminology and in the acceptance of available statistical data for purposes of measurement of magnitudes taken as operational counterparts of his theoretical constructs (such as national product at market prices, with the given distribution of income).

11. Values of the economist as adviser or persuader which influence him in substituting his own value judgments, chiefly those of the supposed interest of society, for those of his actual or symbolic clients, but without deliberate falsification of his data or conscious bias in his findings.

12. Values of the economist as adviser or persuader which influence him to use inappropriate or fabricated data, employ improper methods of calculation, and give false evidence, either in an attempt to secure material advantages for his clients and himself or, alternatively, in the hope of persuading people or governments to take political action in the supposed interest of society.

While the verdict is absolutely clear regarding the last item, we must ask which of the other values or value-concerns might contaminate the economist's product and violate his value-neutrality.

THE ECONOMIST'S SCIENTIFIC OBJECTIVITY

We need not feel nervous regarding the first five items. These values, either assumed or revealed through actual conduct, are part of the subject matter with which economists deal: they are data needed for the analysis of various kinds of problems.

Item 1, the values of household and business managers, which influence their decisions to buy, sell, hire, lend, borrow, and so forth, are "given" to the analyst, who employs models of decision-making and of supply and demand to explain changes in prices and quantities of goods and services. When the economist speaks of subjective-value theory, it is not his theory which is subjective. He deals objectively with the subjective values of the economic decision-makers whose actions or reactions produce observable changes which the economist has to explain. Whether the subjective values, the preferences of the acting decision-units, are (behaviorally) revealed or merely (postulationally) assumed is a question which may concern the radical empiricist (logical positivist), not because of any suspicion of a transgression into the normative domain, but only because of the nonempirical nature of merely assumed values.

Item 2 enters only rarely into economic analysis. It may become relevant in analyses of policy measures or of events likely to incite political reactions. The analysis of problems in which political reactions play a significant role can be perfectly objective, absolutely neutral with regard to the values behind the observed or predicted reactions.

Item 3 is important chiefly in problems with strong infusions of sociological elements, such as the effects of advertising, patriotic or educational campaigns, or changes in fashion or other habits (alcohol, smoking, drugs), to mention only a few social (moral) influences on people's preferences. Valuations that change valuations are subjects of study, and have in fact been studied, without inviting deviations from value-neutrality.

Item 4 hardly needs explanation. To give only one example, the effects of legal or ethical prohibitions upon decisions regarding production, employment, supply, and demand can be analyzed without any normative (evaluative) undertones or overtones.

Item 5 is quite similar. The "official" valuations which, for example, cause the U. S. Government to impose a tax on the purchase of foreign securities but exempt securities issued by less developed countries or by Canada and Japan are data which the analyst can accept and take into account without being deflected from his scientific objectivity.

Item 6 brings us closer to the danger zone, for we are now looking at an economist working on policy recommendations for government, special-interest organizations, business firms, or other clients. Of course, such recommendations cannot help being value-directed. Yet, if the values are not too complex and can be stated in the form of specific objectives, like the tasks assigned to an engineer, chemist, or physician, then the economist's analysis is not basically different from straight causal reasoning. Instead of inquiring for the effects of some action or measure, he has to inquire what actions or measures would cause the effect desired by the client. This procedure, which, following Adolph Lowe, we have called instrumental analysis, does not involve the analyst's value judgments and is not normative in character.

Item 7 is quite problematic, for in this case the "client"—a symbolic client—does not specify his objectives or value-function. The economist arrogates to himself the role of judge of what constitutes the public interest. To be sure, he has many clues that tell him that the community likes a larger income, more employment, faster growth, more equality of income and wealth, better schools, cleaner air and water, better roads, bigger parks, better fishing, and more freedom. If he had only one objective to worry about, he could do his instrumental analysis and maintain his innocent value-neutrality. But with a multitude of social objectives and no specification of an indifference map that would give him the community's marginal rates of substitution between competing goals, "objective" instrumental analysis is impossible. We conclude that this kind of economic analysis—welfare economics—is normative. But let us take this as a rebuttable conclusion, to be reconsidered in the next section.

Item 8 presents no problems to us, though only because the problems involved were authoritatively treated and definitely resolved by Max Weber sixty years ago. Since not every writer has studied and understood Weber's arguments, there have been occasional recurrences of suspicion. Myrdal, for example, thought he could reopen the case and renew the charges that the values which influence a scholar to become interested in a certain topic and particular problem, and to formulate his first hypotheses, would inevitably produce a bias in his analysis. These charges cannot be sustained unless the entire notion of scientific objectivity in any area of inquiry is to be discarded. For the same situation exists in all sciences, the physical and biological included. There is necessarily a valuation behind the choice of topic and problem, and a preconception behind the choice of preliminary hypotheses. But this does not imply anything concerning a lack of scientific objectivity in the analysis itself, in any of the sciences—physical, biological, or social.[9]

Item 9 is analogous to item 8. No scientist can help being influenced by his valuations of alternative methods of research and analysis. In many instances strong preferences for particular techniques, usually developed in the investigator's earlier training, may have a role even in his choice of problems to be researched. No doubt these values on the part of the analyst exist and may effectively influence the choice of his rules of procedure. To admit this, however, is not to admit any insincerity in his endeavor to reach correct solutions. To be sure, some of the favored techniques may hinder or prevent him from getting "true" findings, but this does not imply violation of his value-neutrality with respect to the results of his inquiries.[10]

Item 10 presents more difficult problems, chiefly because an economist's value judgments regarding choice of terminology and acceptance of available statistical data sometimes prevail over the analyst's zeal to obtain and report unbiased findings. The use of value-loaded language is perhaps less treacherous than the use of value-blended statistics, because any design to persuade with emotive or prejudicious words is more easily detected than an attempt to lie with statistics. However, the situation is not quite as serious as it may appear from these comments. The persuasive or emotive effects of value-loaded words may wear off with time or may be removed by proper cautions. And the use of value-blended statistical data may be disclosed or exposed by critical notes. (I am not referring here, incidentally, to fabricated data or to deliberately improper uses of data, both of which belong to item 12. The statistics referred to here as value-blended cannot be cleansed of their value contents. For example, any assemblage of goods, such as the national product, can be measured only in terms of prices or values; whether one uses current market prices, officially fixed prices, prices of some base period, hypothetical prices that would result with a different distribution of income, labor-cost prices, or another standard, some prices have to be used, and the decision may be influenced by value judgments concerning the "right" system.) [11] We

---

[9] Professor Ludwig von Mises used to tell his students about the value judgment that induced chemists and biologists to do research on insecticides. The researchers' interest in these problems stemmed from an obvious bias: they were not impartial in siding with man and against the bugs. But this did not vitiate the scientific character of their endeavor. In the social sciences, research on means to preserve peace is guided by a preference for peace and a clear bias against war. Does this vitiate the research—apart from possible wishful thinking by some of the researchers?

[10] For a good discussion of items 8 and 9, see T. W. Hutchison, *"Positive" Economics and Policy Objectives* (London: George Allen & Unwin, 1964), Chap. 2.

[11] See Fritz Machlup, *The Political Economy of Monopoly* (Baltimore, Md.: The Johns Hopkins Press, 1952), pp. 459–461.

may conclude that transgressions into normative territory are possible on these counts, but that the implied threats to scientific objectivity are not serious enough to make even the purist fret and squirm.

Item 11 is closely related to item 7 in that the economic adviser (or pleader) often is not given sufficiently full specifications of the objectives to be attained and has to fill in with his own value judgments where the specifications leave blanks. The resulting bias may be, and usually is, unconscious, since most people innocently believe that they know what is wanted, either by their clients or by the community. The normative character of this sort of advice will be examined more closely in the next section.

Item 12 presents the most obvious instance of valuations leading to conscious bias and even deliberate fraud. To speak here only of a lack of scientific objectivity is unduly charitable. But let no one think that economists, or social scientists in general, have a monopoly on cheating. Hoaxes, fraud, biased testimonies, and cases of false evidence occur in all fields: in the physical and biological sciences, the engineering sciences, and even the humanities. I have supplied examples elsewhere.[12]

ADJUDICATING CHARGES OF BIAS

The point-by-point treatment of types of valuation calls for a brief summary, preceded by a restatement of the essential issue.

The issue is not whether value judgments *may* intrude into the economist's analyses and reports, or if they *may* impart a bias to his work, destroying his scientific objectivity. There is no question that this may happen and does happen. The real question is whether this is in the nature of all economic analysis or, perhaps, of certain kinds of economic analysis, and if it is therefore *unavoidable* in either all or some kinds of economic analysis.

The values or value-concerns enumerated in items 1–5 are quite irrelevant to the issue. While concern with valuations of this sort distinguishes the social sciences from the natural sciences, none of these value-concerns has any bearing on the issue of value-neutrality and bias.

The values described in item 6, the stated objectives assigned to the economist as an "engineer" in instrumental analysis, present no danger to his scientific objectivity in his work. He is given the task of solving certain problems and of reporting to his clients how they can get what they want.

---

12 Fritz Machlup, "Are the Social Sciences Really Inferior?" *The Southern Economic Journal*, XXVII (1961), 175–176. Reprinted in *Philosophy of the Social Sciences: A Reader*, ed. Maurice Nathanson (New York: Random House, Inc., 1963), pp. 163–164.

Whether he himself approves of their objectives or dislikes them may affect his work, but need not. Ethical conflicts may arise if he has qualms about the social desirability of his clients' or employers' objectives. I can even imagine some zealot supplying wrong answers in an attempt to thwart their "evil" designs. In such cases, however, it is the substitution of his own value judgments for those of his clients or employers that changes the character of his work, transforming it from instrumental into normative.

Almost the same problem arises in cases of incomplete specification of the objectives sought by the advisees—cases under item 11. The economic adviser, not having been given exact and complete instructions about the advisees' valuations of side effects, alternative means, and conflicting goals, has to use his own judgment. In this case, his value judgments are not substituted for those of his clients, but supplement them in more or less essential ways. Where he can do it in an explicit and unambiguous manner, he merely writes the missing part of the specifications of his assignment. If so, no harm is done to the scientific objectivity of his work. Often, however, the value system that supplements the simple set of objectives furnished by the clients or advisees is too complex to be unambiguously specified. In this case, the economist's analysis and report cannot help being colored by his hidden valuations and, thus, are no longer scientifically objective.

The suspicions and charges relating to items 8 and 9—concerning the choice of problem and preliminary hypotheses—were dismissed. Adjudicated long ago, they can worry only those who have not done their homework and have skipped the required reading.

Regarding item 10—value-loaded terms and value-blended figures—we merely advise caution on the part of both producers and consumers of economic reports. Where our language provides only value-loaded words and our statistics furnish only value-blended measurements, reports may have persuasive effects, intentional or unintentional. To deny the scientific objectivity of economics on these grounds would be a vast exaggeration.

This leaves the value problem of item 7 as the most sensitive of all. It is the problem of the normative nature of welfare economics, which we have resolved to consider once more.

THE NORMATIVE CHARACTER OF WELFARE ECONOMICS

Where the objectives are fully and unambiguously specified, the analysis of the best ways to attain the objectives is instrumental, not normative. But where there is any deficiency or ambiguity in the specification, the analyst cannot provide answers without (consciously or unconsciously) filling the gaps *ad hoc* according to value judgments he himself entertains at the moment. This is an undertaking that is hardly compatible with scientific objectivity. The findings of what is "better" or "best" for society under the circumstances become a function of the analyst's predilections.

We have to find out just what it means to have a full specification of social objectives. But before we try to answer this question, it will be helpful to show how a specified map of social preferences would be used in an analysis that determines the social optimum or, more modestly, an improvement of the given state of affairs.

If there were only two social goals, a two-dimensional map with indifference curves would show the acceptable trade-offs between them. The trade-off rates, or marginal rates of acceptable substitution,[13] would of course be very different for different combinations of goal achievement. Assume, for example, that the two goals are "present consumption" and "rate of increase of growth of national product." The acceptable trade-off rates (represented by the slope of the indifference curve) in a range of low consumption and fast growth would be quite different from the acceptable trade-off rates in a range of high consumption and slow growth. Although this should be obvious to the trained economist, it does not tally with his frequent references to a "given hierarchy" of social goals.

The social indifference curves have to be brought together with social possibility curves for the same two goals. The slopes of these curves tell how much of each goal would have to be given up in order to get a little more of the other. In other words, they show the rates of required sacrifice. Again, these rates will be quite different for different combinations of goal achievement. They can be regarded as marginal rates of potential substitution.

The social possibility curves are opportunity or transformation functions, showing the *required* trade-offs between alternative goal achievements—that is, the *cost* of more of one in terms of less of the other. The social indifference curves are preference or welfare functions, showing the *acceptable* trade-offs between alternative goal achievements—that is, the *utility* of more of one in terms of less of the other. The optimum solution would be that combination at which required and acceptable trade-off rates are equal.

To ascertain the required trade-off rates is one of the most important tasks of the economist. To pretend knowledge of the acceptable trade-off rates between social goals is the heroic assumption of welfare economics. Even for only two social goals, the assumption of knowing the acceptable trade-off rates for all possible combinations of goal achievement would

---

13 "Acceptable marginal rates of substitution" may be the preferred expression. I said "marginal rates of acceptable substitution" in order to indicate that all points on such a curve are equally acceptable, and that movement along such a curve represents an "acceptable substitution."

be rather extravagant. To assume knowledge of all acceptable trade-off rates among a multitude of social goals for all possible combinations is well-nigh fantastic.

Even if we think only of the most commonplace menu of social goals offered to the voter in political platforms, we must be overwhelmed by the enormity of the task of imagining, let alone ascertaining, the trade-offs acceptable to just one representative citizen. For there are not only the full arrays of rates of employment, consumption, private investment, public expenditures, growth of GNP, foreign aid, income equality, and so forth—to mention only quantifiable goals—but there are also questions of the composition of these aggregate magnitudes. The same rate of employment may be the composite of several different distributions among regions, occupations, age groups, and racial and ethnic groups; the same rate of consumption may be the composite of different distributions among consumer groups (social groups, income groups) and among consumption items (food, housing, automobiles, entertainment, alcohol, tobacco); the same rate of investment may mean very different outlays in different sectors (agriculture, mining, manufacturing, public utilities, transportation); the same rate of public expenditures may comprise substantial variations in the appropriations for different purposes (defense, research, education, health, highways); and analogous illustrations could be given for each of the quantifiable goals.

If we think of the nonquantifiable objectives our agony increases, for there are innumerable combinations among all sorts of psychic income. Most important are the legal and institutional arrangements to increase or reduce various kinds of economic, political, intellectual, and religious freedoms, many of which conflict with one another as well as with other objectives, such as employment, production, investment, equality, etc. There are also activities to increase national prestige, with acceptable trade-offs against the achievement of other objectives.

The usual reflections on welfare economics have concentrated on measurable increases or decreases in total output or income, and on associated changes in the distribution of income. By making ingenious assumptions concerning side payments through which gainers would compensate losers, the relevance of income distribution for the evaluation of particular measures or changes was eliminated, and total income was made the sole determinant of economic welfare.

With a single social objective and a single constraint—increase in aggregate income with no reduction in any individual incomes—the problem of assessing alternative public policies became manageable. But as soon as one recognizes the existence of several partly conflicting objectives, the possibility of a unique solution, even the determination of the direction of change, disappears—unless the value system of one man can be represented as that of the community. That man can only be the economist himself, and the social optimum is then clearly a personal opinion which cannot be proved right or wrong. In addition, this Grand Arbiter of Social Welfare would probably be incapable of specifying his preference functions fully and in advance; many of his findings would be *ad hoc*, for particular occasions, improvised and not predictable.[14]

An illustration may help to make this clear. The Congress of the United States has been working on a new copyright law extending the term of protection to the lifetime of the author plus fifty years. Although it has not occurred to any legislator to ask for an economic appraisal of the effects of this provision, let us assume that an economist is commissioned to advise. He may be able to say something about the probable movement along the possibility function. He may predict that the increase in incentives for publishers and authors will lead to the publication of additional books (including five novels per year, eight mystery stories, six books on sex, and seven new textbooks, two of which will be on elementary economics with poor chapters on welfare economics); that the prices of books, especially those published long ago but still selling in considerable quantities, will go up by 10 per cent; that private consumer spending on books will be only slightly affected, as consumers will buy fewer books with a somewhat larger outlay of money, but that the budgets of public libraries and libraries of educational institutions will have to be increased; that the appropriations to education departments of states and public-school districts will have to be raised because of the higher prices of most textbooks; that these expenditures will be met partly by raising taxes and partly at the expense of other educational outlays, including teachers' salaries; that expenditures for lawyers' fees and court costs will go up because of the increase in litigation of copyright cases; and that the chief redistributive effects will be from book readers, researchers, teachers, and taxpayers to the grandchildren of the authors of the (very few) successful books. Now all this is on the possibility or transformation side of the prediction. What about the evaluation of the changes involved?

The welfare economist will have to decide how much "society" will delight in the publication of the additional titles (including those on sex and economics); how much "society" will resent paying higher taxes; how much it will appreciate the decrease in teachers' salaries and increase in lawyers' incomes; and, especially, how much it will relish the thought that

---

14 This can also be said of particular decisions on problems of individual households and firms, but with different implications. It means only that their reactions cannot always be correctly predicted and, unless odd decisions cancel out, predictions of reactions of aggregate supply and demand may be less than accurate. The problem is quite different with regard to a single Grand Arbiter of Social Welfare.

some fortunate heirs of authors will receive royalties on the literary products of their late grandfathers or great-aunts.

The use of value-loaded language in the exposition of this piece of applied welfare economics may have revealed the value judgments of the present writer. Whether these judgments agree with those of the majority of the people or of the legislators in Congress is not known, but is quite unlikely. The best that I can say in support of my value judgment is that I presume that most other people would agree with me if, but only if, they thought about the problem hard enough.

The point of my illustration, however, was not that my valuations may be peculiar prejudices not shared by others; what I intended to show was that my value system could not possibly have been specific on the merits or demerits of potential gifts to unknown grandchildren of authors of books that still enjoy sales long after their publication. This spot on my social-welfare function was completely blank until the problem arose and I had to fill in the relevant valuations for the occasion. I could, of course, assert that my appraisal of the legislative action represents a logical inference from my value system and that I can *now* give the necessary specification for others to check my logic. I still doubt that this will meet the objections that the whole procedure is "unscientific."

One more difficulty should be considered: the welfare economist's valuations of future benefits derived from present sacrifices, and of present benefits obtained at the cost of future sacrifices. Some welfare economists are very generous toward future generations and are prepared to give away much of the income of their own contemporaries. Others are quite stingy and resent making sacrifices for the yet unborn great-grandchildren of their friends and fellow taxpayers. ("Why should I do so much for posterity? What has posterity done for me?") Any social indifference map presupposes given sets of rates of time preference (generosity or stinginess *vis-à-vis* future generations), and thus is the result of entirely subjective inclinations.

It may seem that a way out of this and all similar difficulties would be not to specify just one social-value system, but to give the client or advisee (that is, the representatives of society) a large set of alternative systems from which to choose. This is not really practicable, however, simply because there are an infinite number of possible preference systems. It is not feasible to propose a sufficiently large number of alternative value systems to do justice to the existing variety of tastes and preferences. It is not feasible to tell those in the seats of government that they have a choice among millions of different value systems and that, corresponding to each, there may be a different answer to their specific questions. The welfare economist, if he is very conscientious, will at best specify a small sample

of alternative welfare functions and, in limiting the open choices in this
way, will again have engaged in normative economics.

STAYING PURE VERSUS COMING CLEAN

Having concluded that welfare economics is normative in character, the
purists among us may cry, "Unclean! Unclean!" whenever they see a
piece of welfare analysis. This would be unfortunate. Even if welfare
economics is impure, it is a necessary part of our work.

The recent fashion for "cost-benefit analysis" represents a healthy recognition of the danger of choosing blindly and of the advantages of making
choices on the basis of a rational consideration of alternatives. It is true
that the considerations include estimates of benefits that rest on more or
less arbitrary valuations, but this does not imply that we would be better
off if we avoided all "unscientific" estimates and made our decisions without considering what the effects might be and how we would like them.

Honesty demands that we be frank about the evaluative nature of our
appraisals and recommendations. But this does not mean that we must
write long methodological introductions to each and every policy memo-
randum. If we did, we would only increase the percentage of memoranda
reaching their final destination—the files—without being read by those to
whom they were addressed. This would be too bad. A great deal needs
to be done to improve the quality of economic policy advice. We can meet
the demands of honesty by discussing and justifying the value assumptions
made in the analysis and, even better, by showing how the findings would
be affected if we varied the value assumptions. As a rule, we probably will
indicate which value position we regard as the most "reasonable." Most
of us will do this in a rather unmistakable way, since we are usually convinced that our own ethical values are more ethical than others.

SOME THOUGHTS ON LOWE'S INSTRUMENTALISM

Now that I am through with the analytical semantics of the terms and
the methodological analysis of the issues involved, I may take up Dr.
Lowe's commitment to instrumentalism and examine it in the light of my
findings.

In order to guard against misunderstandings, it may be well to say
that Dr. Lowe's instrumentalism is neither identical with nor closely
related to John Dewey's philosophical position by the same name, which
is usually regarded as a species of pragmatism. Nor is Dr. Lowe's instrumentalism related to that of Adolf Lampe, the late economist of the

University of Freiburg, who thought of it as advocacy of an economic
system that would evolve as a compromise between liberalism, the economic system steered by free-market prices, and socialism, the centrally
directed economy. Dr. Lowe's instrumentalism is meant to be a type of
analysis, differentiated from both positive and normative analyses.

The trichotomy—positive, normative, instrumental—follows the proposal of John Neville Keynes, except that Keynes used "practical," not
"instrumental," to denote the third type of economics. For Keynes, moreover, the third type was firmly based on the results of positive and normative economics. Dr. Lowe, on the other hand, views instrumental analysis
as independent of positive analysis, which he distrusts as inapplicable
to the industrial economies of our time, and independent also of normative
analysis, which he regards as meta-scientific.

THE INSTRUMENTAL INFERENCES

The scheme of things in the framework of Dr. Lowe's analytical setup,
in a form in which the knowns are stated as premises and the unknowns
as questions, looks like this:

1. If you are in macro-state A (the "initial" state), and
2. If you want to *move* to macro-state Z (the "macro-goal"), and
3. If L, R, and G are general laws, rules, and empirical generalizations,
   respectively,

then

1. What *path* is suitable to that movement?
2. What *patterns of micro-behavior* are appropriate to keep the system
   on that path?
3. What *micro-motivations* are capable of generating suitable behavior?
4. What political *control* can be designed to stimulate suitable motivations?

Most economists, unacquainted with Dr. Lowe's work, would see in
this arrangement of premises and questions nothing that is different from
their own procedures in applied economics. The second premise, stating
the macro-goal, is evidently the result of normative economics, and the
third premise comprises the results of positive economics—the general
laws, the institutional rules and constraints, and the empirical generalizations. This, however, is not what Dr. Lowe has in mind. Although he
admits that macro-goals are "the results of normative judgment," [15] he
does not tell us how such judgments are justified, which would be norma-

---

[15] See pp. 18, 24.

tive economics. And the third premise, according to Dr. Lowe, does not state the results of positive economics but only those of natural sciences, engineering, and psychology. For in Dr. Lowe's framework, my notation L stands for "laws of nature," R represents "engineering rules," and G stands for empirical generalizations "concerning sociopsychological relations." [16] Thus, Dr. Lowe's instrumental analysis, as he sees it, is not based on either normative or positive economics. He holds that "only after reality has been transformed through such [Control] action" (namely, "measures of public Control suitable to bring about that conformance" of structural, behavioral, and motivational conditions which assure goal attainment) "can the instrumental inferences serve as major premises in a deductive syllogism." [17]

I submit that these contentions cannot be sustained. As soon as there are several goals and several paths toward their attainment, instrumental analysis needs normative economics, because the choices among the alternative paths and the many possible combinations of goal attainments cannot be made without complex systems of values (preferences) which cannot be assumed as objective data given to the instrumentalist. Likewise, the questions regarding the "suitable" path toward goal attainment, the "appropriate" patterns of micro-behavior, the micro-motivations "capable" of generating the required behavior patterns, and the political controls designed to stimulate the right motivations cannot be answered except on the basis of full knowledge of theoretical laws, institutional rules, and empirical generalizations about economic relations—that is, on the basis of positive economics.

THE NEED FOR POSITIVE AND NORMATIVE ANALYSES

Judgments about what is suitable, adequate, capable, and so forth, imply predictability, which in turn presupposes either law statements (positive theory) or firmly established correlations (significant regression coefficients). It is logically impossible to infer the suitable instruments from the "given" goals if there exists no reliable positive knowledge of the type, "If A, then B," which is the type commonly found in positive economics. (This says nothing about the way such knowledge was acquired. More often than not it may have been by way of a search for the unknown cause, A, of an observed effect, B. But this need not be "instrumental analysis.")

The inevitability of normative economics within (and not only before)

---

16 *OEK*, p. 143.
17 *OEK*, p. 311.

instrumental analysis is a consequence of the impossibility of knowing in advance the choices that have to be made among alternative paths, alternative behavior patterns, alternative control measures. It is not just a matter of postponing decisions until we have to "cross the bridge"; it is rather complete ignorance of what bridges there may be to cross. The instrumentalist—the political economist—cannot possibly know what benefits and sacrifices may have to be compared, what compromises to be made, and therefore what values to be applied to the choices among alternative "instruments." Hence, he does not arrive at the many bridges with a ready-made evaluation kit or social-preference map for guidance in the necessary choices. The relevant preferences will have to be mapped out and justified *ad hoc* at every one of the indefinite number of questions whose existence is unknown to the chooser of the best or second-best instruments.

One may ask whether there really are quite that many alternatives to choose from for one's policy recommendations. Things would be easy if there were only one path to the desired macro-state (or even none), or perhaps only two or three, with foreseeable cost-and-benefit comparisons for which all the needed value data can be read off the prepared preference map. Such simplicity cannot be expected; I have always been able to think of countless alternatives in any problem of economic policy with which I have been concerned. For example, when the removal or reduction of the U. S. payments deficit was "given" as a very urgent macrogoal, I enumerated forty-one different types of measures capable of steering behavior along suitable paths—with an indefinite number of variations in degree of application and of possible combinations—each of them restricting to some extent the attainment of other macro-goals. And I doubt that any two of the consultants had the same comparative evaluations of the benefits that would be secured or sacrificed by the alternative courses of action. In other words, justification of values—normative economics—is part and parcel of the job of the policy adviser, the man engaged in instrumental economics.

THE CRITICAL BOUNDARY

The reader, or *this* reader at least, repeatedly frightened out of his wits by all the talk of goal-choosing and control-imposing by the authorities, is finally reassured: Dr. Lowe has us "restrict the choice of our substantive goals to such states and processes as can be brought into agreement with the strivings of the large majority of micro-units." [18]

---

[18] *OEK*, p. 318.

He explains this by accepting the old liberal tenet that "micro-autonomy is vindicated if it is suitable to promote political freedom, and if such freedom takes precedence over any conceivable principle according to which production and distribution can be organized." [19] However, "it is the *well-understood interest* of the micro-units that must agree with the macro-goal, rather than their crude strivings. To enlighten the individual marketer about his true interests by reducing expectational uncertainty and by suitably patterning action directives is the very function of manipulative controls." [20]

We are now definitely in normative territory. Alas, "however hard we may try to avoid choices based on value judgments pure and simple, we cannot run away from an ultimate decision as to the relative significance of the economic and the political sphere or as to the ranking of rivalling political goals." [21] Dr. Lowe justifies the invasion of normative territory by granting that "liberty . . . must be adopted as a 'provisional value' if those among us who believe in absolute values are to be allowed to continue fighting for them." [22]

Dr. Lowe thinks he crossed the boundary into normative or evaluative economics only when he granted priority to political freedom over some "economic" goal or goals. This may strike us as rather strange, since he has again and again allowed some chosen macro-goal to overrule and restrain the wishes of the "micro-units." Perhaps he relies on the widely held thesis that goals and values are subjects of value judgments only when they are compared with other goals and values or when they remain concealed, but are admitted as legitimate data in positive analysis as long as they are clearly stated and are examined only in relation to the means suitable for their attainment.

The trouble with this view is that not only the choice among alternative techniques of control but also the unquestionable "plurality of macro-goals" will always force us to engage in value judgments. The preference scales (or indifference maps) of macro-goals in the value systems of the

---

[19] *OEK*, p. 319.
[20] *OEK*, p. 320.
[21] *OEK*, p. 320.
[22] *OEK*, p. 322. I cannot help setting Dr. Lowe's view in juxtaposition to a statement made by Frank H. Knight, many years before Lowe's plea for instrumental economics: "In the field of social policy, the pernicious notion of instrumentalism . . . is actually one of the most serious of the sources of danger which threaten destruction to the values of what we have called civilization. Any such conception as social engineering or social technology has meaning only in relation to the activities of a super-dictatorship, a government which would own as well as rule society at large, and would use it for the purposes of the governors" [Frank H. Knight, "Fact and Value in Social Science," in *Science and Man,* ed. Ruth Anshen (New York: Harcourt, Brace & World, Inc., 1942); reprinted in Frank H. Knight, *Freedom and Reform* (New York: Harper & Row, Publishers, 1947), pp. 225–226].

Goal Selectors cannot be identical and cannot be fully specified. The elasticities of substitution among additional tenths of per cents of unemployment, total output, total consumption, growth, and all the rest, are too complex and too unstable to be admissible as a "given" assumption of a supposedly scientific "instrumental analysis."

At several points Dr. Lowe tries to escape the normative task of instrumental analysis by making "the implicit assumption that the different aspirations of a goal-setter are mutually compatible and can be translated into a consistent and realizable set of targets." [23] The assumption of a given "hierarchy of goals," where some goals may become means for other goals but where "the precise nature of these interrelations poses a genuinely scientific problem unencumbered by any value judgment or norm," [24] serves the same purpose. But these assumptions are legitimate only as part of a logical demonstration designed to show (1) under what conditions instrumental analysis *would* be nonevaluative, and (2) that these conditions are contrary to fact. Dr. Lowe's hope that the tasks of goal-setting and policy-choosing can be separated and that those engaged in instrumental analysis need not as a rule—except where possible infringements of political freedom are involved—cross over the "critical boundary" [25] into the territory of normative analysis is, in my opinion, not justified.

However, I am neither apprehensive nor critical in any way of such crossings of the border between the Domain of the True or False and the Domain of the Good or Bad. I would do away with all prohibitions, customs duties, and passport requirements between the domains. Of course, I would want all imported or produced values to be declared rather than concealed. But, and this is my point in this context, I do not believe that an honest declaration at the frontier of instrumental analysis would be at all possible or helpful. The customs officer may ask the traveler—the peripatetic political economist—the usual question: "Have you anything to declare? Have you any values or norms in your bag?" And the traveler may declare all the values and norms he is aware of having brought with him; however, he cannot declare those values that he will work out or develop only long after settling down, when he finds that he has to make choices for which none of the evaluations that he has ever thought about are relevant.

---

23 See p. 19.
24 *OEK*, p. 316.
25 *OEK*, p. 321.

7
ABBA P. LERNER

ON
INSTRUMENTAL
ANALYSIS

Professor Machlup, while making it very difficult for me to add anything to his painstaking analysis of the numerous ways in which economists and philosophers have used and misused the words "normative" and "objective" and their various synonyms and antonyms, has greatly facilitated my task of examining the significance of Professor Lowe's instrumental analysis. For this I am extremely thankful, but nevertheless I cannot avoid risking the appearance of base ingratitude by observing that in his careful concentration on labeling all the flowers, Professor Machlup may have been somewhat distracted from seeing the garden as a whole; thus he may appear to have paid insufficient attention to the degree of novelty and significance of Professor Lowe's clarification of the changing role of economic science in today's society.

From a vantage point thus privileged, which enables me so much more easily to view the garden as a whole, I can sketch the view in very rough lines and declare the "objective–normative" issue as being essentially one of honesty. Objectivity turns out to be not the avoidance of concern with what is *desired* in a pure concentration on what *is*, but merely the avoidance of smuggling in an advocacy of desired objectives, without making it clear that this is being done or without making it clear whose are the desires being considered. "Scientific" and "objective" have thus come to mean almost the same as "straight," while "normative" and non "value-free" have come to mean almost the same as "crooked."

It is, of course, not clear that investigators concerned with the efficacy of methods of achieving desired ends have to be, or even tend to be, more dishonest than those concerned with research in pure or basic science, where the usefulness of any discoveries for achieving desired ends is not immediately apparent (other than the end of satisfying curiosity, or perhaps awakening it). They may be more liable to be misled into attributing their own preferences to others, perhaps without being clear that they were dealing with preferences at all—going astray, as it were, rather than being crooked. But pure, objective science is not free of such dangers and temptations either.

Professor Machlup has brought out and emphasized the temptation for the researcher to permit his own preferences to play an unwarranted role in filling out incompletely specified objectives. It is, perhaps, the freedom of the pure or basic researcher from this particular temptation that is responsible for the confusion between concern with value judgments and departure from scientific propriety. What Professor Lowe has undertaken is to show that this realm of suspected departure from the straight and narrow path is precisely the arena where the useful work of economists is more and more to be concentrated.

The normal response to a novel idea is first to dismiss it as nonsense, then to reject it as wrong, after a while to pooh-pooh it as being of little relevance, thereafter to admit and even exaggerate its importance, and finally to declare (and believe) that one has held the new position all along. My own response in the present case was almost the reverse of this. My first reaction was to declare that instrumental analysis was nothing but another name for the welfare economics that I had singled out as the kind of economics which was of the greatest interest to me even before I began my economic studies—and certainly before I proposed to write a Ph.D. dissertation on "the economics of control." I next was rather shaken by Professor Machlup's carefully contained concern, and Professor Lowe's own warnings, on the encouragement that instrumental economics could give to authoritation inclinations. Finally, I have come to see the justification for the emphasis brought by a new terminology to an existing trend which has increased so much in importance that it deserves to be considered as a change from quantity into quality.

The most objective and the purest of researchers cannot be really free from some connection with value judgments if he has any idea that his discoveries may provide something more to fellow humans than the kind of intellectual exercise provided by achievements in chess or go. The purest of pure researchers betrays a preference for knowledge over ignorance, while the medical researcher displays a clear valuation of the lives of humans over those of the deviant cells that he dubs malignant cancer. Yet such researchers are rarely accused of guilt by association with value judgments because there is so little chance of the insinuation of an undeclared or hidden value judgment. All seems to be "straight" and aboveboard.

A second category of researchers who are held guiltless consists of people like astronomers, who are protected from being involved with the possible furtherance of hidden objectives because they are not able to recommend any action that would have a significant effect on the heavenly bodies and that could therefore facilitate the achievement of any human objectives. They cannot be involved in policy matters.

Economists could achieve immunity from suspicion of value distortion (or *bad* advice) and could be considered to be as free from value involvement as the astronomers if they could avoid giving any advice after the manner in which astronomers avoid astrology. Extremely "classical" classical economists have sometimes appeared to have achieved such sterility. Overreacting to naïve planners who are ignorant of economics, they have tended to see in the automatic market mechanism an instrument of such perfection and delicacy that any attempt by mere humans to improve on it could only result in disrupting it. Just as astronomers remain pure because they give no advice, good or bad, to men who *cannot* do anything about the stars, so the extreme classical economists have remained pure by refraining from giving any advice to men who *should not* do anything about the economy because whatever they do can only do harm.

This is, of course, a wicked caricature of laissez-faire economics, but its recognizability, even as a wicked caricature, indicates the change that has taken place in the degree to which the need arises and is recognized for conscious social responsibility in human management of the economy for a great diversity of objectives. This is the change from quantity to quality that justifies Professor Lowe's emphasis on the change in economics from a discipline basically engaged in explaining the automatic working of the price mechanism (with occasional excursions into policy suggestions for correcting untoward accidents or preventing dangerous interferences, especially well-intended ones), into a discipline that concentrates on guiding the economic authorities in continuous endeavors to maintain high employment, prevent ruinous inflation, moderate income inequality, curb monopolies, and engage in an ever increasing number of activities for correcting divergencies between private and social benefits, by restricting socially harmful activities and encouraging socially beneficial ones.

Professor Machlup has amplified Professor Lowe's warnings of the dangers of insinuating hidden value judgments and of encouraging authoritarian developments through pressure to achieve consensus in the face of conflicting interests and preferences. But recognition of the dangers should not blind us to the change that has brought them about. It should only serve to put economists even more on the alert to avoid hidden value judgments and expose authoritarian dangers in working out programs for acceptable trade-offs between the conflicting objectives.

Professor Machlup seems to fear that Professor Lowe's thesis tends too much in the direction of calling for social planning, with its attendant authoritarian dangers. To me, it seems that Professor Lowe is in greater danger of being too much of a classical economist in the sense of the wicked caricature. Perhaps this is so only because of his natural emphasis on the distinguishing features of his main thesis. But I see too easy an acceptance of the myth of a previous state of society, before it became necessary for instrumental analysis to replace "objective" economic analysis, when the economy worked so automatically that it could be studied usefully from the outside, like astronomy.

Just as we do not believe that history will come to a stop after a Marxian elimination of its driving force—the class struggle—so we do not really believe that the free-market system sprang full-bodied from the brain of Adam Smith. A more explicitly evolutionary approach would remove some of the abrasiveness of Professor Lowe's thesis.

The basic machinery underlying the price mechanism consists of a complex series of institutions which did not drop from heaven, but which were the result of the ingenious inventions and adjustments by unknown social engineers that have survived through natural selection over many centuries and, indeed, millennia. I refer to the inventions of private and public property, of contracts and methods of their enforcement, of the use of monies of various kinds, and of techniques of measuring and accounting and the like—all of which were essential for the development of efficient market economies.

This economic evolution was not the result of blind accident as was the evolution of the first organic molecules and their selection by virtue of their stability in their environment, or of chance events such as the haphazard chemical or radiological mutations of the genes of plants and animals which, together with natural selection of differentiated individuals, resulted in biological evolution. There was undoubtedly much that we would call accidental in the specific improvements in these institutions by specific individuals in specific tribes or villages, but as the institutions became more complex, the changes must have been more and more the result of planned experiments based on some understanding of how the institutions worked. There was still room for natural selection to operate by causing those tribes, villages, or cities to grow and survive which had made changes that increased their productivity or otherwise raised their survival power, but the experiments and the resulting institutional changes, both those that survived and those that perished, were the result of instrumental analysis. The social revolution that calls for moving instrumental analysis to the head of the class had been developing long before Keynes heralded "the end of laissez-faire." To apply Marshall's quotation, *"Natura non facit saltum,"* nature did not make a jump.

There is also a lesson for the future. As the number of independent societies with their own sets of economic institutions increased in size and diminished in number, the power of natural selection became weaker and weaker (just as, for somewhat different reasons, it became much less operative in human, genetic evolution with the development of modern medicine, which resulted in the survival of many who, under previous conditions, would have been selected out as "unfit"). Further development is now hardly at all possible through the survival, by "natural selection," of whichever of the several current forms of social organization develops the more efficient economic system. Development, rather, takes the quite different and a thousand times more rapid form where each economic system consciously learns not only from its own, but from its rivals' experiences. So we now see the capitalist countries developing social responsibilities that used to be called socialist, and the socialist countries developing uses of price, profit, and interest calculations, to say nothing of accounting and management science techniques that used to be called capitalistic.

This symmetrical development on both sides of the curtain should serve to warn us that instrumental analysis may look rather like a rejection of free economy and the price mechanism in favor of central planning with its overtones of authoritarian dictatorship; this, naturally, can frighten liberals out of their wits. But that is only what it looks like on this side of the curtain, where market mechanisms have been developed far more fully than centralized, nonmarket institutions for providing public services, economic security, and other social objectives. On the other side of the curtain, instrumental analysis leads rather to decentralization and the more rapid application of the price mechanism.

The most important lesson of all, however, which seems to spring from whatever current social topic we touch, is that until recently it was still conceivable for a conflict to decide by natural selection whether the capitalistic or the communistic system would survive, and that in this decision the relative development of the economies of the two systems, by the application of instrumental analysis, played its part. Now it is becoming clearer than ever that neither system would survive such a conflict in a form that would leave very much of anything. The game of selection and evolution by survival of the fittest is at an end. Only through the conscious application of instrumental analysis can there be any hope of further development or even survival of the economic or any other aspect of modern society.

8

CARL KAYSEN

MODEL-MAKERS
AND
DECISION-MAKERS

Economists and the Policy Process

This essay organizes some reflections on the relations between economic analysis and the processes of policy formation in government, and the corresponding relations between economists and policy-makers. Offered as a tribute to Adolph Lowe, it shares both his skepticism of economic theory and his optimism about what economists might do, although perhaps on somewhat different grounds from his in both cases.

In what follows, I write in terms of American political institutions. These are such as to underline and in some cases exaggerate the conflicts of value inherent in any policy decision, and to exhibit in sharp form the constraints the political process places on consistency and rationality in policy-making. This is especially true of the division of powers between the Executive branch and the Legislature, which is the most striking feature of the American government as compared to that of the other industrial democracies. Nonetheless, the same underlying problems of policy-making are present in all democratic societies to a sufficient extent to make these observations widely applicable.

In recent years, a formal theory of economic policy has grown up, largely under the intellectual leadership of Jan Tinbergen and his collaborators in Holland. Perhaps its most sophisticated version is that presented by H. Theil in *Economic Forecasts and*

Policy.[1] The central feature of this theory is a complete formal model of the economic system under consideration on the basis of which its present state can be described and its future evolution forecast at least over the time horizon relevant to the policy decisions in question. The variables of this system are divided into two classes: *controlled variables* or *instruments*, whose values the policy-maker can choose directly within some constraints, and *uncontrolled variables*, which can be influenced only indirectly through the policy-maker's choice of instrument variables. A subset of the variables is composed of the *targets*, whose values the policy-maker seeks to influence; he is assumed to have a utility function by which he can characterize the relative desirability of alternate combinations of the target variables. The policy-maker's problem then becomes that of choosing the instrument variables that will result in the maximization of the utility function, subject to the constraints imposed by the system.

The model is clearer if the sets of target variables and instrument variables do not overlap, so that the instruments are "neutral" in policy terms. In this case we can, by suitable restrictions on the functions involved, find a reduced form of the system, in which, for any appropriate future date, the target variables are shown as functions of the instrument variables and the predicted values of the other uncontrolled variables of the system. But this restriction is not necessary; the model can also deal with the more general case in which some of the instrument variables enter into the policy-maker's utility function as target variables.

Although in principle a policy-making model of this general type can be constructed for any economic policy problem, in practice this conceptual structure has developed in the context of short-run macro-economic stabilization policy. This is to be expected: it is in this area of policy that economic analysis has made its largest contribution in the last two decades—if not indeed in its whole history—and it is in this area that the possibility of successful policies has been intimately dependent on the technical quality of the economics available to the policy-makers. Here also, the political significance of economic policy is greatest, and political decision-makers accordingly are most sensitive to the possibilities of finding help.

Conceptually, in terms of a model of this kind, the role of the economist and that of the policy-maker can be sharply distinguished. The policy-maker has to specify his utility function, showing what values he places on various alternative combinations of target variables; he may also specify constraints on the range (or even the admissibility) of par-

---

[1] H. Theil, *Economic Forecasts and Policy* (Amsterdam: North Holland Publishing Co., 1958).

ticular instrument variables. After he does so, the rest of the job belongs
to the economists and econometricians, and, in concept, is a politically
neutral one. Indeed, Theil characterizes this separation in colorful terms
when he talks of the "decision animal" and the "information animal."

The task of building usable forecasting models is both intellectually
and practically difficult, with problems ranging from the theoretical specification of a system and the statistical estimation of its parameters, to
the securing of appropriately timely data. For all the difficulties, however, enough progress is being made in dealing with these problems to
encourage the profession to continue its best efforts. It is precisely the
combination of intellectual difficulty and some success in dealing with
the problem that characteristically stimulates scientific efforts. This stimulus is further reinforced both by the degree to which the task appears
to be politically neutral and by the fact that it is demanding enough of
the specialized skills and training of the economist so that the significance
of his contribution to it—in contrast with the contributions of general
wisdom by politicians and men of affairs—is clear to all.

This model of policy-making for short-run macro-economic problems
stands in sharp contrast to the character of economic policy advice in
more traditional areas, such as the "classical" problems of free trade versus
protection; equity and efficiency in taxation; or monopoly, competition,
governmental privilege, and interference in the market. Typically, in
these cases, economists offer advice within a partial rather than a general equilibrium framework, and, on the whole, much more in qualitative than in quantitative terms. These characteristics are not all logically
inevitable; they reflect in part historical and present limitations on conceptual tools in relation to the difficulty of the problems and data available. To some extent these are underdeveloped areas of analysis to which
the newer conceptual and statistical technology of economics is just beginning to be applied. However, many of the intellectual intractabilities
involved lie very deep indeed, and may simply prove to be insoluble in
the terms in which they are usually posed. The total inability of welfare
economics to say anything cogent about "second-best" alternatives, where
the usual allocative conditions for optimality cannot all be met, is a
pervasive limitation on well-specified quantitative policy models for
problems in all the areas listed above; it does not appear likely to yield
quickly to new ideas.

I

The striking fact, however, is that these limitations have done little
or nothing to inhibit economists from giving policy advice on this range

of problems. In fact, the opposite is the case. The absence of all the difficulties and obvious limitations of models involving checkable quantitative forecasts appears to lead to vigorous and confident policy prescriptions and, indeed, to a wide degree of professional agreement on these prescriptions. All, or nearly all, respectable economists are for freer trade and more competition, though few or none are prepared to estimate the gains from some specific reduction in trade barriers when substantial barriers remain, or the value of increasing the degree of competition in some sectors of the economy while accepting as inevitable a high degree of market power in other sectors.

In both cases, the confidence of economists' policy recommendations is essentially ideological: it rests on their commitment to the competitive market as an ideal, and on the consequent belief that any step in the direction of the ideal is a desirable one. While this, in my judgment, is the main ingredient of economists' policy recommendations on these points, it is clearly not the only one. There are, in addition, more directly and self-consciously political grounds for preferring more to less competitive domestic markets, and less to more restricted international trade; i.e., arguments articulated in terms of political liberty rather than economic efficiency. Typically, however, these are not the arguments of the majority of the profession.

The role of the economist in policy formation in these areas is almost diametrically opposed to that envisaged in the formal theory of policy-making referred to above. He functions primarily as a propagandist of values, not as a technician supplying data for the pre-existing preference functions of the policy-makers. Some of his propaganda is directed at those participants in political decision-making to whom the advisers are directly responsive, and is aimed at shaping their values in the direction of the adviser's own. Much of the propaganda is directed through his political superiors to other participants in the political process, including the general public; the adviser becomes, in fact, a supplier of arguments and briefs that seek to gain greater support throughout the society for the economists' value goals.

In some cases, of course, economists have not succeeded even in the first step of converting significant decision-makers to their values. Then they cannot act as advisers in shaping policy in some detail, but only as critics urging that its basis be changed. The outstanding American example of this situation is, of course, the agricultural price support program with its related apparatus of complex restrictions on output. Most competent professional economists view this program as badly designed even in terms of its own goals, and, worse, as directed in large part at inappropriate goals. But more than two decades of criticism, conducted in pubic forums outside the government and, less persistently, in private arenas within it, have failed to change the views of the relevant policy-makers on what goals are important, or what instruments are appropriate.

To be sure, in all these areas of policy-making, economists also engage in purely technical activities, in addition to their prime task of value-advocacy. For example, in the antitrust and regulatory areas where policy is made by a process of case-by-case adjudication before administrative and judicial tribunals, both the selection of cases to investigate and prosecute and the development of arguments for deciding them in one way rather than another can benefit substantially from the technical advice of economists. Traditionally, these activities have been the province of lawyers, and it is only recently that economic advisers have begun to play any noticeable role. Even within the present broad framework of these policies, greater reliance on high-quality economic advice in applying them could achieve substantial gains in their effectiveness. The use of modern econometric methods of cost-and-demand analysis has hardly begun in these areas; their wider application would be one important source of such benefits.

The relative weights of technical and value components in economic advice on policy problems are strongly influenced by their places on the scale of "settled" and "live," in political terms. Antitrust policy is at the relatively settled end of the scale. The broad scope of the law, which determines the limits of the policy, has remained surprisingly stable over time. Since the passage of the Sherman Act more than three-quarters of a century ago, only three major changes in law have been made—in 1914, 1937, and 1950. In absolute terms, the size of the enforcement effort has grown only slowly in the last three decades; in relation to the size of the economy, it has shrunk. The nature of the enforcement process, with its dominant emphasis on response to complaints by businessmen who consider themselves injured by the activities of their supplier, customers, or rivals, has likewise changed little. This situation, in turn, reflects the underlying balance of political forces that sustains and limits the policy. On one side are the strong continuing attachment to competition as a symbol of American virtues which pervades the society; the persistence of populist sentiments among farmers and, to some extent, trade unionists, which is reflected by their representatives in Congress and reinforced by a general widespread suspicion of "big business" and "monopoly"; and the political power of small businessmen and their organized group representatives. On the other side are the productive achievements of the economy, which are widely perceived as the achievements of the handful of large firms whose names and products are household words; the pragmatic unwillingness of nearly all American politicians to engage in "crusades" to improve what functions well; and the political power of big business, especially through the mass media.

This balance incorporates to some degree the economist's commitment to competition as a value, but of course in a crude way that diverges widely from his professional understanding of its significance. Otherwise, it draws on only a small part of what economists have to say about the structure and functioning of markets. However, except to the degree that an economist's views on the virtues of competition may serve to reinforce the existing balance and the "settled" character of the policy, there is little political market for professional urgings of a significantly different policy, especially the more vigorously procompetitive one that students of these problems usually espouse.

In such a context, the policy role of the economist tends to be small and its technical elements relatively important within that narrow scope. As a crusading critic, he is unlikely to have much impact on policy. As an insider, he is generally confined to technical tasks within the given policy framework. The value of these tasks, of course, can be far from negligible. Within the confines of a broadly settled policy, there is still room for change. In this particular area, policy change comes about in large part through the influence of the enforcing agencies in selecting cases and framing issues for courts and commissions to decide. These are processes to which economists have contributed, and, as I have already argued, they can contribute more. Yet this kind of influence has sharp limits within the present policy machinery. The productivity of the marginal dollar spent on antitrust enforcement—which applies to sectors producing substantially more than half the gross national product—in relation to that of the marginal dollar spent on the regulation of the Federally regulated industries—which account for less than one-sixth of GNP—would not suggest that antitrust's present share of the total budget for improving and guiding market processes approaches the optimum.

II

By contrast with the relatively settled issue of policy on competition, we can examine the recent and current situations in international monetary policy. On the political scale, the issue has been one of the liveliest problems of economic policy for nearly a decade, both in the United States and internationally. To the professional economist, the issues turn around the adequacy or inadequacy of the present gold-exchange standard as an international monetary mechanism; the workability of the U. S.

role in that mechanism (in particular, the fixed dollar price of gold and the role of gold as a reserve asset); and the urgency of making fundamental changes in the system. The overwhelming weight of professional opinion—though not all of it—views the present role of gold in the system as irrational. However, there is a wider spectrum of judgments on such questions as how urgent a change in the system is, what the desirable rate of growth of international liquidity should be, and what particular institutional mechanisms would be preferable to the admittedly highly imperfect present one. There are particularly sharp differences of opinion on what the effects on international trade and investment would be if the present regime of quasi-fixed exchange rates for the major trading nations were supplanted with a regime in which at least some major rates "floated."

But it is not these matters on which the question of economic advice useful to political decision-makers currently turns. Rather, it turns primarily on the simple fundamental question of the dispensability or indispensability of gold as a basis of the international monetary system. Next in importance is the only slightly more complex question of the significance of gold to the U. S. position in the international economy, and the nature and consequences of any change in that position. On both of these points, political decision-makers have shown a very strong attachment to the indispensability of gold and a belief in the near-disastrous consequences for the United States of any change in its role. The very terms in which the public statements of government spokesmen and their political critics are framed—"defense of the dollar," "stopping the hemorrhage of gold," and the like—are revealing. For nearly a decade, the major policy measures of the United States have been aimed at "correcting" its balance-of-payments deficit in order to "maintain the stability of the dollar," and the measures taken have become increasingly stringent in the last part of this period. The major task of professional economic advisers, consequently, has been to try to shift these preferences, and to argue that the consequences for the United States and the international economy of a change in the role of gold, including, possibly, its total disappearance, are not at all serious in the appropriate scale, and are much to be preferred to the possible outcomes of a continuance of the kinds of "defense" measures the United States has been taking in the recent past. In this, they have had very modest success indeed.

This failure, in turn, reflects the stubborn attachment of policy-makers to their own ideas of the importance of gold less than it does the political strength of the forces supporting the present arrangement. These include both a domestic and an international component. Within the country the financial community, especially the part of it heavily involved in international markets, and the large business firms with world-wide activities have been the main supporters of the sanctity of the existing system. Their views have been voiced within the government chiefly through the Federal Reserve System, especially by the Chairman of the Board of Governors and the President of the New York Bank. The Secretary of the Treasury, too, must to some degree be responsive to these groups.

The commitment of these groups to the present international system involves at least three distinct elements. The first is the desire to limit the policy-making powers of the Federal government in the economic sphere. The continuing balance-of-payments deficit has been an important and often decisive argument for "restraint" in the pursuit of monetary and fiscal policies directed at full employment. Under present institutional arrangements, this restraint is enforced by the market, and the spokesmen for the financial community play the roles of forecasters and interpreters of what the market will tolerate. Second is the belief that earnings of banks that are active in the international market are closely dependent on the present system. The group argues that the widespread and increasing use of the dollar as a currency of settlement in international transactions, and the large volume of banking business connected with it, are the product of the dollar's status as a reserve currency, which in turn rests on its special tie to gold in the form of the United States' commitment to buy and sell it freely (in international markets) at the fixed price. The final element is a strong ideological attachment to the gold basis of the international currency system, and a belief that it is in some sense "natural," and that alternative arrangements, by contrast, would be "artificial."

Internationally, the first and last of these arguments are both important. The power issue, in international terms, has a double aspect. First, the banking community in Europe is even more suspicious—if possible—of the policy-making power of governments than is the banking community of the United States. Further, the central banks of the continental countries are more independent and stronger, vis-à-vis their corresponding governments, than is the Federal Reserve System; they are also identified even more closely with the private financial community. In addition, however, there is a second element: conflict with regard to the international distribution of power with respect to monetary policy between the United States and other nations. Here it is the institutional interests of the present custodians of U. S. policy in the international monetary sphere—the Treasury, the Board of Governors, and the New York Bank—which are at stake. To a significant extent, arguments within the government in the recent past about the desirability of various changes in the international monetary system have turned essentially on the question of who shall have decision-making power, rather than on how most effectively to improve the functioning of the system as a whole. These issues run not only to the power of the United States *vis-à-vis* that of other countries and the International Monetary Fund as an institution, but just as much or even more to the power of the present custodians of U. S. policy as against possible new claimants to that custody. Thus, for example, a large part of the explanation of the elaboration in recent years of "swaps," "Roosa bonds" and such schemes in preference, for example, to explicit gold guarantees for official holders, or formal agreements through the I.M.F. on the proportions of gold to be held as reserve assets, has to be made in these terms.

An ideological and emotional attachment to gold as the "natural" basis of money probably has even stronger roots in Europe than in the United States. Experiences with large-scale inflation have been more widespread, frequent, and painful there than here, and these lead to stronger and more pervasive fears of its repetition. Thus the conservative posture of continental private and central bankers reflects widespread popular values.

In this context of emotional beliefs and institutional interests, the economic adviser must rely on the power of reason. Where the issues are analytical and empirical, perhaps this power is sufficient, at least in the long run. Thus, for example, the extent of the dependence of the earnings of the international banks on the role of the dollar as a reserve currency can be analyzed and, to some degree of approximation, quantitatively estimated, and a demonstrably wrong view cannot persist indefinitely. However, where the issues are more nearly pure matters of conflicting values, the economic adviser can at best point at the availability and consistency of alternate value judgments. Where the existing constellation of value preferences has a strong institutional embodiment, such exhortation alone is a feeble instrument. If, however, the alternative value scheme can be identified with a constituency of potential political significance, the possibility for advisers to influence the preferences of their political clients is much greater. Here there is a clear parallel between the present difficulties with international monetary policy and attitudes toward gold and recent difficulties—not entirely surmounted—with domestic full-employment policy and attitudes toward budget deficits. The willingness of the leaders of the Administration to shift their own attitudes, and to give less weight to Congressional and public fears, lay at least as much in their increasing evaluation of the political gains of a significant decrease in the level of unemployment as it did in the growth of a conviction that the size of the deficit in the administrative budget, *per se*, was of no economic significance. To date, no equally powerful connection has been made in respect to gold and the balance of payments.

III

The pair of issues we have contrasted above in terms of their position in the live–settled spectrum in politics, the international payments problem being a live one and the antitrust problem a relatively settled one, might be ranked differently in terms of economic knowledge. The basic elements of one or more effective and stable international-payments systems are well understood by economists; in none of them need gold play a part. Choice among them turns on the kind of political issues sketched above. On the other hand, some important economic issues in the design and application of a procompetitive policy are still subject to a significant degree of controversy, which can be settled only by more empirical work. This is especially true of the problems of social economies of scale in marketing, research, and finance, and of the relation between market structure and economic performance in the dimension of innovation. But increased knowledge itself is unlikely to result in any significant change in this area of policy, unless it is accompanied by some change in the political equilibrium which now determines it.

The kind of issue that is live in both political and professional terms often presents wider opportunities for the economic adviser. In such a situation he may be able to shape the way the political and the intellectual issues are framed, and thus try to make knowledge and policy somewhat more responsive to each other. Thus, for example, the problems of incomes policy, or wages and prices, are currently live in both dimensions. In intellectual terms, the problem is to explore the nature of the interrelations between the level of unemployment and the degree of price stability in the short run. Both theoretical and econometric work directed toward measuring and explaining these connections have been growing rapidly. In political terms, the problem is how low a level of unemployment can "safely" be set as the target for stabilization policy. Can the target rate be reduced below 3½ or 4 per cent of the labor force without facing either an unacceptably high rate of price increase or something even worse? This, of course, depends on preference among possible alternatives. Is a 2½ per cent per annum rate increase in the Consumer Price Index acceptable, while 3 per cent is not? Is 3 per cent preferable to wage–price guidelines, while the latter are preferable to 3½ per cent, which in turn is preferable to formal price and wage controls, which are themselves preferable to cutting the tie between the dollar and gold and allowing the dollar to float?

In relation to a problem of this degree of complexity and novelty, the efforts of an economic adviser will generally involve two conceptually different aspects, one technical and one political. Technically, he will try to formulate the trade-offs among all the potential alternative policies, and, perhaps more significant, to bring new alternatives into the discussion. Politically, as we have pointed out before, he will be examining the preference rankings of alternatives, and urging his views on what they should be. While conceptually distinct, these two aspects of the adviser's efforts are inextricably intertwined in practice.

In the first aspect of his role, an adviser on incomes policy might point out the dependence of an evaluation of "acceptable" rates of increase in the price level on the balance-of-payments position of the United States, the status of the dollar as a reserve currency, and the relation between the dollar and gold. These relations, in general, would not be obvious to the political decision-makers, who might then have new alternatives to evaluate. The same process might lead the advisers at least to point out that a floating dollar instead of one tied to gold could make a 3½ to 4 per cent rise in the price level tolerable, and to ask whether or not such a rate of inflation would be acceptable if it would also lead to a reduction to 2 per cent of the target level of unemployment, which in turn could lead to a halving of the unemployment rate of unskilled Negro males.

Or to take another alternative, the argument can be made that the essential mechanism of the wage–price interaction is the attempt by the strongly unionized workers in capital-intensive large-scale industrial enterprises to convert the transient extra profits of the upswing into permanent wage gains via the mechanism of collective bargaining. On this basis, some change in the corporate income tax to capture these transient gains through taxation might prove a key element in preventing their permanent incorporation into the cost structure and might make a system of informal wage–price guidelines workable over a wider range of demand pressures than it would be otherwise. Such a scheme would inevitably contain features similar to those of an excess-profits tax, a kind of taxation viewed with strong distaste by policy-makers, businessmen, and economists alike. Yet, as an alternative to some form of more direct price and wage controls, such a tax device might appear attractive to at least some of these groups. In that context, the economic adviser might wish both to persuade the policy-maker that this was a superior alternative, and to help persuade the policy-maker and, through him, the public that the goals of lower unemployment and "reasonable" price stability were worth the price of an additional and, to some powerful groups, especially obnoxious tax.

The economic adviser may seek or be forced to seek even more direct confrontation with the ultimate value issues on which policy judgments in these areas turn. The general level of unemployment and the problems

of the Negro ghetto are intimately related. It is clear that for the Negro
the period of recent history in which his economic status advanced most
rapidly was the period of war-induced labor shortage and repressed inflation from 1942 through 1946. Then the kind of recruiting, training, and
upgrading programs which the Department of Labor and the Job Corps
are now doing on a pitifully small scale, and that Congress is paying for
most grudgingly, were being carried out on a large scale and many times
more effectively by business firms, impelled by the necessities of labor
shortages. An economic policy which maintained, over as long a period
as proved possible, an average effective rate of unemployment that was
zero or negative in the relations between job vacancies and unemployed
workers, and which relied on direct price and wage controls to repress
inflation, would do more to reproduce the economic and social benefits
of that earlier period for the Negro than any special-purpose programs
directed only to the Negro community which may be within the bounds
of feasibility, no matter how optimistically they are viewed.

Direct wage and price controls are extremely unpopular. Businessmen,
trade union leaders, and economists are united in denouncing their evils.
To the former two groups, they are government interferences with "liberty" that are unwarrantable except perhaps under the circumstances of
total war; to the economists they are so obviously replete with allocative
inefficiencies as to be undesirable except in circumstances where no other
policy instruments are believed to be available. They are admittedly
cumbersome administratively and difficult to enforce, especially if price
controls should extend to the retail level. Yet the social gravity of the
problems of Negro unemployment and poverty is clearly such as to justify
examination of such a program, with re-evaluation of the goals of economic policy it implies. Economists in general, and those with access to
political leaders in particular, are the best placed to initiate such a re-
evaluation and to provide the reasoned framework of analysis and argument which helps to make the sharp changes in the relative importance
of competing policy goals involved in such a policy comprehensible and
acceptable. Whether political leaders would be ready to accept the necessity for such a re-evaluation is another question, but in my judgment
the political context in which it would be made either exists already, or is
rapidly coming into being.

IV

There is a wide range of less apocalyptic problems, which are currently "live" in both intellectual and political terms, in whose resolution
value judgments as well as the technical advice of economists will play

an important part. Examples which exhibit two different kinds of economic value judgments—both, to be true, embedded in technical questions of great complexity—are provided by problems of urban planning and the finance of higher education.

The interrelated set of questions involving urban renewal, urban planning, and transportation planning raises questions that go right to the heart of the usual value assumptions of the economist. The whole field is dominated by the existence of externalities; it is clear that there is no simple meaningful sense in which this range of decisions can be left to market forces. It is further clear that our past methods for dealing with the major externalities are increasingly inadequate, if they ever were adequate. Zoning by a fragmented set of competing jurisdictions, highway planning uncoordinated with zoning and land-use planning or without comprehensive urban–suburban transport planning simply fail to meet the issues. What kind of alternate decision-mechanisms are available? The natural bias of economists is toward believing that consumers "ought" to get what they want, in some ethical sense of the word. Economists accordingly tend to resist, as a matter of fundamental principle, changes in decision-making processes that substitute planners' choices for consumers' choices. Yet, in the face of what consumers' choices are leading to, some such substitution appears inevitable. At the very least, planners will determine, much more narrowly than present processes do, the range of alternatives from which consumers may choose. The key question then becomes, "By what political mechanism are planners' choices reviewed and controlled?" Economists possess both habits of thought and analytical tools that can be put to good use in designing these processes. They will be able to do so, however, only if they share and, indeed, urge the value premise that such processes are desirable. Otherwise, they will emerge as largely futile critics of policies shaped by others, whose objections are viewed as captious or doctrinaire.

In higher education, rapidly rising unit costs and enrollments have given new urgency to the interdependent questions of how much higher education should be provided, how it should be financed, and to whom it should be available. These problems have been one of the stimuli to a greatly increased interest in the study of education by economists. Here again their value premises, often inarticulate, lead economists to address the policy questions in particular ways. In general, education is viewed as an investment, estimates are made of both private and social rates of return on this investment, and problems of admission and tuition policies are seen basically as pricing problems, complicated by the difficulty that the output in question has elements of a collective as well as a private good. In this context, the choice between extending the present state university system with its very low tuition rates and commitment to provide places for all high school graduates who want them, and moving toward an essentially full-cost-tuition market-allocation system, combined with a subsidized loan fund and possibly with repayments geared to subsequent income, is seen primarily as a choice between an "irrational" and a "rational" pricing system. This is certainly a relevant aspect of the difference between the two systems, but it may be far from the centrally significant one in view of the fundamental social issues of distribution of status and income that are involved.

V

The common theme of all these examples is, of course, the centrality of changes in values to policy decisions, and, consequently, the presence of an indispensable ingredient of value-advocacy, along with technical economic analysis, in the advice that the economist offers the policy-maker. This point can be seen in a more systematic context by looking briefly at certain key features of the process of public-policy formation in a democratic society. This examination will make clear why the picture of a policy-maker with known (at least to him) preferences, advised by professionals who present the set of all possible alternative policies and their predicted outcomes, from among which he chooses, is of little use as a conceptualization of the relation between economic adviser and policy-maker.

Policy-making in a democracy is typically a response to pressure on the government to "do something" about a social problem. Changing circumstances to which the social machinery—including the machinery of government—is imperfectly adapted create the problem. If the problem is sufficiently large in terms of some measure of political importance—numbers of people or powerful people or symbolically important people or dollars—and sufficiently persistent, it registers as a "crisis." Such crises typically are not well foreseen, and, even to the extent that they are foreseen, they are usually not attended to in anticipation. Democratic governments are primarily organized to respond to external pressures, rather than to seek out potential problems and initiate action in relation to them. Whether they can or should behave otherwise is an important question, but one which it would take us too far afield to pursue here.

The largely responsive rather than anticipatory character of government policy-making leads to three further interrelated characteristics that are important to our inquiry. The first is what has been called "incrementalism": policy moves a step at a time, and usually a small step at a time. Second, decision-makers fashion policy changes with a sharp eye to the breadth of the support for their proposals and the narrowness of the opposition to them. As a consequence of these characteristics, finally, only a low value is placed on consistency in any large-scale sense as a criterion of policy. Responsiveness to the problem at hand and feasibility in political and operational terms far outweigh any measure of "fit" into "grand designs" in terms of ends or instruments.

Ongoing governmental policies are crystallized in the bureaucratic machinery that is responsible for their application. This machinery in turn is coupled with, and is in some measure responsive to, the interests involved in the policy. Thus the balance of values reflected by existing policies has an institutionalized expression in the assumptions, conceptions, and working rules of those who apply them. The existing policy machinery inevitably acts as an obstacle to changes in policy, since these would require changes in the structure of the habits, rules, and ideas it embodies. To be sure, this machinery usually is capable of some degree of adaptive response to changes in its environment, but as we have pointed out, the need for new policies arises from unanticipated changes going beyond the adaptive range of existing policy means.

Thus changes in policy require not only that policy-makers strike a new value balance, but that they reshape the existing bureaucracy to give effect to that new balance. This is a difficult task, and one which reflects back on the underlying problem of finding an acceptable new policy, since the people who apply and, so to speak, embody the existing policy are usually strong and skillful advocates of its continuance. A political decision-maker in this situation finds the ability of a technical adviser to assist in the tasks of advocacy, which are indispensable to effect changes, an important element of his usefulness; as we have already argued at sufficient length, these are usually tasks of persuasion about value preferences as much as they are the more technical tasks of forecasting the outcomes of alternative policies.

In our governmental structure, the problems of advocacy arise at several levels—within the Executive branch, the Legislature, and the public, including special publics relevant to particular issues as well as the general public. Policy advisers are not necessarily involved at all three levels to the same degree or in the same way. In general, their efforts are most important within the Executive branch, but their ability as effective advocates for wider audiences often has an important bearing on the appeal of their advice to the decision-maker who must bear the final burden of persuasion at all levels.

Looked at in these terms, it is not hard to see that the technical adviser of the formal model would be of little use to the political decision-maker, since his whole output consisted in forecasts of an "if this, then that" type in which the "this's" covered a large range of alternative policies, and the "that's" were, as nearly as possible, politically (value-) neutral descriptions of the distribution of possible outcomes.

All this is not to say that there is nothing but value-advocacy in the role of the economist as policy adviser. On the contrary, the fact that he does command some genuine positive science, that he can analyze events and predict the outcomes of alternative actions with more success than the "statesman" or "man of affairs," is indispensable to his claim to give any advice that is worth listening to, or, over time, that is in fact listened to. In this respect we may look at the economic adviser as essentially playing the role of a filter. He is to select from the whole range of possible alternative policies that "positive" knowledge of the profession can offer at a given moment for a particular policy problem, those few which are relevant to the perspective in which his political client operates, and, in dialogue with him, finally that one which embodies what both see as a workable new value balance.

A large part of the effectiveness of economists as policy advisers comes precisely from the circumstance that the analytical framework of economics provides, among other things, a language and training for the articulation of value preferences over a wide range of important social issues. It is precisely this component of the economist's skills that fits him peculiarly well to the task of helping the policy-maker articulate his own value preferences. This aspect of the comparative advantage of the economist as a policy adviser can be brought out by contrasting him with the specialist in operations research trained in purely technical terms. In, say, a problem of military tactics or logistics, where ends are well defined, the economist has no advantage over an equally well-trained operations-research specialist. But in a broader problem, whether of economic policy or large-scale strategy, where questions of what ends can and should be form a central part of the problem, the economist usually shows to advantage.

It seems unlikely that in our society, with its complex division of labor and rapidly changing technologies, the goals of economic policy will become sufficiently well defined and widely accepted so that the role of the economist in policy-making will sink (or rise) to the level of the purely technical adviser, at least in the foreseeable future. Rather, to the extent that this happens in particular policy areas, other areas now outside the domain of systematic public action can be expected to become the focus of policy concern and debate. Some of these newly emerging areas of policy, such as urban redevelopment, education, and health, are likely to involve important problems that fall outside the more traditional interests of the economists. All of them involve problems for which individual choice within the framework of market institutions is likely to be an inappropriate mode of social decision-making.

The profession may then face the question of the extent to which it can and will adapt its analyses to encompass a wider range of social goals and policy instruments than those conventionally the concern of economists, or leave primacy in these areas of policy-making to other kinds of advisers. But perhaps these are problems of Utopia, and we must spend more time struggling with the still current and unresolved issues of stability, growth, and equity before we can think about them.

9
HENRY C. WALLICH

INSTRUMENTAL ANALYSIS
AND
THE DECISIONAL PROCESS
A Critique

I

Adolph Lowe is undoubtedly right that capitalism is always changing. To diagnose those changes, to see the emerging shape of things on a grand scale, is one of the great challenges of economics. Great recognition is to be won by those who have the right vision. Sometimes it can even be won without being particularly right, as the example of Karl Marx demonstrates.

It is this big game that Adolph Lowe has undertaken to play, and his gambit is an attractive one. If I understand him correctly, the changes of capitalism do not necessarily spell its doom, as so many seers appear to conclude. There are ways of saving it, and particularly of saving the freedom with which, in the minds of many, it is identified. Thus if hereafter I should find myself voicing dissent more often than agreement, we nevertheless have in common the belief that capitalism is viable.

Three aspects of Professor Lowe's great structure of thought I found particularly challenging: his reading of the facts of past and present capitalism, his "instrumental analysis" relating instruments and targets, and his view of the role of government.

155

The Facts

Anyone looking for changes in capitalism since the Industrial Revolution will certainly find them. So will someone looking for continuities. To some extent it is a question of finding a cup half full or half empty.

But the issue is not change as such, but whether behavior patterns of firms and individuals (principally firms in Dr. Lowe's thought, I believe) have become more unstable and less predictable over time. I am troubled by the danger here of lapsing into impressionistic argument. Surely some of the evidence should be testable. Not being an economic historian, I do not know how much of it has been tested. Have economic fluctuations become wider or narrower in time? Have price fluctuations, measured about an average or a trend, narrowed or widened? Have failure rates of businesses risen or fallen? Has the gap between profit rates and the risk-free return on capital, reflecting mainly the entrepreneur's risk premium, widened or narrowed? My intuition, unsupported by research, leads me to suspect that in all these regards instability and risk have been diminishing. This may not always improve the equilibrating functions of markets, but surely it increases predictability.

In lieu of time-series evidence, similar information often is conveyed by cross sections of firms and of countries. Without having examined the evidence, I would think that failure rates among small firms are much higher than among large ones. If it is true that the average size of firms rises over time, this would suggest that risk diminishes and predictability increases.

I have done some work with cross sections of countries, including both industrial and underdeveloped countries. These cross sections relate primarily to monetary behavior, such as the effect upon the income velocity of money of per capita income, inflation, interest rates, and other factors. The findings show that the less developed countries reveal a poorer fit—i.e., less stable relationships—than the developed countries. Given the much more imperfect nature of their financial markets, this would hardly be surprising. From what one knows of developing countries generally, income and price fluctuations, risk premiums, and the uncertainties facing a firm are generally larger than they are in developed countries.

In terms of maximization, too, a case can be made for assuming an increasing predictability of firms' decisions over time. In the early days, firms were largely owner operated. There was a close relation between the finances of the firm and those of the owner. Therefore, relatively more firms probably were utility maximizers and fewer were profit maximizers than is likely to be the case today with the greater separation of ownership and control. The utility maximizer, being in general risk-averse, does not invest for the highest expected return. He trades off some expected return for reduced risk. His investment decisions therefore are not predictable in terms of expected return—i.e., of the marginal efficiency of the investment schedule, which conceptually, at least, is observable. They are influenced also by his utility function, which is not observable. The investment decision of the profit maximizer, who by definition is risk-neutral, is predictable on the basis of expected return, given the cost of capital, which is also observable. The reduction in the ownership-control nexus and the growing predominance of profit-maximizing risk-neutrals enhance the predictability of investment behavior.

Some modern developments that seem to imply a growing indeterminacy of business behavior may simply reflect a growing sophistication of analysis that admits a wider range of possible behavior. Oligopoly reduces predictability. But stronger emphasis on oligopolistic behavior need not mean that competition has declined. It may mean simply that economics is more capable of taking into account market imperfections. The elements that have made for diminishing competition are well known— chief among them are higher concentration ratios than those of 150 (but perhaps not 50) years ago, more rigid prices, labor unions, and large-scale investment. The main factors on the opposite side are also well known —more interproduct competition, more international competition, and more rapid technological change that results in instability in a technology-based monopoly. I am perfectly willing to be convinced that on balance competition has declined, but I would like to see quantitative evidence.

Recognition of satisficing behavior likewise may reflect growing sophistication of analysis as well as an increase in this mode of behavior. Satisficing reduces predictability, since only maximizing behavior is predictable. If satisficing is the result of a lack of information on which to base maximizing, its importance should be declining. If family firms are more inclined to satisfice than professionally managed firms, the shift toward professional management should have the same result.

The growing recognition of uncertainty in decision-making, finally, is another instance where our methods of analysis may have changed rather than the conditions of capitalism. In stochastic models, the analog of perfect knowledge is knowledge of the probability distributions facing the decision-maker. Whether the world has become more or less predictable depends on whether these distributions have become better known, and whether their variances have narrowed or widened.

To conclude these very unsatisfactory remarks on changing predictability, let me make some even less satisfactory general points about the environment in which capitalism now operates. We know that the world can come to a sudden nuclear end today. Yet this does not seem to have reduced the customary maturity of bonds or kept large corporations from trying to plan increasingly far ahead. Neither has widespread fear of inflation or of government invasion of property rights.

Instead we are increasingly able to estimate many future variables— GNP, demand structure, technological changes. Better data, better methods, more professionalism, and more stabilizing public policies all contribute to predictability. The system is becoming more rigid in many respects—prices, wages, and the specificity of capital are prime examples. Rigidity makes adjustment more difficult. But to say that it reduces predictability seems a contradiction.

Instrumental Analysis

I next turn to Dr. Lowe's interesting discussion of what he calls "instrumental analysis," which I take to mean, broadly, the appropriate relation between instruments and targets. Here I find much to agree with. I must confess, however, that I have not succeeded in bringing it to bear on the issue of changing capitalism. I hope someone else will correct that deficiency.

Dr. Lowe argues that Traditional Economics reasoned from known principles, or states of the world, to particular consequences. This is deductive reasoning. His instrumental analysis reverses the direction. The final state of the world, or the desired objectives, are known. What is sought is the initial state, or the values of the instruments by which the desired objectives are to be attained. This is induction.

In terms of a system of equations, Tinbergen refers to the first procedure (Traditional Economics) as the "prediction model." The values of the instrument variables and certain exogenous data are known, as is the structure of the relationships. The system therefore can be solved for the target variables.

Tinbergen would call instrumental analysis the "decision model." The same set of equations is now solved for the instrument variables, the targets being given. Assuming there is to be an equation for every unknown instrument, and implying that there is also an instrument for every target, the system is determinate. It will supply answers to the questions of traditional or instrumental analysis—we just must decide what we want to know. Perhaps Dr. Lowe might question the reliability of the structure in a world of diminishing predictability, or the reliability of the exogenous "data," but that would do equal damage to both forms of analysis.

If we wish to pursue the analogy with inductive and deductive reasoning, we may treat the instruments as the "general principles" and the targets as the particular facts following from the general principles. Intuitively one thinks of a single principle influencing a large number of facts. There is no difficulty in representing this in the equation system. Each target has a partial derivative with respect to any one instrument, and each instrument influences a number of targets. Some recent work assigns particular instruments to particular targets.[1] But this is only a question of comparative advantage, not of any exclusiveness in the relationship.

The analogy becomes more troublesome when we think of several instruments being brought to bear on a single target. Several general principles now affect a single fact. This is nevertheless quite plausible if the decision-maker operates under uncertainty and seeks to reduce his risk by using a diversified "portfolio" of instruments,[2] or if he wants to equate the probably rising marginal cost of employing various instruments.

Targets and instruments may both be unknown and mutually determined under an optimizing procedure.[3] Different instruments now must be combined to produce an efficient frontier along which different targets are traded off against each other. On this target transformation curve an optimum will be found where the marginal rate of transformation among targets equals the marginal rate of substitution among these targets on some social indifference curve. The analogy with inductive and deductive reasoning now breaks down, however, and I am unsure how instrumental analysis would fit into this framework.

In short, the principles underlying instrumental analysis fit in well with some, though not all, of the policy-making models. But these models have not, to my knowledge, been interpreted as implying or suggesting a bridge to a new way of looking at the capitalistic system. I hope that such a bridge can be built.

The Role of Government

Dr. Lowe's stress on the greater role of government within his framework certainly captures well the activist spirit of contemporary economics. This seems to be the essence of his Political Economics. As he

---

[1] Robert A. Mundell, "The Appropriate Use of Monetary and Fiscal Policy for Internal and External Stability," *IMF Staff Papers*, March, 1962.

[2] William C. Brainard, "Uncertainty and the Effectiveness of Policy," *American Economic Review*, May, 1967, pp. 411–425.

[3] Jürg Niehans, "Monetary Policies in Open Economies Under Fixed Exchange Rates—An Optimizing Approach," *Journal of Political Economy*, July/August 1968, Part II.

points out, the economist today is not satisfied to observe and measure economic phenomena. Typically he wants to intervene.

I think Dr. Lowe is right in arguing that this interventionist spirit reflects dissatisfaction with the functioning of a laissez-faire economy, and particularly with its instability. It does not follow from this, however, that capitalism today is more unstable than it was 100 or 200 years ago. It may simply be that, with growing wealth, our standards and demands upon the economy and its stability have risen. Greater concern with income distribution and less faith in the divine rights of property may also enter in. Furthermore, an increase in overall instability, if it has occurred, need not be the result of the greater instability or unpredictability of any particular types of firms. It may simply result from a shift in the composition of "firms," from a predominance of agricultural entrepreneurs who could sit out depressions on the farm, to an industrial society that cannot.

Today, in fact, a contrary view is coming into fashion that sees the private sector as essentially stable and the government as injecting instability. Milton Friedman sees the Depression of the 1930's as generated principally by a reduction in the money supply for which he holds the Federal Reserve responsible. He and others oppose efforts at "fine tuning" the economy, suggesting that dials be set to stay and minor fluctuations be ridden out.

Also contrary to Dr. Lowe's and others' doctrine that the growing maturity of capitalism calls for more government action, is the attitude of developing countries. Here the demand for strong government action is based mainly upon the inadequacies of an underdeveloped economy and the alleged inability of early capitalism to produce a predictable and adequate rate of growth.

Finally, I have some difficulty with the operational content of Dr. Lowe's demand for a Political Economics. He argues that government should influence micro-behavior patterns in order to make behavior more predictable. How far are household and firm preferences to be altered? Would taxes and interest rates be the means, or are more direct methods thought of? Should government try to manipulate consumer preferences, as Galbraith believes corporations to be doing by their advertising? Are firms to be guided by a kind of indicative planning along French lines, or is their range of decision to be circumscribed more forcefully?

These questions must be answered more fully before one can agree or disagree with the policy implications of Dr. Lowe's analysis, whatever one may think of their analytical foundations. As for the latter, I admire the intellectual power that has gone into building this view of modern capitalism on a grand scale. Few men could have performed such a feat of synthesis. Nonetheless, I doubt that the world really looks that way.

II

I now turn to the thought-provoking paper presented by Carl Kaysen. Dr. Kaysen shares with Dr. Lowe the belief that the economist must become engaged. The economic adviser, at any rate, will not get far if he limits himself to advice that is neutral with respect to values. This is a view that I, too, share. Having the powerful authority of these two papers to fall back upon, perhaps I could simply take for granted that the value-neutral adviser is a buckpasser, and go on from there. But because I am troubled by some of the conclusions to which Drs. Lowe and Kaysen both proceed—from the premise that the economist must make choices—I would like to examine for a moment the conditions in which an economic adviser might be value-neutral after all.

Value Judgments

The adviser might offer his client alternatives: If you want result X, do a; if result Y, do b. It is not at all clear that the client might not at times prefer this type of advice, though often it might be frustrating. Nor does this mean that an impossibly extensive array of alternatives would have to be presented. However, the giving of economic advice is a very competitive business. The adviser who does not press his advice is sure to be outmaneuvered by others who do. Thus, if offering alternative choices is not inherently wrong, it is almost certainly a waste of time.

The adviser might also regard himself as value-neutral if he can claim to derive his values completely from the law under which he operates. The new German Council of Economic Advisers (*Sachverstaendigenrat zur Begutachtung der Gesamtwirtschaftlichen Entwicklung*) claims to be operating in this fashion. One might question the extent to which its law really exempts the German Council from value judgments, but conceptually the possibility exists. No one, however, would assert that the American Employment Act of 1946 gives anything like this sort of guidance to the members of the President's Council of Economic Advisers.

Finally, the adviser might claim to be value-neutral if he fully adopted the preferences of his client. That, in fact, is what a loyal civil servant is supposed to do. But the literal application of this precept carries great dangers. Adolph Eichmann claimed that all he did was what he was told to do. Many of the German technicians who worked for Hitler no doubt could use the same alibi. It is clear that, under certain circumstances, an adviser has a duty to assert his own values.

Some Characteristics of the Modern Adviser

Carl Kaysen illustrates this thesis about the engagement of the economic adviser with references to a number of particular policy issues and goals. I realize that these are purely illustrative—although it might not be easy to find many more illustrations of this caliber. It would be a mistake for a commentator to enter into the substance of the issues he cites—full employment policy, inflation, balance of payments, international monetary reform. But the issues posed by Dr. Kaysen, together with some of those posed by Dr. Lowe, lend themselves admirably to bringing out what seem to be certain characteristics of the value-oriented economist as the two authors see him. These are (1) his time horizon, (2) his attitude toward rationality, and (3) his attitude toward risk.

Time Horizon

The modern adviser—the practitioner of Political Economics, to use Dr. Lowe's term—seems to have a very short time horizon compared with his predecessor, the traditional economist. The traditional economist was concerned with the forces determining prices, production, income shares, and living standards in a timeless environment where in fact equilibrium usually would be reached at best over long periods of time. He viewed these forces as largely beyond human control, and was satisfied to observe their workings and to limit his advice to cautioning against interference with them.

The modern adviser is an activist. He believes he can improve things, and of course he wants to improve them now. In doing so, however, he seems to rely on forces and relationships so short-run in character as to be saying, "After my period in office [the length of an academic leave], the deluge."

Prime evidence of this high time preference of the modern adviser is the prevailing belief in trade-offs between employment and growth on one side and price stability and payments equilibrium on the other. A growing group of economists has been arguing that this trade-off does not exist in the long run. Recently, Milton Friedman, in his presidential address before the American Economic Association, added his powerful voice to this group. The trade-off represented by the Phillips curve, for instance, is stable only so long as people do not discount future inflation. Various of Carl Kaysen's propositions involve this trade-off. But if people ever catch on to the game the economist is trying to play with them, promising them a higher real wage increase than inflation eventually will allow them to have, they will stop playing. The Phillips curve shifts upward as inflation is increasingly discounted. For fully discounted inflation, the curve is simply a vertical line above the equilibrium level of unemployment—the level at which wage increases equal productivity gains, plus or minus such changes in income shares as may occur.

The same applies to the trade-off of price stability and growth. Inflation may lower the real interest rate temporarily, stimulating investment, just as it lowers the real wage and so aids growth through forced saving. Once inflation is discounted, the money rate of interest will rise enough to nullify this advantage. It may be argued that inflation reduces the portfolio demand for money and increases the demand for physical assets. But except for currency, interest can be paid on money and, in sustained inflation, probably would be, thus maintaining the demand for money.

A second instance of the modern adviser's high time preference is his willingness to burn the barn to roast the pig. Examples are Dr. Kaysen's proposal to push unemployment to 2 per cent in order to sharply reduce Negro unemployment. Obviously, in the light of what I have just said, inflation could not accomplish this objective for long. Direct controls on wages and prices would be required, as Dr. Kaysen himself says. This would mean basically changing the economy in order to improve the lot of a small minority. Surely a long-run-oriented adviser could find a better way. In Dr. Lowe's case, the barn-burning takes the form of introducing a control-and-command economy in order to speed up what—even if he were right about diminishing determinacy—is for the most part only a slowing of the rate at which equilibrium is approached. In another area, impatience with the slow and painful process of balance-of-payments adjustments, and a preference for junking the slow movement toward a one-world economy, once more document the modern economist's high time preference.

Let me cite one last example of high time preference—the quantitative emphasis on raising GNP as quickly as possible, with what seems to me inadequate concern for qualitative factors. This humanitarian hurry seems to rest upon what might be called a cross-sectional view of income. Comparing rich and poor families, or rich and poor countries, the urgency to lift up the poor does indeed seem great. A time-series view, looking, say, at U. S. GNP over the last 200 years, reduces the urgency. Are we seriously to suppose that in George Washington's day people were as desperately badly off and unhappy as their per capita incomes in present prices would suggest? Obviously there are values other than per capita income.

The economist–adviser's clients typically are politicians. In a democratic environment—as opposed to a monarchy—all political figures except for very farsighted statesmen are bound to have a short time horizon; there is a sharp discount on everything that will happen after the next election. One would expect the adviser therefore to try to correct this bias; the market rate of interest tells him, after all, that even time-distant assets and incomes have substantial value. Unfortunately, that does not seem to be the advice the client is likely to get under a Lowe–Kaysen regime.

Rationality Assumptions

Because I find myself in agreement with so much that Carl Kaysen says, and particularly with his basic premise about the engagement of the adviser, I am compelled to run the risk of nitpicking to find points for debate. But I cannot help being struck by the differences between the assumptions concerning people's rationality that underlie Dr. Kaysen's implicit proposals for curing unemployment, and those underlying his proposals for reforming the international monetary system. The proposal to reduce unemployment through inflation rests heavily on money illusion. People without money illusion—i.e., rational people—will not respond to the promise of high-money wage increases, the real value of which always turns out to equal productivity gains. But in demonstrating that the world's monetary system can be run very well without gold, Dr. Kaysen appeals to their rationality. There is nothing, indeed, that gold can do that paper money cannot also do. Yet, people do cling to the barbarous relic. Why then does Dr. Kaysen want to build an employment policy upon an irrationality that seems to be rapidly fading? Why does he take a different attitude with respect to the irrational attachment to gold, which seems to be firmly rooted?

I do not want to particularize on these matters. All I want to do is to put in a plea for consistency in our rationality postulates.

Risk Aversion

My last comment relates to the adviser's risk aversion. Intuitively, I would say that risk aversion and imaginativeness are negatively correlated, and that responsibility and risk aversion go hand in hand. This hypothesis would explain much of how academics talk, and how policy-makers act.

If the responsible policy-maker is risk-averse, he will typically take action on a smaller scale than that required to reach his objective, so long as the effect of the policy action is a random variable unlike Theil's model, where the stochastic state of the world can be replaced by a certainty equivalent while the coefficient of the policy variable is known with certainty.[4] The risk-averse policy-maker will sacrifice some part of the (diminishing) utility of approaching his goal in order to reduce the (increasing) disutility of uncertainty accompanying policy action on a growing scale. The farther the adviser is removed from responsibility— an academic tenure job is one sort of extreme—the more nearly risk-neutral he is likely to be. Some widely visible academic or journalistic advisers and forecasters whose success depends on differentiating their product may be positive risk-seekers.

I should think that differences in the degree of risk aversion between a policy-maker and his economic adviser might be as important as differences in their value judgments. Drs. Lowe and Kaysen have told us much about value judgments. Perhaps the next step in the analysis should be an examination of the consequences of attitudes toward risk.

---

[4] Brainard, *loc. cit.*

10

ADOLPH LOWE

ECONOMIC MEANS
AND
SOCIAL ENDS

A Rejoinder

The essays assembled in this volume raise a number of challenging questions. Limits of space make it impossible for me to discuss all of them in an adequate manner. Therefore, I will apply myself in the following observations to a few fundamental problems, on a satisfactory answer to which the theoretical soundness and practical relevance of a Political Economics as outlined in my introductory paper may well depend.[1]

My ideas as originally formulated in the book *On Economic Knowledge* have certainly not escaped the fate described by Professor Lerner—that of being rejected on the one hand as quite wrong, and, on the other hand, being played down as affirming only what is general knowledge and accepted practice. But whereas these critical responses usually follow each other as time passes, I have been exposed to them simultaneously. I shall try to defend myself to the best of my ability against the first charge.

---

[1] In doing this I will not confine myself to commenting on the papers printed here but also, at least implicitly, I will refer to the discussion that followed their delivery at the two Symposia. It is only natural that my rejoinder should deal mainly with my critics, referring to affirmative voices only occasionally when they improve on my own argument. The text itself follows the line of several statements I submitted during the proceedings. But it tries to present the issues in a more systematic fashion independent of the chronology in which they arose at the time and also of the order in which they are taken up in this volume.

The second, however, about the absence from my "message" of any revolutionary discoveries, I have myself stressed from the outset. Apparently the detailed description in my book of the gradual emergence of a Political Economics in the history of economic thought has not sufficiently clarified this point. So I should like to state once more and most emphatically that, notwithstanding certain reservations against conventional techniques of analysis and traditional economic policies, my entire undertaking aims at little more than a systematic formulation of the major trend in contemporary theory and practice. To make this implicit trend explicit, and to generalize and deepen the insights that we owe to the "new economics" of Keynesian provenance, to the decision models of the Dutch school of econometrics, and to other modern toolmakers—these are the intentions that underlie my project.

As indicated earlier, even this modest endeavor is far from accomplished. It is the significance of these essays that they contribute notably to the furthering of this task, especially by scrutinizing closely my methodological approach, by pointing out the deeper implications, political and philosophical, of my position, and by the general fairness of their critical stance. As I did on the original occasion, I wish again to express my genuine gratitude for so productive a response to my ideas.

THE PROBLEMS UNDER DISPUTE

In order to locate the principal points at issue I will take my bearings from a comment with which Dr. Machlup introduced the oral presentation of his paper. He found it characteristic of my approach that I am, at one and the same time, concerned with both the science of economics and the actual state of the Western economic systems. It is indeed true that I see the realms of economic theory and practice more closely interrelated than is customarily recognized. Of course no one denies that theoretical knowledge translated into rules for the framing of policy greatly affects economic reality. But there is a reverse and less obvious relationship, in which the actual states and processes of an economy influence our capacity for theorizing.

As I said above,[2] the link in this reverse relationship is the notion of *order* in the inclusive meanings of regularity of state and motion on the one hand, and of a satisfactory and stable level of provision on the other. The former trait defines a "positive" concept of great generality, since it states a precondition for theoretical reasoning—that is, for generalizing explanations and predictions—in all sciences. The latter is a "normative"

---

[2] See pp. 4–7.

concept and, as such, is limited to social research where human actions and their purposes are in the center.

This difference in the logical status of the two constituents of economic order seems to suggest that they are also causally independent of each other. Certainly, as I pointed out earlier, one can conceive of regular and thus predictable economic movements which would result in what by modern standards would be regarded as unsatisfactory provision levels. However, the converse is by no means true, because, when judged by the same standards, satisfactory provision, far from being independent of "orderly" motions within the system, is conditional on a high degree of regularity and thus of the predictability of such motions.

This condition holds for all types of economic systems, centralized or decentralized, but it has a particular relevance for market systems. There predictability is a concern not only of the scientific observer but, before that, of the economic actors themselves who, in the absence of authoritative guidance, must be able on commonsense grounds to foresee the tendencies in their fields of action. Therefore, in an uncontrolled market, movements must be regular enough to enable the individual marketer to predict, at the least, all major changes in their *direction*. In the absence of such autonomous regularity, stable provision perforce depends on the contrived adjustment of these movements with the help of public control. But in order to choose, in a given instance, what measures of control are appropriate, we must be able to predict their effect—a task for the framer of economic policy and his scientific helpmate, the economist. Thus we arrive at the general conclusion that only economic systems whose movements are or can be made sufficiently regular to permit the prediction of major changes, will be efficient engines of provision.

On this basis we can now summarize the gist of Political Economics in the following propositions:

1. The autonomous markets of industrial capitalism lack the required minimum of order. Their uncontrolled movements are too irregular for the individual marketer to predict major changes correctly and thus to achieve the interlocking patterns of behavior which assure stability of aggregate provision.

2. As a consequence, these markets have been progressively subjected to public control, however without as yet displaying a satisfactory degree of stability.

3. The main reason for this failure is the limited range of conventional market controls. These controls confine themselves to altering the micro-units' field of action by opening or closing marketing opportunities, without, however, controlling their responses. I shall call such controls "primary."

4. If orderly states and processes are to be brought about, to safeguard the viability of a system based on decentralized decision-making, addi-

tional or secondary controls must be introduced. These must bring the response mechanisms of the marketers in accord with the behavioral requirements for stable aggregate provision.

5. In order to discover what controls are likely to bestow order in any given instance, the first step is to specify the level and composition of aggregate provision to be obtained in a consistent set of macro-goals. From the knowledge of these macro-goals, of the initial state of the system, and of certain technological constraints, it is possible, with the help of a particular research technique called "instrumental analysis," to determine the goal-adequate movements of and within the system, as well as the goal-adequate motivational and behavioral patterns on the part of the micro-units, and the goal-adequate public controls that may be needed.

6. The findings of instrumental analysis in terms of goal-adequate controls must then be applied as measures of economic policy, so that the actual motion of the system is transformed into goal-adequate motion.

7. To the extent to which such transformation is successful, the practical demand for a satisfactory and stable level of provision will be met, as will the theoretical demand for such regularity of motion as permits generalizing explanations and predictions.

In the preceding essays, almost all of these propositions have, in one form or another, come under critical fire. They therefore offer a convenient framework for my defense. I will begin by restating the *facts* (propositions 1 and 2) that call for a transformation of traditional theory and practice in the direction of a Political Economics. Next comes a brief discussion of the nature of *macro-goals* and of the manner of their political stipulation, succeeded by an elaboration of the methodological principles underlying *instrumental analysis* (proposition 5). This will be followed by a review of the relationship between primary and secondary *controls* and their practical application (propositions 3, 4, and 6). Some reflections about the ultimate *criteria of goal-setting*—a topic only lightly touched upon in Chapter 12 of *OEK*, but thoroughly explored in some of the foregoing writings—will bring my apology to a close.

THE FACTUAL BACKGROUND

My advocacy of a Political Economics and of instrumental analysis as its principal research technique derives from a particular evaluation of certain strategic facts. These facts concern the tendencies of the autonomous movements of modern industrial markets, which seem to me in conflict with the requirement of order in the sense defined above. In fact, in my book and in my position paper [3] I have gone farther by suggesting

---

[3] See *OEK*, Chap. 3, and pp. 11–14.

that, owing to the gradual relaxation of certain natural and social pressures and to the disappearance of some automatic escapements, and in the wake of the progressive immobilization of the industrial structure coupled with ever more rapid technological changes, these "disorderly" tendencies are on the increase when compared with the competitive era of expanding capitalism.

It stands to reason that my diagnosis of the present state of affairs cannot be refuted by a different reading of the historical trend. Yet I readily admit that, as far as the latter is concerned, not only is the available factual material scanty but, as Dr. Wallich rightly stresses, much that appears as "new" may only reflect the growing sophistication of modern analysis. Perhaps my hypothesis will sound more plausible if one keeps in mind that it refers to the tendencies of *uncontrolled* industrial markets and should therefore not be judged by the manifestations of organized capitalism after the Second World War. Do we trust the "self-equilibrating" market enough to acquiesce confidently in the abolition of all the micro- and macro-controls that have been installed since 1929?

But since historical evidence is inconclusive, let me concentrate on modern experience, especially since I include the recent past in my pessimistic diagnosis in spite of the widening range of public controls.

The case for a high degree of stability and predictability in modern business behavior has been stated above by Dr. Wallich,[4] and there is no better test for my own views than a confrontation with his. For this it is important that we seem to agree about the facts themselves, our disagreement beginning only when it comes to their interpretation.

A growing variety of action directives, among them the progressive substitution of "satisficing" for "maximizing" behavior; uncertainty of expectations; prevalence of oligopolies and generally monopolistic manipulations and, as a consequence, a narrowing of price and wage fluctuations; rapid technological progress—all these characteristics of the modern scene which Dr. Wallich stresses also underlie my own argument. Dr. Wallich concedes that some of them, in particular oligopolies and satisficing tendencies, reduce rather than enhance the predictability of business behavior. But he sees compensating factors at work in the advance of professional management, interproduct competition, and other antimonopolistic forces. And if administered prices and wages make the structure of the market more rigid, this should in his view only facilitate prediction.

If Dr. Wallich and I draw such different conclusions from similar premises, the likelihood is that we focus on different aspects of the same phenomena. His is mainly a micro-economic discourse which studies the effect of the modern market organization on decision-making in the in-

---

[4] See pp. 156–158.

dividual firm. More precisely, his emphasis is on the professionally managed corporation, and he aptly describes the behavior of what Professor Galbraith has labeled the "Technostructure." [5]

There is no reason to impute to Dr. Wallich the exaggerated notion Galbraith has of the significance of these oligopolistic corporations in the totality of modern business organization. If we give its due to the stratum of middle-sized enterprises, for whom the corporate form is little more than a legal convenience and whose transactions remain market-bound, the range of managed predictability of costs, prices, and sales shrinks considerably. More important—and this is my major objection to Dr. Wallich's optimism—business planning, even at its most comprehensive, is still inadequate to establish *macro-economic* order.

The decisive point has been well stated by Professor Meade in his review of Galbraith's book: [6] "Professor Galbraith asserts that each modern corporation plans ahead the quantities of the various products which it will produce and the prices at which it will sell them; he assumes . . . that as a general rule each corporation through its advertising and other sales activities can so mould consumers' demand that these planned quantities are actually sold at these planned prices. But he never explains why and *by what mechanism these individual plans can be expected to build up into a coherent whole* [my italics]. . . . In short, if all individual plans are to be simultaneously fulfilled they must in the first instance be consistent." [7]

In a competitive system it is, of course, the market mechanism, operating through price changes, which is supposed to bring about this consistency of business plans. Unfortunately this result can as a rule be achieved only *ex post*, and the respective adjustment processes are themselves a main cause of aggregate instability. Moreover, with the elimination of price flexibility and the weakening of competitive pressures, this adjustment mechanism is rendered inoperative, without there being any substitute as long as corporate behavior is left to its own devices. And this all the more so since, as even Professor Galbraith admits, "there is no *a priori* reason why the policy pursued by any two mature corporations will be the same, for there is no reason to assume that the goals or intensity of commitment to goals will be the same in any two cases." [8] Therefore, in contrast with a widely held opinion also voiced during our discussions, a privately planned capitalism is by no means superior to a competitive

---

[5] See J. K. Galbraith, *The New Industrial State* (Boston: Houghton Mifflin, 1967).

[6] J. E. Meade, "Is 'The New Industrial State' Inevitable?" *Economic Journal*, LXXVIII, No. 310 (June, 1968), 372–392.

[7] *Ibid.*, pp. 377–378.

[8] See Galbraith, *op. cit.*, p. 159.

market organization so far as predictability and macro-economic stability are concerned.

The remedy is, of course, public control, to which Dr. Wallich refers only in passing. This now leads to the cardinal question of whether existing controls, mainly derived from the "new economics," have succeeded in overcoming the difficulties inherent in the modern industrial structure. With my critics I would agree that nowhere in the Western world has the economic process during the last generation exhibited the excessive fluctuations characteristic of the era preceding the Second World War. Moreover, a major share of fiscal and monetary controls in this achievement cannot be doubted, though rising military expenditures may have been the principal force of stabilization. For this reason neither national nor international experiences during the postwar era give any cause for complacency, not to mention the fact to which Dr. Wallich and others have rightly pointed—namely, that as public insight into the man-made nature of most of our economic ills grows, we become much more politically sensitive to their social impact.

I have dealt with the relevant postwar events at length in my book,[9] and I want to refer here to only one further instance which may still be topical when this book appears. Earlier I discussed the serious gamble that was involved in the Kennedy tax reduction.[10] We are now engaged in the reverse experiment of the surtax of 1968. In rising protests over the tardiness of Congress in enacting the necessary legislation, it has been widely forgotten that, up to the end of 1967, economic experts were deeply divided as to the wisdom of a tax increase, because they could not agree on whether the likely consequences would be stabilizing or deflationary. And even now, in the summer of 1968, he would be a bold man indeed who dared to predict the ultimate effects of this surtax on the level of output and employment in 1969, leaving out of consideration any exogenous influences arising from military developments. But what I wish to stress is that this uncertainty on the part of scientific observers, as well as of investors, arises from the unpredictability of the responses of producers and consumers to this type of control. This uncertainty of response is the very basis of my argument.

As was shown earlier,[11] the same obstacle hampers experimentation with econometric prediction models. If it is true that the weak link in these models is their behavior equations, no refinement in research techniques can yield a serious improvement in scientific macro-prediction.

---

[9] *OEK*, Chaps. 2 and 3.
[10] See p. 10.
[11] See p. 8.

Only a modification of the research object itself—that is, the regularization of market behavior—can achieve this professed aim of Political Economics.

THE NATURE OF MACRO-GOALS

Regularization of market behavior is a function of public control. But one cannot exert control without being aware of the specific aims these controls are to attain. This introduces macro-goals as the fulcrum of the analysis, and leads to the "inversion" of the conventional procedure in which terminal states are treated as unknowns to be derived from known patterns of behavior. Now, however, order-bestowing behavior patterns and the controls that are to establish them have become the major unknowns, which can be established only in relation to a stipulated terminal state or macro-goal.

I shall revert to the details of this "regressive" method of analysis and its methodological justification in the following section. Here, in enlarging on my earlier remarks,[12] I should like to add some comments on the general nature of macro-goals, on the question of whether "ends" can be stipulated independently of the "means" with whose help they are to be realized, and on the different categories of possible "goal-choosers." Discussion of the most fundamental problem—namely, the ultimate criteria that are to guide us in selecting the "right" macro-goals—will be taken up later.

1. My first concern is with dispelling a misunderstanding in Dr. Machlup's rendering of my views. It relates to the question of whether pronouncements on macro-goals should be placed in the category of "positive" or of "normative" statements. Fortunately there seems to be agreement between us as to what the two critical terms are to mean in order to be useful in scientific discourse. To me the most plausible distinction between the two, which apparently Dr. Machlup also accepts,[13] refers to statements about "what is" as contrasted with statements about "what ought to be," leaving alone for the moment the further questions of from whom the "ought" is to issue, and of the criteria for his choice. In this interpretation we can also speak of the difference between factual statements and value judgments, one essential characteristic of the latter being that they "cannot be tested by empirical procedures and cannot, therefore, be admitted into the body of positive science."[14]

Now in the face of what I thought were unambiguous formulations to

---

12 See p. 34–36.
13 See p. 103.
14 See p. 111.

the contrary,[15] Dr. Machlup takes me to task for overlooking the "unquestionable plurality of macro-goals," choosing among which "will always force us to engage in value judgments." He also questions my treating these goals "as legitimate data in positive analysis as long as they are clearly stated and are examined only in relation to the means suitable for their attainment." [16]

The core of the misunderstanding is obviously the notion of "data" and the precise sense in which value judgments and the macro-goals derived from them cannot be "admitted" into the body of positive science. If Dr. Machlup means to say that determination of the "rightness" or "wrongness" of a macro-goal is no task for positive science and that such rightness cannot be the subject of observations to be tested in accord with acknowledged scientific procedures, we are in full agreement. This does not, however, exclude any macro-goal, once it has been stipulated by some "nonscientific" procedure, from serving as a "premise" from which scientific reasoning can derive testable conclusions. Its logical status is then no different from that of any proposition serving as an axiom in a particular realm of knowledge. This, and this alone, is the use which instrumental analysis makes of the "datum" macro-goal, a procedure that in Dr. Machlup's own words "does not involve the analyst's value judgment and is not normative in character." [17]

This does not, of course, preclude further examination, logical or otherwise, of such axioms, by submitting them to the critical principles of some different field of knowledge, and as I have made clear earlier,[18] I fully agree with the call for such a "vindication of goals." However, in line with a tradition which, I thought, had been abandoned as a result of the work of Kenneth Arrow and others, Dr. Machlup assigns the function of a "justification of values" and thus of the establishment of criteria for a choice among rivaling goals and means to a realm of knowledge called "normative economics." There indeed we disagree since, as I am going to explain in the last section of these comments, vindication of economic goals must be based on criteria which are relevant for every kind of social action and which therefore far transcend any field of inquiry that could legitimately be labeled "normative *economics*." Still, remembering Dr. Machlup's skeptical verdict on welfare economics earlier in these pages, I wonder whether, notwithstanding our verbal contradictions, we are not in substantive agreement after all.

2. In some remarks of Drs. Edel, Nagel, and Wallich, another doubt

---

15 See pp. 18, 24, and *OEK*, Chap. 12.
16 See p. 128.
17 See p. 116.
18 *OEK*, Chap. 12.

has been cast on my procedure of treating macro-goals as "givens" in means analysis. Do we not, in our policies, as a rule, simultaneously pursue several macro-goals, whose feasibility and compatibility cannot be taken for granted? Do not such goals frequently change their role, so that what appears as an end in one context becomes a means in another? Moreover, do we not also apply value judgments to the selection of *means* irrespective of the instrumental test of their suitability? And more generally, does not the interdependence of all social phenomena nullify all specialist borders, thus on principle depriving the ends–means distinction of operational significance?

I have dealt with some of these questions before,[19] and will confine myself to indicating the direction in which the answers must be sought.

No doubt a set of macro-goals cannot be stipulated, as either a scientific premise or a political act, unless their feasibility and mutual consistency is assured. Mathematical programming was cited above as one of the techniques for investigating the feasibility of goals relative to the available resources, and thus as an auxiliary tool of instrumental analysis. The question of consistency raises subtler issues. To tackle them one must realize that, in the realm of economics, macro-goals are rarely incompatible in any absolute sense. What often makes them appear so is our reluctance to apply the specific means necessary for their joint realization. Take as an example the stipulation of full employment coupled with price stability, two goals which in our experience have so far proved irreconcilable. But were we willing to introduce severe wage and price controls accompanied by rationing or, in the extreme case, by the nationalization of key industries, the apparent contradiction might disappear. So it is ultimately our negative valuation of certain instrumentally adequate means that creates the semblance of incompatibility.

For this reason the real issue is how to relate the value judgments that we attach to certain means to the value judgments that underlie the selection of our goals. This is the *locus* of most practical conflicts, conflicts that can be resolved only by *another* value judgment—that is, which is of greater significance in a given instance: attaining the goal or preserving the integrity of our original evaluation of the means. Differently stated, the value criteria for means selection enter as criteria of optimization into the stipulation of the macro-goals themselves.[20]

Feasibility and compatibility studies are thus indispensable preliminaries of goal stipulation, and as such are a legitimate part of Political Economics. However, at the present stage in the development of social research, I expect little help in this or any other pursuit of Political

---

19 See *OEK*, Chap. 12, especially for the reversibility of ends–means relations.
20 *OEK*, pp. 260–261.

Economics from what is widely advocated as "interdisciplinary" work. In this respect I associate myself with a communication received from one of the participants in our discussions who himself is an advocate of a "synthetic" approach. According to him, "we do not appear to have a viable language or translation devices by which the different social sciences can be brought together into systematic cooperation." This is not to deny that economic processes are embedded in a comprehensive social and cultural system and are interdependent with the latter's motion, nor that the eventual scientific conquest of this wider territory should enable us to extend and refine our specialist investigations. At the same time it should not be forgotten that all so-called meta-economic influences can affect economic processes only through the channel of market behavior. In other words, by ascertaining and controlling motivational and behavioral patterns as they operate *within* the economic sphere, we implicitly take care of the effects exerted by meta-economic factors. Therefore, concentration on these intra-systemic phenomena is a legitimate shortcut.

3. A shortcut of a different kind becomes necessary when we have to decide to whom we are to entrust the stipulation of the macro-goals. We are indebted to Dr. Machlup for having shown once more in his lucid summary of the basic tenets of modern welfare economics that any attempt at deriving such goals from the social preferences of the individual members of a larger community must fail. Even the "heroic assumption" that we could determine the trade-off rates between all conceivable social goals acceptable to each member cannot bridge the gap between conflicting objectives. Therefore, a political decision must be "imposed" in some sense —except in the case of a more or less perfect *consensus*, and even then the achievement of such a *consensus* is mainly a political task.

Dr. Kaysen has presented us with a comprehensive survey of the political processes through which macro-goals are actually established in the framework of American institutions and, in particular, of the various roles which the "economist as adviser" can play in this context. His paper fills a serious lacuna in my own work, and I gratefully accept it as an exemplary demonstration of the manner in which the level of abstraction of a theory can and must be lowered if it is to serve the framing and implementation of policy. But there are some issues in Dr. Kaysen's paper on which I should like to offer a few supplementary rather than critical comments.

The first concerns the distinction between the stipulation of overall goals, such as full employment or a certain rate of growth for the system at large, and the specification of such goals, if possible, in terms of concrete, quantifiable targets. Dr. Kaysen describes from experience the role, more often than not a clandestine one, which the professional economist plays in his capacity as adviser to promote overall goals. Frequently this task devolves upon him by default, when no other authoritative voice can make itself heard in the crosscurrents of the democratic process. Still, as a matter of constitutional principle, one may doubt that this is a legimate function of an expert who "represents" only himself.

However, no one will deny the economist a major part in translating a politically accepted goal into concrete targets. To decide whether full employment should be spelled out as not exceeding a 4 per cent level of unemployment compatible with price stability, or as a maximum level of 3 per cent even if this has inflationary repercussions, requires an understanding of the remote consequences of both of the two states, as well as knowledge of the means required to achieve them—requirements which only professional competence can satisfy. At the same time we saw above that, in most of these decisions, more than detached analysis is involved—namely, a value judgment on the respective means to be applied. Therefore one must never forget that, even when he acts in what appears on the surface as a purely technical capacity, the economist is likely to step over—indeed, will have to step over—the boundaries of his "positive" science.

All this fully agrees with Dr. Kaysen's views. But the question remains as to what political criteria are to guide the value judgments of the advising economist or, for that matter, of anyone who stipulates macro-goals and specifies targets. Dr. Kaysen himself recognizes a "natural bias of economists . . . toward believing that consumers 'ought' to get what they want, in some ethical sense of the word." [21] A generation ago such may indeed have been the bias of the large majority in our profession, but I am not sure how true this is in an age so conscious of the frequent clashes between social and private benefits, and of the grave undersupply of public services. In any case, at this stage we are not looking for ultimate ethical criteria, but for a lodestar of political decision-making.

The answer seems to lie in another distinction that Dr. Kaysen introduces: the distinction between *settled issues* and *live issues*, with antitrust policy and international monetary policy as his paradigmatic examples. Issues are settled or live according to the degree of public *consensus* concerning the means by which we deal with them, and the economist looks like a merely technical adviser to the extent to which the value judgments underlying his decisions reflect the prevailing political aspirations. Take the example of fiscal and monetary controls. Since both are by now fully accepted by American public opinion, tax increases to fight inflation can be presented as merely technical advice derived from the new economics, whereas control of prices and wages—even if they were

---

21 See p. 149.

more effective as instruments of price stabilization—would still be treated as the offspring of a dubious ideology.

This leads us to the fundamental problem. The distinction between settled and live issues is equally applicable to the overall goals themselves from which all specific targets emanate. To clarify this point I must first introduce another distinction—that between *order-protecting* and *ameliorative* goals. The former express the minimum conditions for satisfactory provision as understood by majority opinion; the latter are propagated by reformers or revolutionaries as conditions for a provision optimum. Historically considered, the distinction is by no means rigid. What in one era is an ameliorative goal of a struggling minority, may well be regarded in the next generation as a minimum condition for social survival. Still, for any given period the distinction seems precise enough to serve as a point of orientation.

In my previous writings I have proclaimed stabilization and balanced growth—that is, the full utilization of available resources and the steady absorption of resource increments—as the major order-protecting goals of our age. No one familiar with the postwar history of the West will doubt that these goals are today settled issues that express the aspirations of the overwhelming majority. Their authoritative stipulation thus seems to be in full accord with our constitutional principles. Certainly this in itself does not confer upon them any "absolute" dignity as expressions of a "general will" based on some ultimate ethical standard. But when judged by the maxims of political practice, a macro-goal supported by public opinion at large can legitimately claim the place of an empirical "datum."

INSTRUMENTAL ANALYSIS ONCE MORE

Datum for what? With this question we re-enter scientific territory which, in submitting my position paper based on the methodological and substantive analyses in *OEK*, I thought I had exhaustively explored.[22] However, the challenging questions Dr. Nagel has raised leave no doubt that neither my own statements nor Dr. Gurwitsch's perspicacious exposition of my views, with which I fully concur, have succeeded in breaking down all barriers to a full understanding. Instrumental analysis being the core of Political Economics, I am most anxious to achieve a degree of clarification of its principles which will not only communicate its aims but also demonstrate its concordance with the accepted tenets of the philosophy of science.

---

[22] See pp. 14–32 and *OEK*, Chaps. 5, 10, 11.

Dr. Nagel asks two questions that go to the heart of the matter. Why should the conventional procedure of scientific inquiry, the hypothetico-deductive method, prove inapplicable in economics, considering its uncontested usefulness in the natural sciences? And second, once we probe the alleged "regressive" procedure of instrumental analysis to the bottom, does it not reveal itself as another version of "progressive"—that is, deductive—analysis?

In trying to give precise answers to these queries I shall also comment on the comparison between instrumental analysis and the technique recently used in constructing so-called "decision models." Furthermore, I want to enlarge on some earlier remarks concerning the "knowledge-action" issue—namely, my contention that at the present stage of development the object of economic research can no longer be grasped by passive observation alone but must be "created" by political intervention into the actual economic process.

1. The reason that I find the hypothetico-deductive method inapplicable to the solution of the contemporary problems of economics is implied in my above diagnosis of the relevant "facts." It is that we do not possess any safe hypotheses or major premises from which we could deduce theorems capable of explaining and predicting the processes of industrial capitalism. This is only a formalistic restatement of the substantive assertion that neither the macro-movements of modern markets nor the underlying micro-patterns of behavior exhibit the degree of orderliness that is essential for scientific generalization.

What this amounts to in terms of scientific methodology can be illustrated by drawing some extreme conclusions from a comparison of economic motion with celestial motion. An analog to the physical force of gravity has sometimes been seen in profit-maximizing behavior. But whereas the strength and direction of the force of gravity are *uniquely* and *invariably* described in Newton's formula, no equivalent statement can be made about the actual forces ruling economic motion. Profit-maximization is not the universal incentive in the era of organized capitalism, nor is its effect uniquely determined even where it operates as the dominating action directive. On the contrary, its effect on overt behavior varies with the simultaneous state of expectations, so that the *identical* profit incentive will give rise to *different* responses—meeting a price rise at one time with an increase in supply, and at another time with a decrease. Nor can this uncertainty of prediction be overcome by inquiring into the determinants of the expectations themselves. For these in turn vary with the technical structure, the size, the financial commitments, and other attributes of the firm. What makes the situation still worse is the fact that expectations cannot be simply correlated with objective states of the environment, but ultimately depend on the manner in which the potential economic actor *interprets* these states and their future changes—a contingency which the student of planets and cells is fortunately spared.

Now Dr. Nagel is certainly right in insisting that in physics the relative strength of different forces also varies from field to field, and that, for example, gravitation is stronger in the solar system than in the atom. It is also true that, contrary to an oversimplified statement of mine, the interplay of several forces is not necessarily summative, but may result in very complex patterns. It is even quite possible that the content of the laws of nature themselves is subject to spatial and temporal variations. However, and this is the salient point, the structural order of these natural forces—though different in physics, electromagnetics, or genetics—is constant *within* any one of these fields, or, if it changes within them, does so at rates that are for all practical purposes negligible.

A logical parallelism would prevail—and from such an analogy Dr. Nagel's queries seem to spring—if, say, nineteenth-century capitalism had displayed *one* ruling type of incentive coupled with *one* type of expectations, while twentieth-century capitalism showed a different but also stable pattern. Though then we might not be able to discover transhistorical laws of economic motion, some laws with a limited historical validity might well be established. But if my diagnosis of the contemporary scene is correct, not one but many patterns of interaction are at work between a wide spectrum of both incentives and expectations, and worse, this continuing situation is without any *ex ante* clue as to which of the possible combinations will emerge in a given situation.

To drive this point home, let me illustrate it by a fictitious example from astronomy. Suppose that on Mars gravitation were to operate inversely with the third power of the distance, whereas on Jupiter it was directly proportional with it. Though we could no longer have a universal mechanics, we could still have a special mechanics for each planet. But now assume that on this earth gravitation were sometimes to operate according to Newton's formula, sometimes inversely with the third power of the distance, and sometimes directly proportional with the distance, and that we could not know *ex ante* which of these alternatives would materialize at any given time. I wonder what sort of generalizations the hypothetico-deductive method could establish in the field of mechanics then. Under these assumed conditions, a "theory" of mechanics would have to be replaced by taxonomic description. But this is not so in economics where, within limits, we can *create* order out of disorder, once we have made up our minds as to what our macro-goals are. For once we have stipulated them, they can serve as the major data from which we can derive whichever of the many possible forces—behavioral and motivational patterns, public controls—are "orderly": namely, goal-adequate.

2. The technique for such derivation is instrumental analysis. In discussing its procedure, Dr. Gurwitsch has drawn an interesting parallel with mathematical analysis. In both cases a certain state of affairs is posited—a macro-goal in economics, a geometrical figure with specified properties in mathematics—and the *quaesitum* is the set of conditions upon which the realization of the posited state depends. In both cases, in contrast to the "progressive" technique of the hypothetico-deductive method, the analysis is "regressive"—that is, proceeding from the knowledge of some terminal state back to its unknown determinants.

But is this true? In raising this question Dr. Nagel advances two seemingly grave objections. The first concerns the construction problem in geometry. To solve it he rightly insists that we must know more than the posited state—namely, the specification by a set of axioms of the properties of the respective figures. Must there not also be, he asks, a corresponding set of "axioms" for instrumental analysis? And if so, what else but some known laws of economic behavior can fulfill this function? This leads to his second objection. For if there are such laws after all, why use regressive analysis? Why not proceed by progressive deduction from the knowledge of the initial conditions and those axiomatic laws to the terminal state?

The reply to the first question, which has also been raised with great emphasis by Dr. Machlup, can only be an emphatic "yes." There is indeed in instrumental analysis an analog to the axioms of mathematics: to wit, the engineering rules that tell us how, within the limits of our technical knowledge, the initial state of the system can be transformed into the goal-adequate state. But this set of technical operating rules is *all* that is necessary. *We have no need to know any laws of behavior.* I have tried to demonstrate this above [23] through the fiction of a fully automated economy in which human action would be entirely confined to deciding the output menu, the technology to be applied, and the programming of the computers: that is, to goal-setting. All production and distribution processes would "move by themselves," so that to plan these motions *ex ante* and to understand them *ex post* would require no more than knowledge of the apposite engineering rules and the underlying laws of nature.

The insights imparted by this fiction are also fully valid for our present economic organization in which behavior enters at strategic points. But the patterns of behavior that may be suitable at these points cannot be known before we know the path the system is to follow. Therefore the suitable behavior patterns are themselves among the unknowns of instrumental analysis that are to be derived from the technologically determined path.

To avoid any semantic misunderstanding I should like to clarify the

---

[23] See pp. 24–25.

distinction between an engineering rule and a law of behavior by referring to an earlier proposition of mine where I stated that "a rise of investment is a suitable means of promoting employment." Dr. Nagel interprets this statement as a law of behavior. This would indeed be so if I were to assert that additional investment *will* raise employment. But all I claim there is that investment—that is, building more working places—will *create an opportunity* for more workers to be employed—a technical potentiality for, but no assurance of, subsequent economic action. In purely formal terms, an engineering rule says: If behavior A—a rise in investment—occurs, a technical state B will follow—namely, more working places. On the other hand, a law of behavior says: If behavior A—a rise in investment—occurs, another behavior C will follow—namely, more workers will be hired. Nothing about behavioral consequents following behavioral antecedents is pronounced in instrumental analysis, and therefore no laws or empirical generalizations of Positive Economics are implied.

This provides me with the occasion for a brief comment on the similarities and differences between instrumental analysis and the modern decision models, to which Dr. Kaysen and Dr. Wallich have alluded. There is indeed a formal similarity insofar as both approaches derive the "means"—controls or "instrument variables"—from knowledge of the initial and terminal states by applying certain "structural relations" as constraints. The difference, and it is a fundamental one, concerns the nature of these structural constraints. In the decision models they are, above all, behavior equations, symbolizing the presumed or observed responses of the marketers to specific events. It should be clear by now that in instrumental analysis the structural relations are of a purely technological nature. True, the total set of all known engineering rules is also abstracted from observation, though obtained in the workshop rather than in the market place. But the criteria by which the *suitable* rules are selected, in any given instance, from the total set cannot themselves be "observed."

3. This now brings us to Dr. Nagel's second question. If it is true that engineering rules are indispensable data for instrumental analysis, why bother with a regressive derivation of the suitable path instead of deducing it in the usual fashion from the knowledge of these rules and of the initial conditions? The answer is simple. Once we *know* which members of the total set of engineering rules are goal-adequate, we can indeed deduce the path in the conventional manner. The first step of instrumental analysis is to provide us with precisely this knowledge.

Thus instrumental analysis reveals itself as a search procedure through which the suitable means to the stipulated end—or, if you will, the suitable causes of a desired effect—are to be discovered. It falls within the category of heuristics or of what Peirce called "abduction," a mental technique of problem-solving which is part and parcel of research in every field of science. Far from being in methodological conflict with deductive reasoning, it is the technique by which the premises of any deductive syllogism are originally established.

Though they are really the source of all scientific knowledge and are unlikely to be displaced by even the most sophisticated computer, heuristic procedures do not at present constitute a major theme of methodological discussion.[24] Therefore it is difficult to deal with this aspect of instrumental analysis in abstract terms. This has been one of the reasons why I have supplemented my methodological exposition in OEK by a detailed description of some test cases in which the regressive technique is applied to substantive issues.[25]

Closer scrutiny of the manner in which, in these examples, the critical paths of the system are traced back to the pertinent technical rules of production, and these in turn to the macro-goal, should provide sufficient proof that heuristics has a logical and not merely a psychological status. It is quite true that there are no formal precepts whose observance would safely guide us to the solution. Ultimately we must "hit" upon it through what Polanyi calls a logical "leap." [26] However, it is not a leap in the dark, but one directed by the nature of the problem, and by more or less rigid constraints which set narrow boundaries to the area within which a solution can be found.

We all have heard of Wolfgang Köhler's ape who longingly stares at a banana through the window of his cage, only to discover finally that if he wants to seize it he must move away from the window to the rear, which has an opening to the outside. In an analogous manner, an economic system in which the total capital stock is fully utilized can achieve growth (understood as an *increase* in the aggregate output of consumer goods) only if, to begin with, the current output of such goods is *reduced* so as to set free part of the available capital stock for expansion. There does not exist any technique of inference through which this conclusion could be reached. But the more precisely we circumscribe our problem—a purely logical task—the fewer the number of alternatives which include the solution for which we are searching.

---

[24] See, however, the enlightening comments in N. R. Hanson, *Patterns of Discovery* (London: Cambridge University Press, 1958), esp. Chap. IV; and the writings of G. Polya.

[25] See *OEK*, Chap. 11, especially the re-enactment of the "discovery" of the circular nature of an industrial structure of production, on pp. 266–271.

[26] Michael Polanyi, *Personal Knowledge* (Chicago: University of Chicago Press, 1958), p. 123.

We have now reached the point where my defense merges with Dr. Nagel's charge. Once the heuristic task of instrumental analysis is successfully completed and the goal-adequate forces, private and public, discovered, the road is free for deductive generalizations of the conventional type. These generalizations extend the results obtained in the case analyzed to all similar cases. For this reason I have labeled my procedure "instrumental-deductive," in full awareness that the level of "theory" is reached only when the instrumental findings can serve as highest-level hypotheses in 'the explanation and prediction of facts other than those which were the occasion for their discovery.

And yet an important reservation is in place. The apparent universality and constancy of forces in the world of nature permits, as a rule, a much wider range of theoretical generalization than is possible in the study of society. In the latter, the multitude of possible macro-goals makes it imperative to re-examine the conditions for suitability whenever a new terminal state is stipulated. It was with good reason that the question repeatedly came up in our discussions as to whether the instrumental-deductive procedure lends itself to the same inclusiveness of theorizing to which we are accustomed in the natural sciences, or whether it yields at best a number of unrelated sets of theorems, any one of which is applicable only to one class of cases.

4. The answer to this question is bound up with what is perhaps the most startling feature of Political Economics—namely, its assertion that only "prior ordering" of reality itself can provide us with a tractable object of theoretical investigation. As will be remembered, I have limited this thesis to the contemporary stage of organized capitalism, claiming that the environmental conditions of competitive capitalism exerted a regularizing influence on the behavioral forces sufficiently strong to render conscious control of their interaction superfluous. But the impression has apparently been created that I regard the new constellation of forces as permanent from now on. Indeed, for purposes of policy-framing, the present generation had better base its analyses on this assumption. But it would be rash to close one's mind to a possible future in which as yet unknown regularities might be discovered underlying the ostensible disorder of market movements, or in which even these surface movements themselves would again assume regular form.

The first alternative concerns an opening of scientific insight into new psychological laws that would permit us, after all, to predict which of the rivaling motivational and behavioral patterns will arise in each instance, and thus to construct an economic theory valid for all conceivable cases. Even such a scientific advance would not do away with the practical need for the discovery of the means suitable to establish order in the real world, and thus for instrumental analysis. But its findings would then acquire a generality comparable to natural-science hypotheses.

The second alternative is even more interesting. It amounts to speculating about a future state of society in which the anonymous forces making for socialization of behavior become strong enough to bring about a spontaneous ordering of the behavioral field that assures the desired levels of provision. Under such conditions, observation of what actually occurs could, as in the natural sciences, lead to general hypotheses from which verifiable explanations and predictions might be deduced. A structure of this kind seems to prevail in traditionalist societies, though Dr. Lerner has rightly stressed the extent of conscious experimentation with institutions and rules of conduct, which defies any romantic notions about a pre-established harmony of interaction in these societies. Even so, there the slow tempo of change allows both actors and observers to take the rountinized patterns of stimulus and response for granted over long periods of time.

The image of such a stationary society has little in common with the political and technological dynamics of the modern world. But as victims of the disruptive tendencies of this dynamics, we are apt to underestimate the more temperate, but in the long run not necessarily weaker, forces of conciliation. The collectivist trend of the age may well bring about a new assimilation of incentives, while successive control of the environment may render expectations both more certain and mutually compatible. At the same time the cruder forms of command control seem everywhere on the wane. West and East show, as Dr. Lerner has properly emphasized, a structural convergence toward a type of social organization in which considerable autonomy of the micro-units is combined with order-preserving manipulative controls,[27] made effective through the spontaneous affirmation of the controlled.

5. These speculations about a possible future have a very practical bearing on the immediate present and, especially, on the usefulness of instrumental analysis as a tool for the framing of practical policy.

It will, I hope, be accepted by now that the suitability conditions for goal attainment can be determined without regard to the real social forces at work. But logically consistent as such a design is, it describes an imaginary world. To make the transition to reality—that is, to move toward goal-*realization*—the real world must be approximated to the imaginary one through political action. But to do this is possible only

---

[27] For the distinction between manipulative and command controls, see *OEK*, Chaps. 5 and 12.

if the last step of instrumental analysis has successfully been completed
—namely, if a link has been forged between the motivations of the
economic actors (incentives and expectations) and the forces of the environment, particularly public control.

As I pointed out before,[28] the forging of this link is obviously not a
technological task. It is a problem of social psychology, of determining
the social nexus through which specific environmental stimuli evoke
ex ante determinable responses. So whenever instrumental findings—
themselves discovered without reference to any *social* cause–effect relations—are to be applied, we enter a border region in which "laws" or
at least empirical regularities of a sociopsychological nature must rule.
It is hardly necessary to emphasize once more that the *regularities in
question are not the alleged laws of economic behavior postulated by
Traditional Economics*. The former are of much wider generality, referring to the effect of environmental stimuli on any type of social response,
economic or otherwise. Indeed, one might say that to exist at all, specific
laws of economic behavior presuppose the logically prior existence of a
lawful order of more comprehensive social relations.

The fact is (and there lies the connection with what was said above
about anonymous forces making for socialization of behavior) that the
study of social causation has not as yet come up with safe generalizations.[29] Again I trace the reason for this failure to the state of the research object rather than to shortcomings of the research technique. At
least in the so-called "free societies" of the modern world, the responses
of randomly chosen individuals to the same environmental stimulus vary
widely, as do even those of the same individual at different times. And
yet no social organization, large or small, can survive without a minimum
of conformity and stability in the motivational and behavioral patterns of
its members. Compared with most of the societies of the past and even
with the contemporary societies outside of its boundaries, the "free world"
appears as an extreme case of "nonconformity." And yet its members, in
their daily performances, continue to "interact." They succeed in doing
so because the psychological heritage from more highly socialized stages
of Western history and new agents of the "public interest" sustain coordination.

In any event, it is this looseness of social structure that is mirrored
in the vagueness of empirical generalizations, with whose help we try
to anticipate the effect of social controls. If it is true that the trend is
toward greater conformity, the chances for more accurate prediction of

---

28 See p. 28.
29 See p. 29.

this effect will increase. To demonstrate that even under prevailing conditions these chances can be greatly improved will be the burden of the following remarks.

THE FUNCTION OF PUBLIC CONTROL

Public controls suitable to transform real economic states and processes into goal-adequate ones belong to two worlds. Their discovery is the final step of instrumental analysis and is thus part of the theory of Political Economics. Their application is a political act—the foremost practical task of Political Economics. But to make the theoretical findings amenable to practical application, the level of abstraction of the analysis must be lowered to the point where the general principles of controls can be specified in concrete measures of economic policy, taking into account the intangibles as well as the tangibles of the prevailing sociopolitical structure. This is an undertaking that calls for talents and experiences of which Dr. Kaysen's paper presents a rare display, but which are not the ordinary equipment of the economic theorist. So it should not cause surprise that both my book and my position paper in this volume show considerable gaps in this respect which I cannot even try to bridge in these summary remarks. Their purpose is rather to spell out in greater detail some of those general principles which underlie any specification of public controls.

1. In my programmatic statement of the major propositions of Political Economics,[30] I have distinguished between primary and secondary controls. My first concern is to give this distinction precision beyond the cursory comments made earlier.[31] There I have subsumed all conventional measures of economic policy—taxation, tariffs and quotas, currency control and interest manipulation, social legislation, etc., as well as the techniques of monetary and fiscal controls as advocated by the new economics, under the concept of primary control. In stressing their inadequacy for goal attainment, I did not mean to imply that Political Economics could in any way dispense with such controls. The contrary is true, and only in the context of these controls does the true problem emerge.

This problem was labeled above as the "response mechanism" of the micro-units of the system—that is, their reaction either to actions of other micro-units or to primary controls imposed by public authorities. Because of the unrealistic assumptions concerning the motivational and

---

[30] See pp. 168–170.
[31] See pp. 32–34.

behavioral patterns ruling in a modern industrial market, traditional theory and policy alike take the responses to such stimuli for granted. Concretely, the supposition is that tax reductions will *always* add to aggregate spending whereas tax increases *necessarily* reduce it, that public spending *always* raises aggregate employment, or that increasing labor supply *invariably* stimulates private investment, etc. It is against such a mechanical interpretation of the effects of primary or conventional controls that Political Economics argues. To put it in more practical terms, these controls are not to be replaced, but are to be supplemented by another type of control which assures that the intent which led to the introduction of the former controls is realized.

It is the function of *secondary* controls to bring this about by eliciting the goal-adequate behavior of the controlled. In speaking of "eliciting," I want to make it clear that we are dealing with a social and not a physical phenomenon, with a challenge that can be accepted or rejected. True, there are certain types of command control which, by threats to life and liberty, may perhaps evoke a pseudomechanical reaction. But, as a rule, responses to controls will be goal-adequate only if the controlled *understand* and *affirm* both the macro-goals pursued and the policy instruments used in their service. This is even true in the case of "restrictive" controls such as taxation or quotas on imports. These erect boundaries which the micro-units cannot overstep. But where actual behavior will settle within these boundaries cannot be predicted *ex ante* unless the responses themselves are controlled. To promote such understanding and affirmation, and thus to give the impact of primary controls on microbehavior direction and strength, this defines the role of secondary controls.

What then are the concrete measures of public policy which promise to improve this causal nexus? It was admitted earlier that we have at this stage no sociopsychological laws to guide us in this inquiry, and that we must rely on certain empirical generalizations and rules of thumb. Generally speaking, techniques of secondary control lie between two extremes. At one extreme there is the ideal but exceptional case in which the stipulated macro-goals and the primary controls chosen for their realization coincide from the outset with the aspirations of the controlled. Spontaneous micro-behavior is then intrinsically goal-adequate, and no secondary controls are required. At the other extreme, we find the situation already alluded to in which, for lack of understanding of or radical disagreement with the macro-goals or the primary controls applied, the micro-units act obstructively. There secondary controls are indispensable, assuming the form of circumventing obstructive behavior through compensatory public action, or coercion, or finally, by altogether supplanting private decision-making in a collectivist regime.

The secondary controls appropriate to the mixed systems of the West, which are committed to maintaining a broad sector of private decision-making, lie between these extremes. Their purpose is to "convert" the micro-units to the realization that both macro-goals and controls coincide with their own long-term interests. In other words, they treat private decision-making as open to a *learning process.*

I have shown earlier that, in particular, marketers' expectations are a highly promising object for goal-adequate restructuring through improved public information, in which the instrumental analysis of the given situation plays a major role.[32] Moreover, I could point to numerous instances in which education in the wider sense of the word, including the formation of a more enlightened public opinion, has profoundly affected the attitude of business and of the community at large toward policies that initially were hotly contested. Recent examples are the universal acceptance of collective bargaining, and of public spending as a means to counteract recessions. Since Dr. Kaysen has placed such emphasis on the role of the economist as public adviser, I should like to stress his function as teacher and educator, a more subtle but over the long run even more effective instrument of secondary control.

How severe secondary controls should be in any given instance may be difficult to gauge from the outset. Incremental application of the respective primary controls can offer an important clue. If, for instance, in a state of depression, small doses of public spending lead to a rapid rise in private investment, the presumption is that the response mechanism in the private sector is goal-adequate. Conversely, as happened during the 1930's, a negative response of private investment demonstrates the need for supplementary secondary controls, a course of action which was not comprehended at the time.

2. From improved information, the enlightening of public opinion, and effective teaching through the numerous techniques of "persuasion" such as guideposts or indicative planning, to compensatory public intervention and finally outright coercion—the arsenal of secondary controls is large indeed. Hence it is not surprising that again and again in our discussions an anxious question was raised asking to what extent these weapons are compatible with decentralized decision-making. More than one voice expressed the fear that once they have such means at their disposal the controlling authorities will be tempted into collectivist adventures.

It cannot be denied that there is always the danger that the insolence of office will grow with the strength of the powers that be. But the real problem, one that goes beyond bureaucratic ambition and misuse of political authority, has different roots. Whether controls, primary or

---

[32] See p. 29.

secondary, will in fact be harsh or lenient is not determined first and foremost by the caprices of the controllers. It is, rather, a functional problem in which the nature of the macro-goal and of the initial state plays the dominant role. As far as the latter is concerned, the prevailing social and technical structure of a society is a rigid constraint for the adjustment processes that connect initial and terminal states.[33] From this it follows that certain goals are incompatible with the maintenance of the structure of the initial state, and can be attained only if this structure itself is altered. To give an example, an egalitarian distribution of income and wealth is not a feasible goal within a capitalist order of property relations. It can be accomplished only after these relations are abolished. This, however, would require the most extreme forms of command control.

Of greater practical importance at this historical juncture are goals, such as radical urban renewal, that in principle fit into the prevailing social structure, but run counter to the interests of powerful strata of society. These goals can be successfully pursued only if resistance can be circumvented, say, by attractive forms of compensation, or can be broken by more direct means. The primary controls required for this certainly lie outside the range of the manipulative controls of the new economics or of other conventional policies, and the secondary controls can hardly confine themselves to applying persuasion.

What we run up against here once more is the difference between "settled" and "live" issues. But now the context is much wider, including the popular attitude not only toward the goal itself, but also toward the means required for its attainment. In this wider context we can now define that difference more precisely. An issue is "settled" when the goal in question and the primary controls associated with it are approved of by a politically relevant majority. It is obvious that in all such cases any secondary controls, if required at all, can be of the lenient kind. It is our good fortune that, as was mentioned earlier, the major order-preserving goals of the present age fall in this category; it can be shown that purely manipulative controls are very likely to assure their realization.[34]

This is by no means true of what I called "ameliorative" goals, most of which are "live" issues—that is, the fighting concern of pioneering minorities. So long as they have not conquered public opinion, such goals can be accomplished only if the sponsoring minority succeeds in imposing its will on an antagonistic majority. If it were only a question of "extremist" groups pursuing sectional aims, the answer would not be too difficult, even in a democratic system. Alas, more often than not such

---

[33] *OEK*, Chap. 10.
[34] *OEK*, Chap. 11.

dissent reveals a serious dilemma. It arises wherever an enlightened minority perceives as a long-term necessity what to a majority blinded by short-term concerns appears as a violation of its interests. In other words, the distinction between order-preserving and ameliorative goals is historically fluid, especially when we remember that our sensitivity to "disorder" increases steadily. Under this aspect it is an open question whether stabilization and balanced growth still fulfill the minimum conditions of satisfactory provision, as I suggested earlier. Urban renewal, economic equality of opportunity among the races, pure air, clean water, and, last but not least, greater distributional equity are today proclaimed as preconditions for social survival by vocal minorities supported by serious experts, in addition to such "international" goals as population control and prevention of worldwide famine. If it is true that our very physical existence is threatened by shortsighted interference with ecological equilibria, can we wait with remedial action for a political consensus to be achieved through the democratic techniques of persuasion, or must such issues be "settled" by other means?

In placing these alternatives before us I am raising grave questions of a constitutional nature. I have never cherished any illusions about the efficacy of lenient (manipulative) controls in underdeveloped societies that are striving for emancipation from the tyranny not only of nature but of oppressive rulers, domestic and foreign. But in writing my book I was perhaps too optimistic in relying on the social consensus prevailing in the mature societies of the West as a safe basis on which Political Economics can build. The symptoms multiply that the mere attempt at preserving our accomplishments for future generations will involve us in social conflicts for the resolution of which many of our present institutions may have to be restructured.

However, we should be aware that in attributing to certain ameliorative goals the function of "preserving order," we have extended the notion of "order" far beyond the original definition we gave it. It is now no longer a question of regularizing "economic motion" and thereby assuring predictability of the system. Rather, the aspect of "satisfactory provision," which was then stressed only as a complementary constituent of order, now takes over, and Political Economics reveals itself as the instrument for the discovery and application of means suitable to the attainment of whatever goal our welfare judgments regard as worthy of pursuit.

CRITERIA FOR GOAL-SETTING

This wider scope of application is implied in the very concept of a Political Economics which tries to supplant what Dr. Lerner calls the economic "process of natural selection" by goal-oriented planning. But it brings to the fore an issue that we could evade as long as we assumed that the stipulated goals were accepted by a more or less unanimous public opinion. Stipulation was then little more than articulation of popular aspirations, and coincided with the legalization of these aspirations in the framework of prevailing political institutions. This is no longer so when popular consensus gives way to dissent over what the "order-preserving" goals are in a given situation. The alternative to a struggle of brute force can then only be an appeal to criteria which, as the ultimate vindication of political action, are themselves above the power struggle.

There lies the crucial significance of Dr. Jonas' radical assault of the agnostic position I have taken in all my writings as to whether there are any *scientific* criteria to guide our choice of goals.[35] This is the position conventionally labeled as "scientific value relativism," of which the work of Max Weber contains the paradigmatic formulation. It is important to stress that the relativism proclaimed there confines itself to what scientific inquiry or discursive thinking generally can contribute to establishing "intersubjective demonstrability" of norms. It remains open, and this is an important proviso, whether or not the choice among values and norms is yet amenable to a cognitive judgment, but in a realm in which we can communicate only by "pointing to," as opposed to the realm of thought where propositions rule—a distinction which, in the words of Wittgenstein, is "the cardinal problem of philosophy."[36]

Now what Dr. Jonas tries to do, and what to my knowledge has not been attempted in any other philosophical disquisition about economics, is to demonstrate that the essential criteria for goal selection can be explicated by rational analysis because they are intrinsic to the nature of economic organization as such. Of course, even if such a scientific explication of the "true" goals proved possible, this by itself could not assure their acceptance as rules of political action. But it would certainly elevate political debate above the mere airing of "opinions" and "subjective judgments," and would provide us with a foundation for a self-contained science of Political Economics.

In my subsequent remarks, I shall have to raise a number of serious objections to Dr. Jonas' demonstration. But I would like it to be understood that, even if he has not spoken the last word, he has addressed himself to the fundamental problem underlying all social research in an age which tries to transform the historical process from blind motion into responsible action.

1. I will begin by briefly restating Dr. Jonas' major propositions: (a)

---

[35] See *OEK*, Chap. 12, and pp. 18, 34.
[36] In a letter to Bertrand Russell. See *Autobiography of Bertrand Russell*, Vol. II (London: George Allen & Unwin, 1968), p. 172.

Rather than being stipulated from outside the economic field, a definite goal-commitment is an indispensable condition for constituting this field. (b) This is so because economics deals with human institutions which cannot even be defined unless we include a "causality of purpose." (c) The intrinsic goals in which this basic commitment manifests itself are two, *provisioning* and *providence*—namely, providing the members of a group "with the physical goods necessary to sustain their lives" and, in doing so, "looking and planning ahead." These basic economic goals are themselves ultimately grounded in two biological constituents: metabolism and reproduction; they express the "basic self-affirmation of life," "an *a priori* option." (d) No extrinsic criteria are required to vindicate these basic goals. Rather they offer themselves as the criteria for the choice of more specific ones, at least by setting boundaries which separate legitimate goals from others. This yields us an "unconditional economic imperative": "Do not compromise the conditions for an indefinite continuation of some viable economy."

In trying to comment on these propositions, I find myself in a strange quandary. I am in complete agreement with Dr. Jonas' conclusion as stated in his economic imperative and, as a consequence, also with his counsel of caution when it comes to pursuing grandiose projects. But I cannot accept some of the premises from which this conclusion is derived, especially those which concern the intrinsic nature of provisioning and providence, as understood by Dr. Jonas, and the treatment of the basic commitment as an "*a priori* option." Moreover, even if the economic imperative is accepted unreservedly, in telling us only what *not* to do, it fails to offer guidance for our positive decisions within the permitted range.

2. To vindicate my second and less fundamental objection, let us consider some of the topical choices among rivaling goals with which contemporary policy-framers are confronted. Is it "better" to reduce unemployment to the zero level even if this implies an actual price rise by x per cent to be borne by the recipients of fixed incomes—or to maintain price stability even if this will keep unemployment above the y per cent level? Or, as another example, "should" a developing country keep consumption near the subsistence level to facilitate investment and a rapid rate of growth, or "should" the present generation be favored with a rising standard of living at the cost of reducing the gains of future generations?

Obviously either of these decisions is covered by Dr. Jonas' viability norm, some provision and some providence being assured in each case. But how are we to evaluate the relative advantages which alternatively accrue to different income groups and different generations? True, my examples do not refer to the category of global goals with which Dr. Jonas is primarily concerned, but belong to what he calls "measured alternatives of short-range planning." But as a matter of fact, the overwhelming majority of goal-choices that arise in Political Economics fall in the latter category, for which both the goals and the means can be spelled out with reasonable precision.

However, the same dilemma confronts our decisions on "long-range, large-scale perspectives." We agree that the new opportunities for communal choices and also the dangers implied in a wrong choice both derive from the same factor: rapid technological change. What then should our attitude be toward further technical progress? The general norm that states: "Do not endanger economic viability," yields no guidance. Perhaps technical progress should be stopped altogether in the interest of safeguarding "human wholeness"—a "value" which, according to Dr. Jonas, should form "a legitimate part of hardheaded economic reasoning," making "viability . . . rather a comprehensive concept in which the technical aspect . . . tends to merge with the humanistic aspect of man's well-being." [37] But how can we decide on this unless we have an image of man in which we can read what human wholeness and the humanistic aspects of his well-being are?

3. This question leads us to the fundamental issue of where to look for criteria—not only to help us choose among rivaling specific goals, but also to give precision to those basic goals: provisioning and providence. I agree with Dr. Jonas that the overall purpose which constitutes economic activity can be formulated in these concepts. But I must disagree with his claim that these concepts provide us with any criteria other than the *successful functioning* of economic activity. And "success" is measured here as the ability to make the "best" of an altogether bad job, that of allocating scarce human and natural resources to our wants, where "best" means "most efficient," irrespective of any "humanistic commitments."

To see this clearly we must disabuse ourselves of the widely held notion that economic activity can be placed side by side with activities such as politics, science, or religion that pursue intrinsic *substantive* goals. When Dr. Jonas speaks of provisioning as being concerned with supplying the physical goods necessary to sustain our lives, he comes dangerously near to the notion of there being a special type of wants called "economic" or "material" that concern *vital necessities:* food, clothing, housing, etc. In reality there are no particular wants that can justifiably be labeled "economic." There is only an *economic manner or technique* by which we provide for the satisfaction of *any* wants—vital, political, religious, etc.—a technique that comes into play whenever satisfaction is conditional on the application of scarce resources. Therefore, the con-

---

[37] See p. 82.

struction of a church or—*sit venia verbo*—of the gas ovens of Auschwitz poses no less an economic problem than does the production of bread and shoes. Or even more pointedly: economic activity is not at all concerned with the actual satisfaction of any particular wants, but with overcoming the resistance a stingy Nature opposes to the satisfaction of all means-requiring wants. Thus economics deals exclusively with the realm of means, and is as such both narrower and wider than the other realms of human action: narrower because it is bare of any substantive goal, wider because it is subservient to all the other realms insofar as they require means.

Now what difference does it make whether we delineate the realm of economics as standing on a par with politics, science, or religion, or as a subsidiary and auxiliary realm of means disposal? The difference is far-reaching indeed, because only in the latter conception does economic action reveal its historical relativity. All the realms pursuing substantive goals—vital, interpersonal, political, moral, etc.—are likely to remain fields of action as long as man walks this earth. They sustain, to speak with a physical analogy, the "voltage" of civilization—namely, the positive forces of human society. Not so economic relations. They are the "ohms" of civilization, measuring the resistance of a stingy Nature to the fulfillment of our positive goals. They symbolize Adam's curse which, all through past history, has compelled men to sacrifice the potentialities of the "good life" to the toil and trouble of procuring the means necessary for our most primitive—namely, vital—ends. But contrary to the Biblical prediction, technology is gradually emancipating us from this bondage, by progressively reducing the obstacles to means procurement. At least asymptotically we are moving toward a state in which the significance of economic activity dwindles relative to the opportunities for pursuing genuine goals.

But so long as it is with us, economic activity as such is *goal-neutral*. The only imperative that can be derived from its intrinsic character commands us to apply the available resources as efficiently as possible to any extrinsically posited end. Even provision, in the sense of that which is to be provided, and providence, understood as the time span over which we are to provide, remain empty boxes unless they are related to a particular "menu" stipulated from without. "Indefinite continuation of a viable economy" may be an item in that menu, but need not be. If Hitler had decided in 1945 to bring about the final *Götterdämmerung*, the complete destruction of the German people and land, then the task of the economist *qua* economist, unmoved by extrinsic considerations, would have been to help in doing so most efficiently.

4. Now in insisting that economics can provide us only with a func-

tional criterion, I am far from proclaiming that in the economic realm "everything is permitted." But when I speak out against *autos-da-fé* and other destructive uses of "means," calling them "mala" in accord with Dr. Jonas, I transcend the intrinsic neutrality of economics by an appeal to extrinsic moral norms. As a matter of fact, such transcendence begins already when I try to define what "legitimate" wants are. True, on the primitive subsistence level, "choices" and thus normative decisions are in practice almost excluded, because vital needs claim all the available resources. I say "almost," because even there, "affirmation of life" and "interest in being" remain a genuine "option" and, contrary to Dr. Jonas, are no *a priori* of economic action. But certainly above that level, the opportunities for choices steadily expand, and with them the need for criteria beyond the functional command of efficiency.

As a matter of historical fact, these criteria are rooted in the dominant system of cultural values, which determines the legitimate range not only of wants but also of means: to a pious Jew pork is no food. Thus only by surrendering its autonomy in favor of the rule of such extrinsic moral, aesthetic, and other values in which "human wholeness" comes to fruition, will economic activity remain within the boundaries of what is "constructive," and will economics be able to fuse its criterion of technical efficiency with the "humanistic aspect of man's well-being."

At the same time it cannot be the business of economics and its adepts to pronounce on these values. In spite of Dr. Jonas' modest disclaimer, this is a philosophical task, more precisely one of philosophical anthropology. Practically, if not in principle, its services might be dispensed with if our age were dominated by one and only one cultural value system. Here our present discussion merges with our prior reflections on the conflict of rivaling macro-goals in Western public opinion, not to speak of the ideological conflict between East and West or between traditional and modern societies generally. Seen in this light even terms such as "humanistic aspect of man's well-being" lose precision because they point to a very singular image of man, as it has been formed through the blending of the classical heritage with the Judaeo-Christian tradition. I sympathize with Dr. Jonas' fear and trembling when confronted with such a Promethean task—but to whom else if not to the philosopher can we appeal in our search for a "just" solution of these conflicts?

5. In conclusion, a word must be said about another objection which Dr. Jonas has raised. It concerns the feasibility of instrumental analysis, an objection which, if sustainable, would be truly crushing. Optimistic as he is when the establishment of ultimate criteria for goal-setting is at stake, he turns into a radical skeptic when these criteria are to be

applied to spell out the concrete features of the terminal state in which
the stipulated goal is to materialize, and also of the intermediate stages
which represent the suitable path. This skepticism arises from our inability to foresee the long-term effects of any action, because any terminus
projected today is "spotlighted . . . out of a darkness of collateral unknowns with which it is inextricably intertwined." Therefore, "in the
last resort, the directed and 'controlled' alternative is cognitively little
better off than the 'automatically' self-realizing one." [38]

It may be useful to emphasize that Dr. Jonas' reservations to instrumental analysis are different from and more radical than Dr. Machlup's
stress of our "ignorance of what bridges may be crossed" in the course
of carrying out our instrumentally established policies. What bothers Dr.
Machlup is not our inability to foresee the long-term effects of our present actions, but the multitude of alternative paths and behavioral patterns through which a stipulated goal can be reached, and between
which the choice can only be made on the basis of a value judgment.
In other words, Dr. Machlup's problem is the abundance rather than
the dearth of our cognitive findings, to be solved by stepping over the
boundaries of positive economics into the realm of what he calls "normative economics." Though, as should be clear by now, I regard a normative economics in which values can be "justified" as a scientific mirage,
I fully agree with Dr. Machlup that we must transcend the realms of
positive economics or of instrumental analysis if we are to find criteria
for such choices.

Dr. Jonas, on the other hand, stops short from the very outset, because
he denies the feasibility of any cognitive propositions on means. Fortunately, he confines his skeptical reasoning to "long-range, large-scale
perspectives," and thus opens the way for Political Economics after all.
This is so because the collateral unknowns of a distant future play a
minor role in the short-range projects with which Political Economics
is mainly concerned. Certainly stabilization and balanced growth, our
paradigms of order-preserving goals, do not refer to a Utopian future,
but point to an ongoing struggle against ongoing threats of economic
dislocation. And the darkness in which even the proximate future may
be shrouded can be lightened by the trial-and-error technique of incremental control. All this has been stated very clearly and convincingly
in Dr. Edel's comments, with which I fully associate myself.

I should even go farther and assert that the typical goals that Political Economics stipulates and the typical measures it advocates are in
strict conformity with Dr. Jonas' cautionary warning, because they are
all in the service of viability, which is only another term for what was

---

[38] See p. 70.

defined above as "order" in the comprehensive sense. On this level it would be a gross misreading of the facts were we to place the "automatically self-realizing alternatives" on the same footing with the planned ones. As the experience of the Great Depression has demonstrated only too forcefully, the former alternative threatens us with the very destruction of economic viability. Even if political control is, and to some degree will always remain, an imperfect tool, it would be a surrender to a negative eschatology were we to prefer the risks of "natural selection," a view which again seems to accord with Dr. Edel's position.

But I must not end in this critical vein. As I said at the outset, Dr. Jonas' paper has opened a debate which is bound to challenge both economists and philosophers for some time to come. I admit that, with all his concern about the intrinsicalities of economics, I still see him wearing the philosopher's crown rather than the bowler hat of the economist. But when he tells us that economics is "interdisciplinary by its nature," [39] dealing with an indivisibly "compound situation" in which the physicist, the biologist, the anthropologist, the psychologist, etc., are also involved, I begin to wonder whether for him that crown and that hat are not really the same. I wrote some time ago that for the solution of its basic problems, economics is in dire need of another Aristotle,[40] meaning a philosopher sufficiently at home with the economic issues of his time to be able to provide it with its ultimate norms. Though for the time being Jonas' answer is not Aristotle's, he has retrieved Aristotle's quest.

---

[39] See p. 83.
[40] "The Normative Roots of Economic Value," *Human Values and Economic Policy,* ed. Sidney Hook (New York: New York University Press, 1967), pp. 170–180.

ADOLPH LOWE SYMPOSIA

First Symposium

February 9–10, 1968

The Relationship of Economic Theory to Economic Practice

Chairman: Dr. Gerhard Colm, National Planning Asociation

Participants:

DR. SIDNEY ALEXANDER, M.I.T.
DR. RUTH NANDA ANSHEN, Editor, *World Perspectives*
DR. ALLEN AUSTILL, Dean, New School for Social Research
DR. FRANCIS BATOR, John F. Kennedy School of Government, Harvard University
DR. DANIEL BELL, Columbia University
DR. ABRAM BERGSON, Harvard University
DR. JOSEPH BERLINER, Brandeis University
MR. PETER L. BERNSTEIN, New School for Social Research
DR. ERNEST BLOCH, New York University
DR. HERMAN BLOCH, St. John's University
DR. MURRAY BROWN, State University of New York
DR. GERHARD COLM, National Planning Association
DR. ALFRED CONRAD, The City College of New York
DR. EDNA EHRLICH, Federal Reserve Bank of New York
DR. ALEXANDER ERLICH, Columbia University
DR. JOHN R. EVERETT, President, New School for Social Research
DR. SOLOMON FABRICANT, National Bureau of Economic Research
DR. VICTOR FUCHS, National Bureau of Economic Research
DR. JOHN GAMBS, Hamilton College
DR. GEORGE GARVY, Federal Reserve Bank of New York
DR. NICHOLAS GEORGESCU-ROEGEN, Vanderbilt University
DR. HARRY GIDEONSE, Chancellor, New School for Social Research
DR. ELEANOR GILPATRICK, The City College of New York
DR. DONALD GORDON, University of Rochester
DR. JOSEPH J. GREENBAUM, Dean, Graduate Faculty, New School for Social Research
DR. ALLEN G. GRUCHY, University of Maryland
DR. ARON GURWITSCH, Graduate Faculty, New School for Social Research
DR. WILLIAM HAMBURGER, Graduate Faculty, New School for Social Research

202   ADOLPH LOWE SYMPOSIA

Participants, 1st Symposium (cont.)

DR. ROBERT L. HEILBRONER, Graduate Faculty, New School for Social Research

DR. WALTER HELLER, University of Minnesota

DR. BENJAMIN HIGGINS, University of Texas

DR. ALBERT HIRSCHMAN, Harvard University

DR. ISSAI HOSIOSKY, Treasurer, New School for Social Research

DR. GEORGE JASZI, Office of Business Economics, Department of Commerce

DR. HANS JONAS, Graduate Faculty, New School for Social Research

DR. ALFRED KAHLER, Graduate Faculty, New School for Social Research

DR. CARL KAYSEN, Director, Institute for Advanced Studies, Princeton University

DR. L. R. KLEIN, University of Pennsylvania

DR. TJALLING KOOPMANS, Yale University

MR. ALBERT W. LANDA, Vice President for Development and Public Relations, New School for Social Research

DR. ALBERT LAUTERBACH, Sarah Lawrence College

DR. LOUIS LEFEBER, Brandeis University

DR. ABBA P. LERNER, University of California, Berkeley

DR. HERBERT S. LEVINE, University of Pennsylvania

DR. ADOLPH LOWE, Graduate Faculty, New School for Social Research

DR. FRITZ MACHLUP, Princeton University

DR. JACOB MARSCHAK, University of California, Los Angeles

DR. PAUL MEDOW, Graduate Faculty, New School for Social Research

DR. GERHARD MEYER, University of Chicago

DR. GEOFFREY H. MOORE, National Bureau of Economic Research

DR. ERNEST NAGEL, Columbia University

DR. HANS NEISSER, Graduate Faculty, New School for Social Research

DR. PHILLIP J. NELSON, Graduate Faculty, New School for Social Research

DR. OSCAR A. ORNATI, New York University

DR. GUSTAV RANIS, Yale University

DR. NATHAN ROSENBERG, Purdue University

DR. WALTER SALANT, The Brookings Institution

DR. PAUL SAMUELSON, M.I.T.

DR. SAYRE SCHATZ, Temple University

DR. DAVID SCHWARTZMAN, Graduate Faculty, New School for Social Research

DR. B. B. SELIGMAN, University of Massachusetts

DR. HANS STAUDINGER, Graduate Faculty, New School for Social Research

Participants, 1st Symposium (cont.)

Dr. Thomas Vietorisz, Graduate Faculty, New School for Social Research

Dr. Henry C. Wallich, Yale University

Dr. Sidney Weintraub, University of Pennsylvania

Second Symposium   March 29–30, 1968

Philosophical Aspects of Political Economics

Chairman: Dr. John R. Everett, President, New School for Social Research

Participants:

Dr. Reuben Abel, Graduate Faculty, New School for Social Research

Dr. Ruth Nanda Anshen, Editor, *World Perspectives*

Dr. Hannah Arendt, Graduate Faculty, New School for Social Research

Dr. Allen Austill, Dean, New School for Social Research

Dr. Norman Birnbaum, Graduate Faculty, New School for Social Research

Dr. Nathan Brody, Graduate Faculty, New School for Social Research

Dr. Robert S. Cohen, Boston University

Dr. Arthur Danto, Columbia University

Dr. Stanley Diamond, Graduate Faculty, New School for Social Research

Dr. Abraham Edel, The City College of New York

Dr. John R. Everett, President, New School for Social Research

Dr. Harry Frankfurt, Rockefeller University

Dr. George Ginsburgs, Graduate Faculty, New School for Social Research

Dr. George Goe, Graduate Faculty, New School for Social Research

Dr. Victor Gourewitch, Wesleyan University

Dr. Joseph J. Greenbaum, Dean, Graduate Faculty, New School for Social Research

Dr. Murray Greene, Graduate Faculty, New School for Social Research

Dr. Emile Grunberg, University of Akron

Participants, 2nd Symposium (cont.)

Dr. L. H. Grunebaum, New School for Social Research

Dr. Aron Gurwitsch, Graduate Faculty, New School for Social Research

Mr. Earl E. Hall, The Vikewood Corporation

Dr. Robert L. Heilbroner, Graduate Faculty, New School for Social Research

Dr. Mary Henle, Graduate Faculty, New School for Social Research

Dr. Erich Hula, Graduate Faculty, New School for Social Research

Dr. Hans Jonas, Graduate Faculty, New School for Social Research

Dr. Paul Kecskemeti, Brandeis University

Dr. Richard Kennington, Pennsylvania State University

Dr. Sherman Krupp, Queens College

Mr. Albert W. Landa, Vice President for Development and Public Relations, New School for Social Research

Reverend Professor J. Quentin Lauer, S.J., Fordham University

Dr. Adolph Lowe, Graduate Faculty, New School for Social Research

Dr. R. M. MacIver, Graduate Faculty, New School for Social Research

Dr. Richard Martin, New York University

Dr. Renate Mayntz, Free University, Berlin

Mr. Immanuel G. Mesthene, Director, Program of Technology and Society, Harvard University

Dr. Sidney Morgenbesser, Columbia University

Dr. Ernest Nagel, Columbia University

Dr. Hans Neisser, Graduate Faculty, New School for Social Research

Dr. Benjamin Nelson, Graduate Faculty, New School for Social Research

Dr. Paul Oppenheim, Princeton, N. J.

Dr. Saul K. Padover, Graduate Faculty, New School for Social Research

Dr. Aage Petersen, Yeshiva University

Dr. Harris Proschanski, U. S. Department of Labor

Dr. J. H. Randall, Jr., Columbia University

Dr. Phillip Rieff, University of Pennsylvania

Dr. David Schwartzman, Graduate Faculty, New School for Social Research

Dr. Hans Staudinger, Graduate Faculty, New School for Social Research

Dr. Arthur Vidich, Graduate Faculty, New School for Social Research

Dr. Thomas Vietorisz, Graduate Faculty, New School for Social Research

Dr. Marx Wartoffsky, Boston University

Dr. Howard White, Graduate Faculty, New School for Social Research

Dr. Dennis Wrong, New York University

24

1393   16